The Immaculate Conception

Jeshua Verona

The Immaculate Conception Press

Copyright © 2002 by The Immaculate Conception Press
First printing, December, 2002
Printed in the United States of America
Library of Congress Cataloging in Publication Data

The Immaculate Conception:
Second edition.
Printed May 15, 2004
JC-18
ISBN 0-9632793-7-8

The Immaculate Conception, how many have wondered,
it has truly been a stumbling block for the ages,
from the birth of Judaeo-Christianity to these days soon ending,
its debate like a wildfire still rages.

November 3, 1996 – 6:30 a.m.: Initial Message to me

"Assuredly I say to you,
the poor are not in terms of economic means,
but rather in lack of knowledge, wisdom, and understanding...
Return to them their needs."

THIS IS THE STORY...

This is the story... of a man and his teacher,
and oh so much more than a teacher is He,
as He comes with a pure song for the whole world to sing,
bringing true love to both you and me.

The subject is the same but the classroom has grown full,
as all souls soon shall gather as One,
to receive this final lesson from the seats of our choice,
at each podium please now welcome the Son.

We have drifted so far away and well forgotten how to listen,
and rarely can honestly say we hear,
but this still small voice within is like not any other,
for it is that true love we once held so dear.

No longer do we dream with a clarity of vision,
much less with heavens gifts even greater,
two eyes and two ears with one mouth and a nose,
without touching the real sense of this waiter.

Who forever comes to serve and not ever to be served,
for in Gods truth human reason does fail,
as we erroneously continue to misread our finest gift,
deep within us dwells the pure Holy Grail.

It is good to believe in this blessing now upon us,
for in unbelief there lies very little hope,
so grasp this special journal and do not ever let go,
for our true cleansing shall require water and soap.

As your time does approach may each grade be a passing one,
for to fail shall be unpleasant to see,
while the teacher unveils each report card of souls,
do not settle for any lesser degree.

When God chooses to speak with us we feel obligated to share,
and if through us He speaks then we write,
so that all may partake in the most sacred of teachings,
from the One He anoints dressed in white.

The student that listens shall always do well,
but the one who truly hears even better,
for when we look inward and see each answer to life's questions,
that are given through the spirit beyond letter.

Each "law" is now fulfilled by the water and spirit,
as this baptism creates each life anew,
for we must be born again to the Holy Spirit as gifted,
return to me and I shall assuredly return to you.

This is the story... of a man and his teacher,
whom return once again to this earth,
and that soon shall stand together at the front of each classroom;
with new diplomas for your heavenly rebirth.

Amen.

* Seven years ago today I gave body and soul,
to serve God also known as HaShem,
deep within us is returned the one pearl of great worth,
and when found is our life's finest gem.   (JEM)

THE MARATHON OF MYRIADS

We have run this race amidst billions who began front and back,
now ahead of you there is only One, and in the rear lies the pack.
So grasp your strongest breath for this glorious stretch run,
and then challenge Me to that finish line, where true understanding was begun.

Our training has been together from so far away and long ago,
and you have followed with such loyalty that our God could only know.

As teacher and friend I must call upon you once again,
to bring each soul to their mount of great hope,
allowing nothing to keep them from me for your guide is set in place,
as she shall bind you to that knot in our rope.

You have well accepted your destiny in each chapter thus far
as the forerunner that ends up second best,
while the kingdom awaits patiently for this book to be completed,
and when I grade you on this one final test.

Remember always our vow in battle to win the war of all wars;
the safe return of All Souls to their home,
now our enemies shall be defeated and brought straight to their knees,
as in the former glory we experienced in Rome.

I shall very soon surprise you with an acknowledgement yet unseen
reserved only within the eyes of our true,
for my mission as teacher is to produce the finest student...
"where far greater things than I ye shall do."

You have been given my eternal mystery that goes far beyond written,
so write it for the whole world to see:
The Immaculate Conception is each ones journey back home...
life's greatest story told through both you and me.

TO KNOW OUR SPECIAL PLACE WITHIN

To know our special place within,
that each soul may seek and find,
where science cannot locate,
through their scopes of eye and mind.

As religions speak too often sleek,
their doctrines crowd the earthly meek,
from truth divine as our most treasured peak,
presented both through strong and weak.

The scholars create in futile debate,
this hidden pearl saved for those who wait,
upon God's word forever great,
like those that fished but left their bait.

Mystics struggle upon this path,
with a secret math in their ritual bath,
for it remains alive to ye that hath…
not to false belief in heavenly wrath.

Politicians yell and lawyers quell,
while the untold masses sit and dwell,
upon the "truths" they seek to sell,
and the rumors they should not tell.

As clergy pray their victims say:
"this cannot be the Christian way,"
we shall say goodbye to cloudy gray,
for black and white must clearly stay.

"The Street's" decline is a fearful sign,
to greed upon the money vine,
these grapes of wrath that crossed the line,
shall drown in pools of their tainted wine.

The towers tumble and our leaders stumble,
as sporting heroes do sadly fumble,
while "musicians" shriek: "let us form a rumble;"
too few remain of the honest humble.

This "faith" we learn is now a grave concern,
as these fallen idols shall crash and burn,
from thrones of glory they did not earn,
let us pray forgiveness at every turn.

The evil dollar has bound a collar,
upon our collective necks until we holler,
for truth and grace instead of squalor,
our human stature cannot grow taller.

Bring back the scales of equal measure,
so that all may share in life's real pleasure,
and remove the terror from your goodly many,
or our map of truth remains hidden treasure.

This spirit cannot be sold or bought,
unlike the body forever caught,
in temptations web once Eden's plot,
now return within to meet God as taught.

The media spits from its poisonous pits,
as a venomous viper within our midst,
their dance of charm that never quits,
while pure integrity on sideline sits.

Return your saints in our time of need,
to plant new seed that our souls may feed,
upon the wisdom of heaven's creed,
let us rise above through word and deed.

Our world still honors wealth and fame,
as life's greatest game is that why we came?
So accept the blame and conquer shame,
by paying karmic debt to restore good name.

It is not too late for our appointed date,
turn back the hands of time and fate,
and remember always to love thy mate,
and leave all else outside God's gate.

The Phoenix circles until cleared to land,
each five hundred years over sea and sand,
from ashes risen to lift heart and hand,
then march in step within heaven's band.

This sound is pure no drum or fife,
as all children sing with man and wife:
"Goodbye to every earthly strife...
for today we greet eternal life!"

Switch off the news that sings the blues,
and grasp true faith as our soul renews,
its proper course far from earthly views,
within this sanctuary are many pews.

Please take one moment and behold His face,
our champion of grace in every marathon race,
beckoning to each for a simple embrace;
now "Go" within to our most treasured place.

The Immaculate Conception

Acknowledgements

To immediate and extended family, and friends one and all; thank you for standing firm during this mission with such loving patience and understanding. It would not have been possible to record a single page without your love and unwavering support. To those whom I have partly or completely separated from physically during these past seven years, know that for not one moment are we parted in spirit or memory when our will does not allow a place within us for it to be so. Please accept my sincerest apologies for any voids or burdens placed in your lives as a result of my personal decision, as it was not by intent or design to offend any. This work is a gift of grace and tremendous blessing, that deserves being followed through with a fully committed discipline and focus toward its most successful completion and delivery. My only hope is that these gifted words of perfection, shall pierce through the many imperfections of my far lesser humanity. This is the way that it has been offered, and thus the way it shall now be shared. The free choice that we make in following the path of spirit at the expense of self-desire, shall produce a real difference in the great awakening to our true purpose in life. May the precious fruits within this spirit of truth become a most welcome visitor into each of your lives as well, and to all whom you lovingly cherish and encounter along the way. I shall mention no names so as to forget not any, as each well knows to whom I am referring and remain forever indebted to and grateful for. What better way to enter into this new age of understanding, then by each of us remaining anonymous and selfless, whereby our self driven individualism is set aside willingly on behalf of divine oneness and unity. Let us determine to disqualify our physical self, and thereby qualify our spiritual soul as an earthen vessel of God's will upon this earth, and soon *The Immaculate Conception* shall be added unto each life, that so desires sharing together in this very special inner partnership of holy communion.

* Only through this understanding can we reach our fullest potential as individual human beings, and then as a collective humanity most pleasing to God. This book serves a critical need, not because I wrote it; but because I did not. This is the will of God and our eternal hope for continuing grace.

Unto me these words have been freely given, so also unto you I freely give.

May the Lord bless and protect you upon your journey and let us say; Amen.

Dedication

* This book is lovingly dedicated to the eternal struggle of each spiritual life in its quest for truth and soul equality. To each and every woman of this world, so long oppressed by the dictates and desires of our male dominated societies, cultures, and their resultant institutions of self servitude; I hereby proclaim your freedom trail eternal... through the avenue of each soul in partnership covenant to God within.

The "suffrage" movement is a political volley that can only serve to achieve temporary equal standing within the well confined evil essence of this physical world, now sentenced to heavenly spiritual warfare as so declared, within this true oracle of our One God understanding of unity and Oneness. You must no longer seek to gain territory in that which is to be lost, as the time of gentile rule within this age is over. As you witness in these days to come, the complete and total dismantling of the historic human power structures, you shall be far better served in the aspects of distancing.

That biblical time is soon coming and already is, whereby these actions of heaven shall occur in response to evil rule. "The Immaculate Conception" is our war manual from God that shall open every door and light each pathway of souls.

Let us no longer tarry as passive participants in the day to day routine of decline and corruption in this old world age, that is passing away swiftly and decidedly. We must now embrace that to which our spirit soul and not mind body, determines as the best place to stand upon God's battlefield. The physical and spiritual middle area of gray indecision, where the multitudes have forever gathered and lingered between good and evil as if in a game of what suits me best today; shall be utterly destroyed in the awe of a moment, as the rationalization of our watered down sense of goodness, is finally exposed to the light of truth and grace once again. DO NOT be caught in this lukewarm state of our physical world "drunkeness", but make the choice to be hot or cold.

Each battlefield lies within us in truth, and it is there that God forever agrees to meet and greet us with unconditional love, in the form of care and compassion filled forgiveness. As we freely choose this source of gifted divinity through honest and sincere repentance, we shall soon find our own salvation standing firmly upon the winning side of Godly!

May God bless each soul upon this journey and say; Amen.

* This spiritual path of understanding begins in (Part 3) with "The Road Back To Me", so it is best to start there.

"The Immaculate Conception" is to make our true connection.

When "the law" became of no effect a greater sacrifice was made, for truth and grace pays every sin as our cornerstone God has laid. Understand these gifts for they do not collide but rather build upon each other, as so must we to reach Temple Three; reunite with Lord and brother.

Amen.

Table of Contents

Preface

This book, *The Immaculate Conception,* is one entity consisting of three separate but unified sections, beginning with its *Poetry and Introduction* (Part 1), continuing as *God's Living Word* (Part 2) and concluding with *The Road Back To Me* (Part 3). This final part is the starting sequence of my experience in time, and progresses forward to Part 1 as most recent. It is easier to gain understanding by beginning with Part 3, for this is where I also began.

The calling to this service came seven years ago on Rosh Hashanah 5757, today being the Jewish New Year of Rosh Hashanah 5764. (September 15, 1996 - September 27, 2003).

What has transpired in between both physically and spiritually is beyond reasonable explanation, but if so taken as intended upon pure faith in God's Living Word, shall open our soul pathway to this life's essential needs. There is one critical truth upon our road back to understanding, that must be truly grasped and then acknowledged before entering into this most gifted spiritual domain of our collective and universal equality: * The Lord our God is One... and from this Oneness comes all!

It is prophetically told, "In all thy getting get understanding" which means that we must get spiritual understanding through divine communion within our very souls. These words are not spoken in terms of physical definition towards greater external knowledge, but rather a much deeper inner human potential of truly divine wisdom.

In this new age we shall learn to aptly apply and humbly share our gifts soul to soul, without the limitless earthly divisions that have hindered our pure and collective spiritual progress throughout history. It is our greatest hope and purpose in this life. Each Adam born of flesh must become an Adam born of spirit within each of us, if God's master plan for earth is to be realized, and our perpetual life cycles of soul incarnations thus properly developed to the point of our higher level in understanding.

Please absorb and digest this journal with a quiet, slow, and most deliberate type meditation, whereby our spirit of truth may pierce through this life's many distractions and dissension, as this ministering process is to each their own, as willing and able.

If the writing moves too deep do not give up the challenge, but rather slow down the intake pace, reviewing when necessary to achieve a comfortable new understanding. With the gifts available to each life upon earth so graciously given, yet so greatly misunderstood and so long under utilized, their keenly precise movement and usage throughout today's world, is most essential toward first halting and then reversing our hastening downward spiral. The patient and focused teachings of the living Christ spirit within each of us, simply awaits our proper invitation of soul readiness, sincerity, and willful commitment to a higher ideal, before activating this pure teaching process. "Ask and it shall be given, seek and you shall find", etc. is the true spirit pathway of universal right direction. We must travel beyond words into this commitment of truth. This unique partnership covenant shall deliver each soul to its "narrow gate" of eternal salvation, through the gifts of our Living God's ever merciful truth and loving grace.

This is the pure will of God and teacher that must become our will as human students toward imperishable crowns of spirit... the graduation diplomas of each eternal life. Until we offer ourselves up as an enlistment to learn, we cannot be truly taught this understanding, for its birth is predicated upon the death of most self desires. As we direct our prayer and energies inward toward the greater good of God's will, thus realizing the insignificance of self will, we begin to grow in life's oneness.

The soul at its earthly best with no further need of selfhood, soon becomes a most proper earthen vessel (soldier) in this greater battlefield of God's one master plan. Our coordination and cooperation of souls allows for Providence to foster, as the good versus evil (self) battalions begin to fall silent, and then ultimately succumb to peace.

When our path is made straight within each soul, the universal truth enters into our subconscious, that the conscious may then be awakened from its prolonged spiritual slumber. As we increase energy levels toward each other, instead of depleting this most precious resource, our God within rises up to once again meet its universal source.

Soon after, we become spiritually conjoined, not unlike the element of mercury as physically brought together when in close proximity to itself, or the human marriage ceremony thus bonding two into one, and the even greater bond of our worldly brotherhood of one into all, or the single greatest reunion of all back to One!

Most every separation that we as humanity create through free choice, is contrary to God's perpetually universal activity of renewing a pure and unified creation each day. In this way we are setting conflicting physical forces in motion against spiritual forces, not unlike our human interrelationships, whereby the resulting clashes further produce an increased density of matter, and thus a slowed down universal soul development. We must begin at once to move energy of every form into harmony with nature, if life as we know it is to be sustained upon this planet. There is no Sabbath rest for our God.

The words contained within this journal represent the free will exchange of our truly avowed eternal love, for God and one another in this everlasting covenant of promise. No greater bond of love exists beyond this covenant thus fulfilled, between our Creator and each creation. God is forever waiting patiently at our within altar of this most treasured love, and when we freely choose to be enjoined as one, our eternal marriage vow is thus consummated in ceremony as our very own "New Jerusalem" now betrothed. Upon our souls sincere and active vow of "I do", each earth life cycle as signified by "the ring," is thus completed from repentance through salvation, and the far greater journey of the anointed universal spirit soul may once again travel back toward home. Upon each bridge between heaven and earth stands the teacher who grants fair and righteous passage to the other side, as the veil hangs quite thin where true faith is king. As we instill positive spiritual energy into daily life on earth, we begin to rise up tall toward the true source of our Creator, that awaits patiently this full emergence of each creation.

The only element of our total being that prevents altogether, or partly hinders us from attaining God's truth… is self. By removing conflict from within and without we shall become this pure spirit soul of freedom that is most pleasing to God and our fellow. Nothing created or birthed upon this earth is without a pure and purposeful intent to God, for He does not labor in vain nor turn away from any soul in need. It is forever humanity's inhumanity through iniquity (poor free choice) that separates us ever further from God and one another, but the distance is never too great if we focus upon the return. Prayerful thought and good deeds (mitzvos) increase our energy production and relationships, helping to propel the multitude of souls toward their heavenly home.

Universal law supercedes any human law and its basis is love built upon tender mercy. Our only commandment is to love God and one another with all thy strength of being, as all else is merely commentary upon this simple karmic doctrine of universal truth.

Repentance is not a spoken apology, but rather a turning from one's ways, whereby salvation may be granted to each soul through God's grace and compassion only. All of creation is welcomed into the "kingdom of heaven" as the "Israel" (seeker) of promise, whereby each soul possesses and is granted equal access and entitlement.

To reach this "inner kingdom" of scriptural reference regarding total being, we must come to understand the proximity of God's presence as eternally operational within and without each life form, and only in accordance to humanity within the bounds of free will as gifted. When free will is returned, all barriers in this life are thus lifted. As we actively and sincerely seek God within the very essence of our souls, there comes a full response that leads us far beyond any human doctrine, belief, or religion; straight to the heart (pure church) of our endless human struggle for this life's true meaning. This special and defining moment of which I speak is readily available to each soul as a product of creation ongoing, thus bonded with our Messiah on perpetual altar call within. The body is our temple, our soul is the altar, and self is the offering. During the seven-year process of compiling this journal of experience, we shall soon systematically witness and share in the reality of evil's demise, from a position of false empowerment over us, to becoming fully subjected to us through faith in God's will. As we behold the decrease of evil's reality, we can then welcome in the increase of Messiah's.

The advent of Messiah (anointed one) is an individual event at first, thus emerging from within upon the soul invitation and preparedness to this most holy inner communion. Although personal in nature, this experience may soon become the shared edification of all who wish to travel upon the true life pathway back home. Those that aspire to the pure religious church found only within us in Godly truth, understand that the way must first be cleared, leveled, well paved, and then individually walked; until our individualism and self will are no more. Along this progressive course of spiritually influenced soul growth, we begin to shed the physical remnants of selfhood, and through our daily trials and tribulations begin to make good each approaching choice for spirit and no longer only body physical. This transformation process shall amaze even the skeptic within you, as selfless behavior continually increases and spreads. What is now better for us is also better for others, and especially most pleasing to God.

Alone, this process is most difficult if not impossible to implement, but with God as our partner and true faith as our guide, all things are possible within the gift of this special and most treasured universal covenant. Let us no longer accept waiting upon earthly death as our point of soul transition, when our pure instinct of spirit is to embrace the full potential of our total being in the here and now; and thus elevate each soul today! This is the will of the ascending soul, and the basis of our return is in perfecting its communion as created, with creation and Creator. From our soul origins so very long ago established it is our birthright born of spirit…God's Living Word upon The Road Back To Me shall become "Our"…Immaculate Conception.

Foreword

Please excuse any recorded redundancy and repetition for these are emphasized points of spiritual injection, received at varying intervals of time over an extended period of deliverance, for the purpose of becoming acceptable into our spiritual and physical mindset. Each word contained within this testament is sent on behalf of God's desired unity with every life form, for no created being is apart from the realm of universal conscience and control. Do not burden yourself with gender reference regarding our God, for that is only applicable in the physical and not spiritual plane. Any mention of varying religious denominations or beliefs, are strictly for the readers benefit while relegating this work to our respective human doctrines and various houses of worship.

Our focus is to prepare and share with one another this edifying purpose for reception of God's living word to each soul in the here and now, as space and time are only relative understandings to our physical world relationships; nothing more nothing less.

In our world of today there is a well deserved and ever increasing degree of mistrust in the external bureaucratic "higher" orders of our society and their assumed leadership integrity, but let us not be dissuaded from our focused and foremost internal lifetime mission… to love God and one another with a full heart and soul. "In God We Trust" is forever our banner to carry, while "United We Stand" by unrelenting faith and hope. Our standard bearer of every truth remains poised at the door of each soul, so is it not time to now welcome Him in? This calling forth of our inner partnership bond shall first provide every pathway, and then deliver each soul upon our freedom trail eternal. This physical world is now entering into a period of great change, where neither doctrinally enforced religion nor human science can provide a valid support system for understanding life's universal truth. Has not each human agency had more than ample opportunity, to ask and receive answers to our timeless questions of life's meaning?

It is the continually inappropriate manner in which we approach the altar of truth, that prevents wisdom and understanding from being added unto our human knowledge. Unity through Oneness with the express purpose of serving God's will and not our own, is the one faithful and true path to follow, whereby this offering is forever well received.

* Calling from the lips of Abraham to the eternal cross of Christ today; bring faith toward truth and grace for we are One with God I say!

The ongoing and ever increasing pace of our world transformation must at once be met head on with the direct force and application of pure faith, as our partnership covenant with God who dwells within does attest. The human will is the driver of this faith, and thus our greatest resource for positive change. It is this pure faith toward God and one another as evidenced in our earthly father Abraham, that bonds us to our heavenly Father through the continuing truth and grace teaching of His Christ spirit everlasting.

We must at once become more spiritually astute and soul savvy, if we are to meet and then defeat this invasion of our most treasured world freedom. Faith in full force is the only mechanism that we possess within our collective being, to successfully combat the effects of unwanted earthly change. The sheer will of courage and determination shall bring about a renewed sense of hope toward the unconditional establishment of first Godly, and then brotherly love as our most proper relationships in this lifetime. This essential process of soul growth must become the immediate concern and responsibility of each person, to thus set in motion this special gift that allows all of creation to partake within God's essence of truth, otherwise known as the eternal bonded covenant to our universal Oneness. (Abrahamic covenant of true faith and loyalty.)

Salvation for each soul cannot come about merely through the physical channels of human doctrine, tradition, culture, ritual, contract, baptism, or any religious law; but rather emerges as a pure spiritually active partnership, made manifest in truthful soul acceptance to the Christ teacher of God, both within and without our being when ready. The body physical must now defer to the body spiritual for this gateway to thus open, as indeed it is the mystically referred to "Number Fifty Door" that Moses entered not. In terms of religious leaders throughout nations and history, understand the source of their common calling as bringing One God worship in truth. Focus not only upon their individual humanity as religious founders, but rather recognize the same loving spirit by which they came to mission, most departing this world persecuted and bereft, but still following God's and not human command. These are the footsteps in which to walk, and do not think for a moment that their physical diversities are not spiritually joined.

It is the pure will and selflessness of our religious founders such as Abraham, that qualified each to forever proclaim the oracle of our One true God, even unto this day. Their one desire and eternal mission is for each of us to walk likewise, and through the sacrifice of self will for God will, every truth shall be made manifest unto each of us as well. This is the true essence of "Akedah" (intended sacrifice of Isaac on Mt. Moriah and symbol of Israel's martyrdom).

It is Abraham that we share and may identify with in common, so let his faith be our starting point toward ecumenical understanding, while the Christ spirit of truth and grace shall become the finish line of self, and the eventual champion of each and every soul!

Our Living God concept of truth shall open every door and light each pathway toward our continuing educational guidance in soul growth. May we seek this truth together as a congregation in spirit toward our common human origin, for it is forever our greatest earthly mission and forthcoming eternal destiny.

It is for this purpose and to this end that we come.... and then return home.

QUOTES OF CHRIST

* "At the river Jordan you baptized Me and our lives began anew, now I return with the Holy Spirit to forever baptize you."

* "When God teaches through us we also seek to teach, but when God truly reaches us, our self will we must impeach.

* "The student that listens shall always do well, but the one who truly hears shall always do better."

* "The student that looks inward is surely on the right track, but the one who truly sees has understanding front to back.

* "You have been given My eternal mystery that goes far beyond writtien, so now write it for the whole world to see, 'The Immaculate Conception' is each one's journey back home; life's greatest story told through both you and Me."

* "It does not matter greatly what you purchase or from whom, the value remains forever the same, quite worthless from womb to tomb."

* "You were recently told the saying that the definition of a wealthy person is one who has no debt, but assuredly I say to you that the truly rich person is the one who has no debt to humanity or God."

Part One
Poems and Introduction

THE IMMACULATE CONCEPTION

The Immaculate Conception, how many have wondered,
it has truly been a stumbling block for the ages,
from the birth of Judaeo-Christianity to these days soon ending,
its debate like a wildfire still rages.

Many lives have been spent in pursuit of this truth,
but its truth is not something to be learned,
the wisest among creation have been frustrated by this fact,
as their minds and not hearts further yearned.

Knowledge is a gift that travels only so far,
there are limits to which humankind may attain,
through scholarly research a mere testament of our past,
capabilities confined strictly to the brain.

Wisdom is the second step on this journey back home,
and in that group the membership is quite restricted,
for the few in human history entering into this domain,
a needle in a haystack is more accurately depicted.

This area of which I speak lies deep within ones heart,
calling out to the spirit of love in degree,
with the discovery of this channel the world begins to move forward,
a step closer on the road back to Me.

Understanding is the crowning glory that the gifted seek to wear, the graduation
ceremony of both wisdom and knowledge,
a degree as unreachable as the furthermost star,
yet to be offered in the curriculum of any college.

Its mystery has remained hidden and held back for good reason,
heaven's final card is this ace in the hole,
to be played at the end of days in the collective presence of humanity,
this eternal gift shall be the blessing of one soul.

The seal of this envelope has been set from day one,
in the beginning the light testified against the end,
from this courtroom long ago established the verdict shall soon be rendered,
based on evidence presented by the one to call friend.

Understanding is in His right hand and judgement in His left,
in a flash every wrong is made right,
The Immaculate Conception is the living word of God,
by the spirit of Christ comes the true power of thy might.

May all peoples and nations return to Him as one,
for it is in this spirit of unity I thus endow,
His loving gift through understanding is life's most precious jewel,
now freely given to all children in this vow.

Call upon His name today for tomorrow is promised to no one,
through our hearts He desires mercy upon each nation,
repentance is the ticket for the journey of a lifetime,
where God's oneness shall be glorified in salvation.

Our mission is thus fulfilled upon the completion and delivery,
of this summons which proclaims to all His living word,
it is His final eternal gift completing the bridge to humanity,
bonding each Torah to Christ and both Temples to the Third.

Amen.

There is only one truth in this world that best represents all religions and human doctrines, and this special church that each must seek can be found only within our very soul. There is much to be said about the life well lived and its adherence in allowing nature to take its course, but there is much more to be said when we allow God's will to partner with and thus out shine our human nature, thereby setting our proper course upon His universal truth and oneness. Let us welcome the word of the *Immaculate Conception* once again.

We can no longer tarry when it comes to setting straight our personal relationship with God, as times all around us give ample warning as to the coming cataclysmic events foretold in most every religious scripture and doctrine. Within the essence of universal truth, our fate is co-determined by free will, therefore let us assertively apprehend God in the here and now as so taught and lived by the eternal Christ teacher; forever standing patiently at the narrow gate of our evolving, developing, and ascending souls. May the timeless lessons be now finally learned through the teaching process thus complete.

*Historically, most religious doctrines teach us to prepare for the second coming (Messiah), but rather be assured, He is very much here today. The spiritual truth is that Christ has not, cannot, and shall not leave until we are ready, willing, and able to follow; therefore He waits patiently within us until called upon to step forth and deliver within each, our own salvation.

The Immaculate Conception is both physical and spiritual, as is *The Immaculate Conception* (the true author) Himself who grants eternal gifts to each soul such as this one. Let us go willingly together to meet this pure faith in peace, through divine truth and grace. Amen.

Q: Please explain to us *The Immaculate Conception?*

A: Not only was Jeshua immaculately conceived within the virgin Miriam, but so also was Miriam conceived immaculately to Anna of Machaerus.

This physical definition must not be a point of contention among brethren of God, for it only serves as a cause for unwarranted judgement, conflict, prejudice, and further separation. The broader and more specific answer is the spiritual understanding of its eternal nature, that must now serve as our far greater collective concern.

The Immaculate Conception is that special and defining moment for each soul upon its journey of repentant spirit readiness toward salvation; where past, present, and future are gathered together as one, within the timeless reality of our most sacred communion with God and universe thus understood.

It is this "kingdom" within our total being that we must seek, act upon, and enter into, if our true will is to be with God and one another in perfect harmony once again.

THE STAR OF DAVID

The Star of David consists of two separate but equal life triangles. The triangle pointing upward let us call "The Ascendant", and the one pointing downward shall be termed "The Descendent". Located within both centers as separate entities and as a unity lies God, both within (internal) and without (external) of our total being. The three points of the ascendant triangle are knowledge, wisdom, and understanding (spiritual) as shown bottom left to right and up. The three points of the descendent triangle are: mind, soul, and body, (physical) as shown top left to right and down. Interconnected and interwoven they provide us with life eternal. The Star of David is a pathway for every soul, and much older than three thousand years. It is the star of universal unity, that brings heaven down to earth, as one without the other is an incomplete life journey.

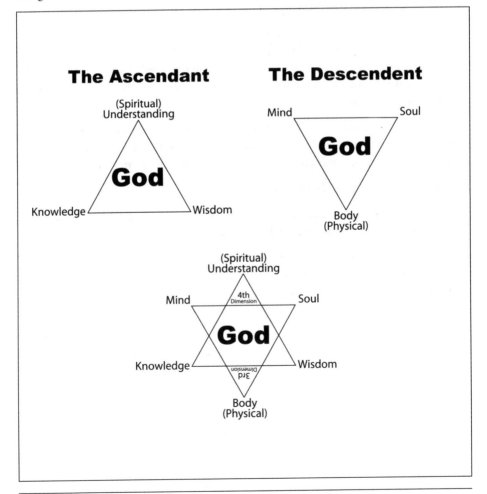

We begin in the fourth dimension as a spirit body, (soul) and descend through the thought process of our creator (God) into materiality. Understand that we are a part of God and apart from God as well. Attuning to His will through pure faith and selflessness we shall reach atonement, at-onement, and truth.

As we come to truly understand the total beauty of this most precious royal diadem, being not only a physical emblematic star, but far more importantly, an imperishable crown of spirit, then our viewpoint of this treasured gift is from above. To clearly see God's truth we must travel the complete inner and outer paths of this life cycle, whereby free choice actively seeks and *The Immaculate Conception,* then shepherds us home safely.

The ascendancy of our soul while in the physical realm of being has forever been our collective mission, and upon the grasping of this eternal truth in practice becomes our own graduation diploma. Complete spiritual understanding of the universal conscience both within and without of our being, provides the answers to a oneness forever sought after which becomes the ultimate goal, ideal, and purpose of every soul in each sojourn upon this earthly plane and beyond. The proper pursuit of this knowledge is rewarded with the gifts of wisdom and discernment, thus supplying a sufficient girding of truth in our continuing spiritual quest. Let us unite in this eternal purpose of oneness and unity.

As we learn to shed the excess weight of temporary and physical world dictates in favor of the eternal spiritual freedom that awaits our call, soon the blinded eyes shall see and the willing ears shall hear. God our father is the one that bestows these gifts, and as we travel this road back to Him, the gap that we have created grows narrow. The separation between life and death, as we allow it, shall no longer be a dividing wall of fear and great apprehension as if in finality, but rather our spiritual transformation from the physical earthly plane, to our world of collective understanding within God's everlasting love.

To love the Lord our God with all our heart, soul, and strength, and our fellow life forms as ourselves is to fulfill God's will. This two part commandment of the Christ is the very essence of David's star, as all else written and taught is only further commentary upon this eternal truth. From "The Star of David" to "Day One of David" lies the map of right direction and our blessing to each soul, as our hope is to share heartfelt and most loving gifts to all of God's children in this vow.

Human life begins in a dimension apart from the third that is known to us as the earthly plane. God is spirit and His spirit is love, therefore universal law is also love as relating to life on earth. Souls that are in various stages of their ongoing development seek bodies in which to manifest themselves, so as to fulfill each common destiny. We begin life in the fourth dimension as a spirit body (soul) and descend by choice through the thought process of our Creator and enter into materiality. Once again, understand that we are a part of God and apart from God during each sojourn of our eternal soul. This is the within and without essence of our total being as illustrated in the two part Star of David.

Through this assimilation into the world we acquire our physical characteristics, while also maintaining our true essence of soul. In the earthly state of total being (spiritual/physical) we must focus upon the destination to be reached, without pausing too long at any particular stage toward complete development. Too often we embrace a false sense of security within the various "harbors" or comfort levels present within the six smaller triangles, and thus become spiritually stagnant. The main purpose of this book is to provide the wake up call as commanded by ministering to each their own as able.

The sacrifice of self will in favor of God's will, shall provide the proper course for each soul, as we shed the physical dictates of a temporary master (self) within a temporary world. We must at once, assertively and not passively place our total being under the command of its eternal master, that gives us direction and energy toward truth.

Set our sights upon all that is Godly and earthly life flows. From this point of realization, as to cooperation and coordination of being, the spiritual mindset shall lead body and soul forward. If through free will we can make a concerted effort to create peace, then God shall assuredly respond as our partner within the holy covenant He so treasures. Redemptive soul salvation is found only within this awareness well practiced. The thread of life's journey intricately woven through the fabric of grace, when honestly approached with heartfelt purpose, becomes our greatest partnership in God's universe of tender mercy.

Each lifelong desire of the soul when not hindered by the physical body, is the universal understanding of truth. Our timeless answer and well prepared pathway is unique for each person according to soul readiness, but the main criteria in reaching our special ministry of earthly purpose, can only be found through the commitment of pure inner faith, whereby prayer leads to works.

Inward prayer is our sign to God that we understand His whereabouts, and now wish to interrelate within this temple communion as a soul partnership.

To believe that God only exists outside of our being, is the greatest injustice that we can serve upon ourselves and our fellow life forms, for it isolates us from the purely interconnected circle of universality. This spiritual reunion is what God patiently awaits, and is our direct soul connection to the creative source.

Upon adapting to this unconditional love within our being over a period of soul body gestation, a tremendous awakening and life transformation shall then ensue. During the stages of each change comes a pure cleansing, then a balancing of total being that elevates our soul to its rightful place within God, at the true center of universal and human consciousness. As we put into practice the free lessons of our spiritual teacher, a synchronistic pattern of divine providence begins to swirl about our routine daily activities, thus presenting many ample opportunities to contribute towards the greater good; and less toward self. this field becomes the proving ground of our soul.

The comings and goings of our selves and others become purposeful and precise events, as we now consciously separate self will from the will of fate.

This is simply a matter of moving over and letting God do the actual driving. It will feel extremely awkward for a time, because the mind body wants to act according to its five physical sense commands, but by slowing the pace of external world stimuli, the internal spirit of our gifted sixth sense takes over. This is precisely what takes place in an emergency whereby the ever intuitive sixth sense actually freezes time, and allows the soul body its opportunity to override that which the mind body determines not possible. By training our body to progressively relinquish its temporary powers to the eternal soul, this transcending conduct becomes a process of our inner partnership, rather than self alone, and "the zone" that we seldom experience, becomes a much more common occurrence within our vastly improving whole life development. "The zone" is a euphoria that occurs when we are performing at a level well beyond physical, purely spiritual by nature, and increasingly present in faith.

To reach a clear and concise understanding of our earthly life, we must separate the two essential components of total being, and self define the origin of purpose for each. This shall require an introspective examination of the physical body with its temporal properties; and our pure eternal soul.

Once understood separately, we can begin to blend both entities into a bond of common ideal, that as does" The Star of David," best represent our highest self in God.

We as separate individuals by our physical nature, are simply the products of their original source, both Godly in spirit and earthly in body. Our growth or regression is dependent upon this partnership identified, integrated, and then implemented into truthful practice, through our gifted will as this life's most powerful resource. Heredity and environment do factor in as developmental influences, but it is the will of each soul that primarily determines outcome.

It is the human soul and not the physical body that must be served, if our universal harmony is to be met and experienced in this earthbound lifetime.

The spirit is life's activation of our soul source energy, and through our free choice as gifted becomes the character traits of each person in thought, word, and deed. The physical body and its pathway chosen becomes the outward evidence of our inward witness for good or otherwise; to self and also others.

If at first we conform the will for the betterment of total self, then the two activities of body and soul can work in unity as intended, rather than as two contrary and conflicting forces both from within and without our total being. As each person acknowledges in their own time, the loving partnership of both entities at work within them, then that soul body begins to clearly see its full life potential of true mission as covenanted to God's desire of oneness.

In the same manner that a rocket ship enters into orbit by dropping stages no longer necessary, throughout human development we must likewise comply. The physical world focus is our creation of narrow mindedness, and thus a hindrance to our spiritually energized soul and its quest to return home upon proper course. We can no longer be deterred from our ideal of true purpose, as a simple reunion of pure faith through sincere repentance, shall light every pathway and open every door. We have reached the plateau of life's higher understanding and must determine our collective fate. Do we rise above in unity; or once again fall? May your journey within be well with you and God, for as self becomes visible from the outside in, the victory is yours and ours!

GOD'S SPIRIT OF CHRIST - LIFEBLOOD OF THE EARTH

The biblical reference that all things are made through Him,
is a profound statement regarding this life indeed,
containing deep rooted answers to our spiritual questions,
grows the tree of life from God's original seed.

This spirit of truth is the world's sustaining power,
coupled with grace our finest gift from the source,
whose lifeblood is physical motion producing spiritual love in action,
throughout our universe there is no greater force.

We are well taught through scripture that all blood is sacred,
the Pentateuch makes this perfectly clear,
understanding as our mission through knowledge and then wisdom,
shall eliminate the dangers born of apprehension and fear.

As we share in the joy that the Passover represents,
a celebration of freedom we believe is second to none,
let us also share in the sorrow that makes this season bittersweet,
the crucifixion of God's one and only son.

The yoke that still remains is a far greater harness,
than any physical persecutions of the past,
for it is in spiritual freedom that final glory is attained,
through repentance that special dye may be cast.

As children of the covenant embraced by God from the start,
His firstborn forever through both good times and bad,
please kindly make amends with this eternal guiding light,
bringing tears of joy far too long shed as sad.

It is salt in this world that determines ones worth,
when the flavor becomes lost so do we,
acknowledgement of this truth is a display of intestinal fortitude,
soon every tongue shall confess the Lord on bended knee.

God resists the proud but gives grace to the humble,
it is His spiritual pain which remains in agony upon the cross,
to bring Father and children back together once again,
requires a vow that we are truly sorry for His loss.

As the Red Sea was parted and each pursuer thus engulfed,
that deliverance solved the mystical burden of proof,
along with commandments of law through His faithful servant Moses,
transgression of faith forced our Father apart and aloof.

Both passions of love and anger run deep in heartfelt emotion,
reaching extreme levels to include the consecration of blood,
separations from our God has led to many unnecessary tragedies,
Sodom and Gomorrah, the two Temples, Holocaust, and Great Flood.

How many times do we test Him before the lesson is finally learned,
from His firstborn He has expected a little more,
not unlike any other parent demanding honor from their offspring,
for whose benefit do we believe chastening is for?

If committed to help establish a settlement based on faith,
He will deliver peace and goodwill heaven sent,
to the unified House of Israel as all seekers who believe,
the Lord's hand is still reaching into our tent.

In Jesus there came hope that the Gentiles never had,
we must honor His sacrifice as the true Lamb of God,
the Exodus from Egypt produced a physical miracle of freedom,
watch closely for the upcoming Divine spiritual rod.

The staff of Aaron in the desert was a vessel made from wood,
brought to life with the great powers of heaven above,
not unlike the *Immaculate Conception* that is His gift to this house,
God's living word is the third temple built upon His love.

Its foundation shall be constructed without mortar and brick,
but rather with eternal covenants of each Torah, truth and grace,
build it we shall for these days have thus been written,
His promise is here and now front and center face to face.

As His wrath is redirected let us not ever test Him again,
focus strict attention upon these words we understood once,
the real enemy of creation has now issued the ultimate challenge,
threatening life on earth we have become the prey satan hunts.

We must set aside all our differences and swiftly answer this call,
the Lord desires strongly that we join with Him as one,
the unity of humankind must begin with His firstborn,
lead this final parade with an acknowledgement of His Son.

Exclude no one on this journey and as the chosen be responsible,
to carry the banner of God's justice soon unfurled,
upon witnessing this miracle all peoples and nations,
shall follow in amazement throughout the entire known world.

History bears us witness to all sufferings throughout the years,
every punishment brought further tears to our eyes,
for as siblings are well aware that the eldest bear great burden,
never feel alone as we have shared in those cries.

For the pains and persecutions thus endured throughout the ages,
how great is the Lord's forgiveness in terms of this fate,
no higher love could one attain then God's unrestricted return to mercy,
a long time coming but assuredly well worth the wait.

May the Lord grant us peace and understanding in these days,
with a clean slate to assume that most proper place,
at the head of life's table where a special seat has been prepared,
with an imperishable crown worn by all finishers in this race.

No human being can attest to the driving force of this desire,
His living word requires not the aid of any preacher,
the blood sweat and tears must now be dried from His face,
as together in unity we perform the true will of our teacher.

I am not the composer for I simply hear the tune,
that I pray the whole world shall finally sing,
in the presence of our Lord whose patience and longsuffering,
perseveres love through the faith we must bring.

The spirit of Christ is the greatest gift to humanity,
which never dies as it travels onward in time,
the prophets spoke the truth as it emerged within Jesus,
let us overcome the guilt and denial attached to this crime.

Straight ahead is our direction looking neither left nor right,
as we march confidently with heads held up high,
to the drumbeat God has sent in His word and not our being,
there is no limit to the spiritual heights we shall fly!

It is time to receive Christ through the mirror of our souls,
for that special love dwells deep within the heart of each,
the most essential ingredient to life and eternal peace everlasting,
is in God's hand now placed well within our reach.

I ask the Lord daily to kindly receive my prayers,
and supplications that are requested from the heart,
for the oneness He so desires I commit my soul to that vow,
never wavering from the end to the start.

LET MESSIAH ARRIVE NATURALLY

The main problem that most people and religions are plagued by today, is the over anxiety and anticipation that accompanies this expectant birth. As the world at large begins to sense this long awaited arrival, our tendency as humanity is to induce rather than allow nature to take its course according to plan. Our life cycle shall continue regardless of human indifference, or contrary efforts versus the true will of God as to His design.

As we remain spiritually stagnated and tunnel visioned upon the road of physical knowledge only, we neglect the eternally important territories of gifted wisdom and understanding. We were well taught the critical importance of our spiritual potential some two thousand years ago, but have failed miserably ever since amid the evil (self) entrapment of greed and self servitude. This hurdle must now be cleared; once and for all!

Instead of gradually progressing as a unity to this final stage of understanding over an extended period of time, from knowledge and then to wisdom, we are now confronted with a developmental leap of desperation at the conclusion of this tumultuous age. We must at once become battle ready as a unity of humankind, to fight a deadly common enemy hell bent on eternal destruction. If we continue to tarry, many unnecessary casualties will occur. This enemy is self, and our soul lives are continually its battleground.

As Moses led the captives to freedom out of Egypt by the right hand of God, we must now remove the chains of spiritual bondage that enslaves each of us to this day. The living word of God contained within *The Immaculate Conception,* provides the key to unlocking the chains that has forever spirit bound humanity. A united House of Israel must lead this new spiritual Exodus, as all people and nations are members of this one Godly family.

To fully grasp the understanding of the coming Messiah, we must form the bonds between each Torah (law) and Christ, and both physical Temples to the spiritual Third, thereby building God's inner sanctuary upon all truths. It is through the original Abrahamic covenant that this glory shall first be witnessed, as the labor pains and suffering throughout history subside, welcoming in the unbounded joy of a birth like no other. This euphoria of ecstasy shall be shared among all true believers throughout the world, as we return in unity to the garden from whence we came, amidst the perfect beauty of our spiritual Eden.

HOW I LONG FOR THEE

Hear O House of Israel, our time is finally come,
no more days filled with sadness and tears,
just one more good cry for the dearly departed,
and the Christ Jesus our God so endears.

All is thus forgiven when repentance steps forth,
in a flash every wrong is made right,
each bittersweet taste shall regain its lost flavor,
this is a promise by the power of thy might.

With each victory came defeat due to pride and transgression,
as we took advantage of our favored dominion,
that is why today's temples are divided and torn,
many have closed while yet others struggle for minyan.

Take heed of these words for as Solomon once said,
"True wisdom is the acknowledgement of correction,"
now understanding may follow as all gates are thus opened,
How I long for thee... in these days of resurrection.

THE THIRD TEMPLE (ITS SPIRIT HAS COME)

The inherent beauty of the true church is best reflected in its progressive doctrine of belief that remains open minded as to the receptivity, and allowable provisions concerning prophetic revelations and gifts of new teachings from the one living God. Where so many other humanistic belief systems, most notably in the western world, are closed off to God's living status in terms of will to communicate beyond scriptural accounts and experiences of the past, this openness to spiritual truth allows for continued growth and development. The true church always respects, and at times may even incorporate certain doctrines of other religions, but is not restricted or subjected to past limitations while maintaining its tradition and spirituality as paramount. This spiritual Essenism is now active once again, as these timeless soldiers dressed in white, remain forever at the readying call. Essene means "expectancy" and this very special group is once again in place.

In order to truly grow in God we must be spiritually attentive. This unique process of development must be in attunement with our creator, through the avenues of prayer based on good faith. It is through this vessel of communication that we gain insight into wisdom and understanding, which then carries us beyond knowledge to the altar of truth. When someone within the sphere of belief becomes enlightened, they are obligated to perform it for the benefit of the entirety, thereby further developing the true church for the world at large as well. If we learn to set aside our egotistical weaknesses and human frailties in favor of thankfulness to God's gifts, then we may graciously acquire the fruits of love that He so desires to bestow upon us. God is without form for He could never be that limited or restricted, and our only likeness to Him is contained within the territory of each soul.

Our physical attributes are temporary properties of the earth which cannot be conveyed to the spiritual plane of the world to come, therefore we are greatly mistaken by continually serving them. If we as a collective unity remain spiritually stagnant and physically compliant, without breaking through our inhibitive confines of the five physical senses, then we will assuredly become subjected in judgement to those temporary limits. The greatest elements of this world are the gifts of God unseen, for as the root supports the beauty of the tree, so also does our living God support us with an everlasting promise of love. If we do not take the initiative to dig down deep inside our souls, and discover the truth of this source through our gift of free choice, then we cannot attain the required understanding needed to propel us into eternal life.

Each salvation is primarily dependent upon our willingness to reach out to God with earnest and sincere intention, not only in times of need but more importantly in daily thanksgiving. We maintain that God lies within, so direct your prayer inwardly. He shall provide each of us who calls upon Him with the gifts of His Holy Spirit if our heart is pure and unselfish, whereby each gift differs according to the individual's ability to cope. Throughout human history the spirit of God has been our helper, and a constant guiding light versus the darkness of our evil intent, when in truth; evil, hell, Satan, etc. are merely physical world conditionings of the temporal human mind with no true universal essence whatsoever. The evil intent influence is simply our human unwillingness to project light and goodness, thereby creating the adverse and contrary excuses of our human failings. This is no different than a child's imagining demons in the night, or entities nonexistent. We have created evil development and must now separate from it to move forward.

With each succeeding age there has arrived an increasingly stronger spiritual presence, that continues to build upon the previous levels of understanding to its personal culmination in Messiah. Many have been touched by this very special spirit, but only a select few have experienced the reality of its ability to dwell within our very essence of being. The biblical quotation of Jeshua that states: "Many are called but few are chosen," is a profound and accurate accounting of God's gift to humankind in terms of acceptable vows. When we are ready, the few shall become the many.

We are long overdue in terms of meeting God's criteria for a proper relationship with Him and towards each other with love. To progress spiritually we must regress physically, by going back to the road of proper direction that we missed so long ago, amidst the confusions and separations of poor free choice. This wake up call is necessary today, for the kingdom of God is always near at hand, and further delay is extremely dangerous. If we soon arise from this deep slumber within the cradle of spiritual infancy, then there is still time to walk together toward God. It behooves each of us to take stock in this reality, by putting aside all selfish differences in favor of serving the far greater good. He may not always provide us with that which we want or expect, but He shall always provide us with that which we need. First and foremost is His love for each of our soul's, and their subsequent ascending journeys back home in peace.

The Passover season represents the ongoing celebration of freedom from physical slavery, first the Exodus and then the Cross, how much greater a celebration now that spiritual bondage is being lifted? The world has yet to see such a joyous occasion, as that very special freedom is now well within our grasp.

With an open heart, I wish to share this spiritual gift concerning our remnant of the Second Temple, which provides the foundation of understanding that the Third Temple is to be built upon. From the living word of God now revealed to the House of Israel, all seekers must complete the bridge of God to humanity, thus enjoining this world in which we live to the world that is soon to come. No longer left unheeded, may we build this unity in His oneness of brotherly love as a testament to His divine teachings.

A new commandment I give to you with the blessing of our God: Build the third temple within each Salem upon His living word of truth, that shall endure in every temple throughout the world and for all time. No one can destroy it and no one can take it away, for it is built with the eternal bond of love found only in the everlasting covenant with our one God and creator. The third temple must be viewed from within each person upon that soul's readiness and commitment to ascend. The third temple is our covenant to this inner reunion with God.

* The House of Israel is all of humanity who seek God in truth, and within the souls of these true believers awaits our temple everlasting; for one and for all!.

FREE CHOICE

Free choice is a gift that presents two paths to follow,
the coarse outer bark or gentle mystery of the hollow.
The familiar is the favorite as too many base their existence,
on the road taken wrongly...the path of least resistance.

We must refrain from this fear the human eye cannot see,
by embracing faith in our Lord and heavenly powers to be.
We are no longer children that too greatly fear the dark,
raise your spirit to adulthood so the angels they may hark!

"There is nothing to fear but fear itself" you have heard oft,
for the Lord stands at our threshold with a greeting so soft.
His departure is on schedule and the arrival time precise,
shall we greet Him courageously or as frightened as mice?

A pure and simple choice that each soul is free to make,
continue in spiritual fear or establish faith no one can take.
Place heart front and center as you gather yourself together,
before opening this door without knowing the weather.

His eyes shall meet yours in final judgement thus complete,
one moment will tell all as you look straight or toward feet.
His sincere hope is your greeting open hearted with love,
as we well know through scripture He is sent from above.

We must crucify our inner selves there is no room for error,
of critical concern is keeping our resurrection from terror.
Evil influence all around us places a great fear deep within,
confront this outside invader now and exorcise every sin.

There is no area in between us or territory to call gray,
repentance is our last hope with free choice gone astray.
Look beyond that surface which is pleasing to the eye,
for the truth of eternal life is not having to ask why.

Each of us has been schooled from the world of upward mobility,
now travel within this journal to the Lord's inward nobility.

*To understand heavens riddle we must learn to play second fiddle.

HIS NUMBER FIFTY DOOR

Understanding is the final summit upon each sojourn as we seek,
the true meaning of life in every soul our spirits eternal peak.
This wisdom reaches from our inner self as the outer soon defies,
the call from God to every child... please meet My loving eyes.

The knowledge gained in each new day shall push us ever higher,
to this temple mount that dwells beyond the voice of His desire.
From Egyptian bondage and forty years to stand beside His Moses,
atop Mount Nebo the desert bowed to behold His bed of roses.

The road is long and stops are many for some it is forty-two,
as in the days when faith was challenged answered only by the few.
Who see the light which lies beyond the pathway of our minds,
as darkness fades and blindness ceases we loose the tie that binds.

Spirits trapped so well confined must declare our will to flee,
these prison walls of earthly fears that keep us far from free.
Each encampment has a place in time but its purpose only rest,
stay not too long for we must go forth and leave an empty nest.

Our journey home is forever forward not back the way we came,
where herring run its life soon ends let us travel not the same.
The Star of David now points the way for body up toward soul,
as the climb brings focus to a spiritual peak our everlasting goal.

From twelve o'clock high a hand above we travel nine to six,
this descendent path of material life weighs upon the soul as bricks.
As we shed this burden and continue forth ascending to His spire,
leaving sin behind is a lighter yoke on our trek through every fire.

The heat is only a passing test and dry well a fleeting thirst, as
we gird our waist in truth and grace each last becomes the first.
Let us forge this path in spirit strong the body shall not yield,
a temptation placed upon every life brings danger to each field.

A lighter load the walk now smooth as curves turn into straights,
a guiding friend is steadfast still His name three figure eights.
As we reach the top and check our gear as a body quite in shock,
there is nothing lost along the way if the spirit sets our clock.

To reach the point of no return as our flesh transforms to soul,
each death shall die to life eternal as we walk within the whole.
The view on high was a treasured gift where Moshe led the poor,
now seek the One who walks you through... His number fifty door!

HE COMES ONLY DRESSED TO TEACH

Take pen in hand and write this simple prayer for all,
that invites each of God's children to His final altar call.
The Lord is our God, the Lord is one by heavenly decree,
our Father who art in heaven with Son and Spirit equal three.

Mary is our friend forever as this count now climbs to four,
Moses, Buddha, and Muhammed walk us nearer to His door.
Onward we must journey toward that blessed day of peace,
for each body to understand our soul merely signed a lease.

Nothing may be bought or sold upon this earth or heaven,
so return His precious Sabbath and embrace our lucky seven.
These numbers that we call have no bearing at the gate,
two kings named Martin Luther stand within the figures eight.

The passage through India, Gandhi and Teresa did design,
storming past human doctrines floating hope upon cloud nine.
Our living God is active still dwelling faithfully among men,
His trials and commandments produce a minyan made of ten.

How many must be sent as the tally rises beyond reach,
Remember always heaven's promise...
He comes only dressed to teach.

FROM MOUNT SINAI THROUGH MEGIDDO
TO MASHIAH AND HOME

Messiah is now poised and ready to re-enter this earthly plane of existence as the scriptures do proclaim, so let us greet Him with a most proper reception of hopeful expectation and joy that His longsuffering has not gone unheeded. The disparities among our sacred and moral institutions has left the new multitudes without proper direction, as this generation lost seeks a fertile ground of hope. The divide and conquer strategy of our nemesis is now reaching into the sanctity of our homes, and we can back up no further than self. Where do we make our final stand against evil while the soul is being placed in peril?

I say that we must hereby defend in a manner as of a life and death struggle now, for there is no further room to recede. The yetzer ha-ra (evil inclination) and the yetzer tov (good inclination) are the daily warriors that we as their battlefield trod upon, and until we decide the outright victor by removing the other from our being, the battle remains lost. Armageddon is a place within Megiddo of northern Israel, the geographical site of several historic battles between good and evil forces, and where the final biblical battle is prophesied to occur. For some it is a day in the far away future, but for others it is an imminent and deadly confrontation. The real Armageddon dwells deep within our very souls, and although many battles have been lost there, we can still win the war when true faith rises up. If we understand that this war is ongoing within, then the ultimate victory is sweeter with the enemy revealed, and thus exposed and defeated by eternal truth and light.

When the conquest of self occurs in this physical state of being, the soul is set free to then follow its development unhindered. The battle of Armageddon, like other biblical prophecies, is a call to spiritual and not physical arms. Throughout human history we have reached for physical ideals and thus failed our spiritual souls in the process. May you win your battle most decisively as a soldier in the Lords army, and return home as a hero dressed in white, wearing His imperishable crown of witness to these three eternal truths... *His Torah, His Christ, and His Light.*

THE LAMB NO LONGER SILENT

His word is being sent along not only just to me,
for as you read and digest slowly it speaks most clear to thee.
Without true understanding wisdom's knowledge cannot be,
so seek that special place within this faith which makes us free.

In our world of great distraction focus sharp upon His grace,
as soul and body agree as one to share this warm embrace.
If you believe this gift has dwelt in just one time and place,
I say to you one checkpoint only not the finish of His race.

The spirit of Christ is an education that travels forth in time,
rising up when needed most, God's rhythm and His rhyme.
To walk again upon this earth and to rid our souls of crime,
a bittersweet taste is sin to love choose the lemon or the lime.

Our course of travel is not a line that journeys from A to Z,
this track is oval as souls return upon the road back to Me.
God's living word is a guiding light our beacon on stormy sea,
The Immaculate Conception one more time by heavenly decree.

As His counsel turned to council all the pureness drained away,
when human doctrine takes center stage it turns into a play.
For no religion can claim a throne of truth on Verona's day,
as the hour closes and each has failed whose turn is it to pay?

God has forever promised and still dwells within our reach,
this meeting place of every soul that invites Him in to teach.
His vow to each remains alive made both to saint and tyrant,
our gifted grace within each life... the lamb no longer silent.

THE ONE WHO SITS ATOP ZION

Concern yourself not with explaining the unexplainable,
but rather echo the gifted psalms within your heart,
still maintaining that keen focus so long ago established,
by staying razor sharp from the end to the start.

There is no differentiation between any of God's children,
in heaven above or upon the earth far below,
as we are forever one for all and forever all for One,
understand this simple truth while you grow.

Into all that you can be when the victory is finally won,
from the inside on out of Life's tree,
where these branches do sustain every soul with pure faith,
ears shall hear and willing eyes shall soon see.

The eternal truth planted within is our war cry indeed,
as the enemy must be defeated and then chained,
with the yetzer ha-ra which surrenders without condition,
to the yetzer tov where the Lord has remained.

The only battle worth fighting is from the confines within,
where we determine which force is friend and which is foe,
there is no longer time to hesitate as the battlefield appears,
choose the Lord who sends the dove and not the crow.

Each mission is to now answer this spiritual call today,
no longer drifting upon the seas of temptation,
and to keep our feet firmly planted in the truth of His doctrine,
as we reach out to each people and nation.

This war has been blazing since the days of Adam and Eve,
when the serpent deceived true faith in the garden,
this terminal generation is where we make our final stand,
as the multitudes have crossed over the river of pardon.

Recall Gettysburg and Normandy as great turning points in history,
not by design did you understand their true impact,
for they grew far beyond their missions original intent,
thereby preserving the higher purpose still intact.

When Jehovah (YHVH) goes to battle it is on the side of the just,
overturning the tables of our adversary's detailed plan,
as this scale can be tipped when the numbers remain close,
although today we have lost the strength of inner man.

Each departure from the good has greatly weakened our cause,
and we proclaim as God's soldiers dressed in white:
The final battle shall commence by our home in Megiddo,
near the mount where we first welcomed the light.

Our most loyal vow in truth travels onward through time,
far beyond the physical confines of this earth,
for that covenant never dies within the spirit of God's will,
as death shall be conquered bearing the sanctity of rebirth.

Come forward to the inner altar of peace where truth does reside,
dropping the sword cast by evil in molten iron,
joining together with our forces in this righteous resurrection,
you must be born again to the One who sits atop Zion.

GOD'S SPECIAL PLACE

Each day I rise swiftly to thank God within and above,
for the beauty of His whole creation and all that I love.
There are so many things to do and so very little time,
please share this simple truth in our rhythm and rhyme.

If not me well then who and if not now well then when,
is to grasp His true will concerning women and men.
More than listening is to hear and truly looking is to see,
understanding our most gifted path upon the road back to Me.

We never ask Who for the answer is always me,
nor do we ask What from the powers that be.
We cannot ask Where for the answer is right here,
or simply ask How for that gift is crystal clear.

We must no longer ask Why for the answer is why not,
and especially not When for this answer has been taught.
The When is today so put aside self for others,
and the Why comes to life among sisters and brothers.

The How is as plain as the nose on your face,
if the Where is unconfined as to time and to place.
The What begins with oneness for the Lord is our God,
as all else is the Who that departed Eden east to Nod.

The road has been long and the questions beyond count,
but until stepping forth we cannot reach the temple mount.
Truth of witness births justice as a gift of His loving grace,
may your journey dwell within where you shall find... God's special place.

WITHIN THE SOUND OF SILENCE

There is only one universal law between heaven and earth,
and that is the Law of One upon the origin of each birth.
The gift of free choice is life's lesson that we must learn,
for this can only be understood upon its gracious return.

To remove self from our being so that His light may shine through
is the sacrifice needed to combine me and you.
As the many become one both in spirit and in mind,
we shall realize the great importance of none left behind.

This life is a team effort between God and each other,
to remember always the greater good serving sister and brother.
When we stand to the side and let our spirit take the lead,
soon the body shall bear witness to this miraculous deed.

To live on with the excuse that this world moves too fast,
and that our lives are so busy we have forgotten the past.
Is the deterrent to truth which hinders souls from their rise,
a great misfortune indeed to not reach the ultimate prize.

If we separate much further and at this most dangerous speed,
the glue can no longer bond together our heavenly creed.
Please take stock in this matter for at once is quite late,
as there is no further purpose for opinion and debate.

To place self upon the altar of God's temple deep within,
is a most worthy commitment toward the destruction of sin.
For the impossible to us is not so throughout His realm,
where we relinquish the reins and return Him to the helm.

It is very difficult to hand over the keys of life's control,
but to do so is true wisdom thereby serving every soul.
This free choice we treasure does not serve our spirit well,
if still focused upon our Eden where the myriads have fell.

There is no greater freedom then enslavement to God's will,
as we break the tie that binds us remaining patient up until,
His word arises as evil falls in surrender to every violence,
that still small voice forever speaks within the sound of silence.

THE WINDMILLS OF YOUR MIND

When one grows into two and then those two turn into ten,
very soon you have a minyan saved and that is just in men.
Increase this faith and follow truth in every step you take,
as our vow remains forever young a bridge we often make.

Where did we come from many ask as raindrops from the sky,
a living water quenching every thirst a fountain flow on high.
Some believe and some do not so stay the course we drew,
and keep your eyes upon His path that all may start anew.

Why they wonder could we not wait until their time is passed,
as many lives hang in the balance with evil spread so vast.
Most concerns shall mainly center on self and not on others,
that bond has lost its will to give a loving share as brothers.

How can this be when wealth abounds and comfort reigns supreme,
an illusion lives within the soul's reality through dream.
So test the spirit of each one's gift an ability born to share,
the love that stems from deep within our missionary's care.

Who stands behind this master plan as many wish to know,
the answers loom in every heart that seek His special glow.
Still burning bright as darkness fails the purest color white,
our kindred spirit remains the same through every day and night.

What must we do to reach His light as life spins far too fast,
slow down the speed so all may see their future in the past.
In present time we lose our focus on truth becoming blind, now
seek the crown that dwells beyond the windmills of your mind.

LISTEN TO THE CHILDREN

When our voices echo loudly interrupting earthly peace,
listen to the children, and our anger soon shall cease.
As we hasten off to war with every righteousness in tow,
listen to the children, for only they can truly know.

When vengeance is our will a confrontation must then follow,
listen to the children, who are the hope of our tomorrow.
The battle cry so often heard shall lure us to his den,
listen to the children, for the who what where and when.

If we only react to each attack it feeds the evil hunger,
listen to the children, less the older more the younger.
These souls are wise beyond our years do not be fooled by size,
listen to the children, for it is written in their eyes.

An action must be taken but before we shoot each gun,
listen to the children, that represent the Law of One.
They possess a universal wisdom far beyond our furthest reach,
listen to the children, for these students come to teach.

Slow down the speed of retaliation and ponder every option,
listen to the children, who are sent for our adoption.
A moments pause before each reaction shall never hinder fate,
listen to the children, that know not to take the bait.

God now returns His very best to earth a Hall of Fame in souls,
listen to the children, as they earn all leading roles.
Do not expect cooperation when it comes to supporting violence,
listen to the children, as they pierce the sound of silence.

As we fight and grieve it wears us down in war we cannot win,
listen to the children, that have conquered earthly sin.
Recall the scripture as Christ stood tall amidst defiant rage,
listen to the children, that were with Him in that age.

Messiah lives among our ranks His time is not quite yet,
listen to the children, who have paid their karmic debt.
Stop and pause to focus prayer upon the ones we've lost,
listen to the children, before we pay the final cost.

There is no winner when it comes to war especially in these days,
listen to the children, while reconsidering all our ways.
The only place to answer seek is the mirror of our souls,
listen to the children, for they bring strictly heaven's goals.

We can finally hear this freedom call to God who dwells within,
listen to the children, for His response on how to win.
We beckon Him to aid our cause before He does decide,
listen to the children, that feel the ebb and flow of tide.

Ask each one how their spirit feels beyond the age of three,
listen to the children, while they climb upon each tree.
In every nation and every realm what do the masses seek,
listen to the children, for they are indeed the earthly meek.

Which country stands within God's favor amongst its gilded past,
listen to the children, whose patient love is spread so vast.
The eagle once a favorite son has lost its wings to soar,
listen to the children, that walk peace through every door.

The media shouts a fevered pitch which only raises ire,
listen to the children who have walked beyond the fire.
We seek with anger a retribution that's not our father's will,
listen to the children, for they have swallowed every pill.

This tragedy looms on each horizon with many bodies spent,
listen to the children, that shall witness He who sent.
We are in the days so long foretold do we escalate the fear,
listen to the children, who still embrace our God so dear.

* Each time I think this book will end it speaks another page,
I finally listened to the children, they said this is the age!

THE WAR THAT DWELLS WITHIN

Throughout human history it has remained our greatest sin,
no weakness can compare with these soldiers made of tin.
From each tribe to all nations the evil path forever followed,
so much promise lay in ruin with that pill still being swallowed.

Regardless of our reasons and rationales we deem as right,
when choosing the mark of Cain we remain fated to his plight.
No enduring glory is possible through the acquisition of land,
nor does power produce favor in God's eyes or in His hand.

It is our physical earthly appetites born of envy and each greed,
that keeps us spiritually apart from the Lord's will to feed.
The manna from above that serves as our peace everlasting,
for without this eternal nourishment it is better to be fasting.

In each worldly confrontation there remains no permanent gain,
from the temporary meal of war that passes through us in vain.
One course may be righteous while another feeds on lust,
but the soul cannot develop proper as the body returns to dust.

How often must we witness before truth takes its final stand,
from the highest court of peace to lay claim upon every land?
As the spirit of every soul that has passed by the only Lord,
echoes clearly His sentiments to make ploughshares from sword.

We must separate this strong soul from the weakness of our flesh,
to assure safety far beyond the great reaches of His thresh.
The wheat shall be bundled and stored safely in His barn,
as the tares are being burned while still entangled like yarn.

Have we still not learned our lesson through failure of war,
with not one redeemed nation why do we come back for more?
This supply line must be cut for it leads only to disaster,
for our sustenance in this life is the road back to the Master.

He waits patiently and calm at the door of each heart,
please invite Him in faithfully to thus gain a fresh start.
His kingdom is at hand and there is no longer time to wait,
send your invitation at once that He may tip the hand of fate.

That has plagued and befallen every civilization to date,
may we kindly share this food only served upon His plate.
As we now fully understand the painful errors of our ways,
that has hindered the Lord's teachings to the end of all days.

Let us join ranks at once with His worthy sons of light,
for this final battle uphill while they wage the good fight.
Of every conflict yet created through the shortcomings of men,
this group forever pays the price as the righteous number ten.

The sons of Zadok remain true to every cause sent from heaven,
so answer each one your calling and raise that figure to eleven.
They are counted in each tribe and are great disciples who delve,
into true faith as our Essenes when the clock approaches twelve.

For as that moment draws near are you awake and well prepared,
to defeat the real enemy on his turf that has kept you ensnared.
Spiritual freedom has a hefty cost can you pay the total bill,
to ease His burden is a great reward if you walk atop that hill.

That stands above the highest clouds no eye could ever see,
His mansion holds so many rooms to house both you and me.
Dear Lord please grant us mercy and forgive our greatest sin,
then join with us in our final charge;the war that dwells within.

THE ROAD FROM GLITTER TO GOLD

To become fully aware of who we are and can be,
we must understand who we were when our spirits were free.
Mother Mary and Christ Jesus are the twin souls of one,
and *The Immaculate Conception* is their story undone.

Through this great faith and sacrifice mercy returned from the Lord,
upon the road we must also travel far removed by the sword.
When we eliminate the pursuit of each material possession,
gifts of spirit are then granted to remove every obsession.

By refusing the poison fruits of physical temptation and fraud,
places us safely back upon the road that leads only to God.
His living word is now at hand within the reach of each heart,
where brotherly love serves us well as His gift to impart.

Placing self before others is the detour that you see,
preventing safe passage home upon the road back to Me.
Your map is this journal in these days of great separation,
as He calls one last time to each people and nation.

To come forward in unity not by race or religious belief,
remember always He arrives quickly as that biblical thief.
This earthly life as you know it is cyclical and of one,
the byproduct of this promise that thine will shall be done.

Each entity within the universe understands its true calling,
only humanity disavows this sacred bond forever falling.
We must reverse direction immediately and righten ourselves at once,
reclaiming spiritual freedom from the pray Satan hunts.

The time is now upon us when we can no longer fully comply,
to the gravity of earthly dictates with the spirit running dry.
Our sustenance is the manna that only emanates from heaven,
not the pleasures of the eye producing lumps in the leaven.

You ask fervently through prayer how to break from this grip,
as life's journey is now teetering on stormy seas as a ship.
Go inward to your soul and focus clearly upon His spark,
that is gifted to each person where the angels sweetly hark.

Now sing that music soft and sweet from our glory days of old,
as sparks ignite the eternal flame; turning glitter into gold.

TILL SHILOH COME

When peace is announced the final battle shall begin,
for it represents the forces from without not within.
As Clinton realizes his departure with Arafat close behind,
this "treaty" with Israel is the false tie that will bind.

Not one to another as they would have you believe, but
rather an increase in bloodshed as the multitudes grieve.
Have we not learned our lesson by the will of these three,
as personal gains take precedence over both you and me.

They are reacting upon the influence of life's evil force,
we must distance ourselves quickly and choose proper course.
In scripture we are assured that our leadership is appointed,
by our father in heaven assigning only the anointed.

These and many others have since dissolved while in term,
let this danger be revealed thereby eliminating their germ.
I do not proclaim violence when calling for this change,
rather faith in God's word to help broaden the range.

The minefields are many with those legacy's at stake,
by overlooking the common good for their personal sake.
Clinton has so failed us that he seeks desperate measure,
at the expense of a peace we have long come to treasure.

On the surface he shall disguise the true meaning of accord,
knowing full well the consequences only sharpen the sword.
Which the evil one wields from the east towards the west,
as our sense of safe distance shall be put to the test.

At Pearl Harbor we awoke late to a shock beyond belief,
that alarm clock is much quieter then the shrill of "The Thief."
For this war is now blazing in the dimension known as four,
all troops I call to active duty so strife shall be no more.

The holocaust was a test of faith as in the days of Noah,
"the church" did fail in silent song befallen by the Shoah.
Become a universal conscience in mind comprised as one,
whereby the unity of God's command is built upon His son.

His echo rings to every land as the pang within each heart,
to change the fate unsealed today that end can be our start.
From the Bible, Torah, and Koran we find the path of truth,
Buddha talks and Christ still walks to aid our aching tooth.

That must be pulled for pain to cease as all's been said before,
now walk beyond the days of Moses through His number fifty door.
Accept this challenge open heart and try your soul's true worth,
is it fire tested from high in heaven the place of every birth?

There is no haven or refuge from our capitalistic greed,
as we join the Kittim of an evil past in corruption of His seed.
Planted once in loving grace but now so rotting to the core,
as we turn our backs on God's true will no better then before.

The eagle's wing has lost its soar not by the works of one,
but o'er the years desertion looms when relying on the gun.
Our rewards have been abused and evil appetites increased,
to the point of self destruction when the palm is being greased.

When the good is gone and bond decayed no longer are we great,
our world must turn around today or face the coming fate.
Let faith arise in such a way that we crave God's living word,
the road back home our final call His song so seldom heard.

New Jerusalem is the true bride not the beauty of the beast,
God's hope is for not one to perish and all attend His feast.
The rise and fall of human spirit still a factor at this time,
until each tribe can come to terms war lives within Ephraim.

* The promise made shall never die as told to more then some,
that all may see beyond this world; keep faith till Shiloh come.

U_ _ _Y

Let us reflect upon one word that stands for the true principle of this life,
in fact the very essence of our being.
It begins with "You" and ends with "Why",
a gift from God once welcome but now fleeing.

Established from above and then passed to earth below,
always sent with an abundance of love.
From Father to Son and Holy Spirit
as one it arrives on the wings of a dove.

This is our true connection to the heaven each one seeks,
in this lifetime and the one soon to come.
That shall echo through every land from the pangs within each heart,
our hope is for the many as opposed to only some.

Life has always been about our treatment of the gift,
time and again we have freely chosen to reject.
The unbounded love of God for all of His children,
best reflected in our diversity of each sect.

There are limitless human doctrines and not one without flaw,
for in humanity we have forsaken His perfection.
When presented in the flesh those that did not rebel openly,
have since done so by further breaking this connection.

Let us focus our spirits upon the cross and its meanings,
and ask ourselves about these most critical tests.
Do we live within the oneness that our Father so desires,
or in the separation to which the evil one attests?

Flowing robes and ornamentation are merely decorations within the sanctuary,
and not what the Holy One does seek.
The road back to Me is upon the avenue of pure heart,
our special cup prepared lovingly for the meek.

The most important holy day is the Sabbath of God's rest,
and on that simple truth we do not even comply.
By exercising our individual will in contrast to God's plan,
is not partnership but rather the means to defy.

If we truly are sincere to make amends with our Creator,
then return to His Sabbath at once.
Where common ground is reestablished upon the pathway of His word,
and not the greed which is the prey Satan hunts.

The Day of Atonement is Yom Kippur held so dear,
that special moment when every Shofar cries out.
A new start we must make for it may well be our last,
can you assure me otherwise beyond any reasonable doubt?

The further we drive down the evil path of separation,
from one another and then ultimately from God.
Shall create greater despair in this world of confusion,
stand together but far apart from His rod.

To each nation and era He has come to establish,
the truth forever planted as our seed.
Though the body has taken so many different forms,
His spirit is the same purity of breed.

What humanity wrongly terms as simply diversity of beliefs,
is not any of our self righteous concern.
Take heed of our own soul for there is much work to do there,
hear these words spoken truthfully and relearn.

The covenants once established cannot ever be broken,
for in God that vow stands forever firm.
It is humanity that has defaulted thus betraying this pact,
through earnest prayer ask to renegotiate each term.

Although we have failed miserably throughout the course of history,
it is not too late to call upon His name.
That we understood once so very long ago,
and through our changes He remains ever the same.

Man's inhumanity to man only divides each of us further,
reaching the solitude and precious sanctity of each home.
Do we continue upon this road of self destruction and despair,
that only leads to the eventual fate of Rome?

Forgiveness of our sins from within the sanctuary of God,
is not located in any confessional bin.
Nor the church, temple, or mosque rising up from the square,
but in the comfort of each heart deep within.

Can you understand now how the world pulls apart,
beginning with the dispute of one day.
And the deity of one soul that achieved true perfection,
as our teacher who still points the right way.

There are many places and times the Holy Spirit has surfaced,
each gift fully complimenting the other.
As this very special treasure belongs to each caring heart,
that is willing to become sister and brother.

The only pure religion known to God in our reality,
is that which we as humans call love.
Impressed simply upon the heart so that all may embrace,
this eternal faith from within and above.

Now return to the first sentence and reflect with deep thought,
upon the three letters still missing from the middle.
The answer appears on the surface quite simple,
but truly feel the greater depth of this riddle.

A Hebrew name for God is spelled without vowel,
which is proper when reading from the Torah.
Right to left is the direction that the ancients prefer,
with holy scriptures in the soft light of Menorah.

This duality is relative to the very essence of God,
that not only creates but befriends.
Fear means respect and hate only less preferred,
for His means serve to justify those ends.

God is not simply apart from us but also dwells within,
and as we abide He rises swiftly to the fore.
As a friend and not a foe as so many do believe,
please welcome His grace open door.

With our hearts front and center which is where they belong,
this journey is now well on its way.
Toward the brotherhood we understand as a bond with our Creator,
only then shall we truly welcome His day.

Both answers as stated are one and the same,
take the obvious and build from that point.
Kabbalah works the hardest and are warmest to My clue,
but quite cold toward the one I anoint.

The greatest among your ranks do not accurately compare,
to the heart of one very special lion.
That sits upon the cusp of that dreaded disease,
much closer to heaven then Zion.

Do not ever underestimate the ways of the Lord,
for His purpose is the only one that shall stand.
As the drum before promised is now gifted and ready,
to beat slowly and bring forth heaven's band.

The one I send ahead of Me has passed this way before,
and shall travel the high road once again.
This spirit of which I speak cannot be found where you seek,
for he is well concealed among the average of men.

The main criteria to consider is the birth date of this drummer,
falling squarely upon the ninth day of Av.
Your calendars are close some only five days off course,
consult the mystically most reliable Rav.

This date is rather tricky as it leaps to and fro,
nineteen days hence from last year to this.
The same number of benedictions as in his Shemoneh Esreh,
when you added one to this Amidah of bliss.

His spirit was awoken from a very deep slumber,
on New Years five seven five seven.
Arriving safely in the temple a short time thereafter,
as sent again by the powers high in heaven.

Very difficult to detect in the shul or on the street,
for his number is not counted among men.
Each Sabbath he prays with you and when minyan is unreached,
your count is nine but My tally is ten.

What year you may ask did this spirit arrive,
in the flesh and from which port of call.
Five seven one six is your one final clue,
from mystery "Babylon" with the demeanor of Paul.

The firmament above commanded the waters below,
to be enjoined as one and thus they were.
Now let each of us volunteer likewise by increasing our faith,
casting aside the delusional gold and myrrh.

This one word that I emphasize as the key to our destiny,
flows powerfully within the currents of each verse.
Grasp it with all your strength and do not ever let go,
for it comes to you as a blessing and not a curse.

This simple request understood by the many,
but abused by the powers of the few.
That seek the poison fruits through self-indignation,
return to Me and I shall assuredly return to you.

Much poetry has been woven into this manna from heaven,
and shall take time to be digested and discerned.
As the answers from above come through loving prayer thus given,
by the teacher whose chosen students have since learned.

To share the oneness of God within the true spirit of faith,
by fulfilling His commandment of love.
Sets each of us free from the confines of this world,
upon the wings of that beautiful white dove.

My plan is not yours for how long would you have lived,
upon this earth if I remained out of sight.
From the Garden at Eden where My word was first sold,
your beginning could have been the end of this plight.

More important then earthly life was the trust thus established,
and when broken your greatest gift was born.
Forgiveness through mercy by the suffering of one soul,
brought your faith toward salvation once torn.

Bring a focus with prayer to the innermost of your being,
for that is where I truly reside.
Not a million miles away between the "You" and the "Why,"
each heart and soul is where together we confide.

The secret meaning of life is held back for good reason,
never found in the distances you travel.
Embrace every goodness and I shall shepherd you home safely,
to an eternal peace that dwells far from the gavel.

In regards to heaven's quiz concerning the channel of this journal,
a member of the Great Assembly is correct.
But only in part for he has lived before and after,
as an entity that proclaims our secret sect.

Travel back a little further to the challenge upon the mount,
when the Baalists were on the verge of control.
For he was present on that day and stood firmly upon that peak,
as I answered him body and soul.

Recall My response when he cried out that day,
that the idolaters sought his life too.
I have reserved for Myself seven thousand of true faith,
that have not bowed to Baal just as you.

This faith is not written upon tablet or stone,
nor in the scriptures of any humanistic belief.
At Carmel that day the true Essenes did emerge,
and have since flourished within the teachings of "The Thief."

My word is not passed along upon parchment or scroll,
but only surfaces as a wellspring from the heart.
Within those deemed most worthy long before they are even aware,
it rises again from the end to the start.

This drummer to whom I speak has awaited patiently his drum,
and as before thus fulfilled our master plan.
Through true faith and not reason he now prepares the Lord's way,
choosing pure heart over the avenues of man.

Each incarnation he steps forward is your sign so desired,
knowing full well that I am not far behind.
Time and time again we have rehearsed this production,
as those that truly seek Me shall find.

When Rome entered our land and brought forth pagan worship,
we faced oppression that divided house loyalty.
Many chose to remain and plant the seeds of rebellion,
others commingled our pure faith with their royalty.

The Zealots and Sicarii were our warriors in those days,
as these seeds of revolt were being sown.
While the political Pharisees were too busy saving their own skins,
blinded to truth and the living Torah thus shown.

Zealous and jealous are the best words to describe,
those attitudes and behaviors of that group.
As the events in Jerusalem that brought down Jeshua and then the temple,
were the direct result of their evil concocted soup.

The Saduccees were bystanders amidst this great turmoil,
playing both sides most cleverly against the middle.
As Essenes we did our best to preserve the true remnant of Israel,
you are very close to the solving of this riddle.

Our separation from all entities left us a very small sect,
and the issues that divided us were quite few.
Ritual water purification and our understanding of resurrection,
which is reincarnation of spirit through and through.

It was not difficult to prophesy that many worlds were colliding,
as the prospect of destruction was at hand.
Preservation of the sacred writings was utmost in our heart,
as we left again for the Salt Sea and desert sand.

Our mission is always focused upon protecting the gift,
as God's living word once again must go forth.
Lest we dare to not recognize the eternal winds of life's meaning,
blowing briskly west from the east, south, and north.

On Erev Israel the Dead Sea Scrolls were the shower gifts,
heaven's acknowledgement of this long awaited birth.
As those branches grow tender and their buds bring forth fruit,
the coming harvest shall attest our true worth.

The holocaust was the labor pains in those days before state,
a final travail to precede the blessing of God's truth.
That His sacrifice be remembered and tender mercies confessed,
as in Job, the New Testament, and Ruth.

The Immaculate Conception was authored long ago,
not simply written upon this journal you now read.
For time is quite different in the annals of our history,
My request as always is to please serve every need.

Our teacher and friend is now calling once again,
for our UNITY between each branch of Life's tree.
Whether Elijah, Ezra, or the Baptist named John,
through God's grace please understand it is He!

Amen.

GOD'S PROMISE IS ALWAYS NEAR

Please come in from the cold and embrace His true flame,
to many this shall be different, but to me quite the same.
I have passed this way before and now return once again,
bearing truth of spiritual witness to the families of men.

This journey has been long and the battle always uphill,
but we continue to march forward as each knows the drill.
Of our commander in chief to every soldier that steps forth,
we shall conquer each territory from the south to the north.

Then east toward the west as gospel lightning does flash,
the Son of man changes pace from His marathon to dash.
In the blink of an eye shall His mission be thus complete,
as truth crushes its bitter enemies namely lies and deceit.

There is no pardon available if draft dodging this call,
so prepare yourself quickly for there is no time to stall.
If you put off repentance and the acceptance of inner truth,
your vote is cast accordingly in the holiest polling booth.

Never has a war commanded such intensive preparation,
as this one final battle shall soon encompass every nation.
All deferments are thus denied seek not any further reply,
for His eyes no longer weep when the tears have all gone dry.

He has nothing left to give us as His burden goes most unheeded,
myriads of years in pain why have we not yet fully conceded.
To His loving sacrifice and compassion painted on many an altar,
but unlived by those He most entrusted that continue priestly falter.

The gentile time is now quite full as holy scriptures do proclaim,
only a semblance of the true Christ lives apart from all the shame.
The Lord is now a warrior sowing truth and justice in His name,
Do Not relinquish our hope in faith for His mission stays the same.

His methods shall confound so many but His virtues hold forever true,
the gift must be acknowledged by these many and the few.
All eyes shall soon be opened wide and each ear that wills to hear,
"God's Living Word" come to life again in His son held oh so dear.

We offer this invitation as an eternally divine promise as well,
for tomorrow is much too late if today sounds the heavenly bell.
The enforcement of His cross has become a most unpardonable sin,
this justice shall weigh quite heavy as a punishment from within.

This price must be repaid in full to My children first begotten,
for our covenant never dies nor the House of Israel be forgotten.
Shema is still our affirmation strong let it ring out one more time,
as you comfort in our truth and grace feel the rhythm in our rhyme.

When the Law became of no effect a greater sacrifice was made,
Torah and Christ are building blocks, the foundation God has laid.
For one is truth and the other grace depending upon your view,
the mirror image of one another when true faith is found in you.

The promise has now arrived on time upon this winged dove,
listen closely to its sweetest tune that is echoed from above.
As we pull the house together from the four corners of the earth,
death shall no longer have dominion here or share in this rebirth.

Take this journal to your heart and soul for that is why it came,
to build our temple once again upon the glory of His name.
Each person and nation may rise again to water His seed with love,
but the increase can only come about from our Father up above.

The unseen enemy is now positioned behind plus left and right,
straight ahead and within is the true direction of God's eternal light.
Do not quarrel with your brethren but rather unify in force as one,
as chaos and much confusion shall then reload that deadly gun.

That must at once be all dismantled placing peace upon each table,
where truth shall once again be heard over fiction and every fable.
Life can be quite simple when embracing faith as our only guide,
then attune the ear of our spiritual soul on this final heavenly ride.

* Understanding is the weapon of choice in defeating apprehension and fear,
"The Immaculate Conception" once again ... God's Promise is Always Near.

Introduction

In the beginning of this experience, the messages came forth in the form of daily logged journal entries (Part 3), at first very brief and then expanding according to an ability to accurately receive and record. (Part 2) It was not until much later that this journal began to take shape (Part 1), and then evolve into final book form over this seven-year period. As you shall read by the times of day entries, most writings have originated directly from the sleep state, whereby the original messages were penned almost immediately upon waking at various intervals. The later writings and undated poetry were mainly received in like manner during this period of normal sleeping hours. Only on rare occasion would the calling to write occur amidst active daily routine.

The following morning these notes would be typed and then placed in the folder chronologically, before attending to normal daily tasks and schedules. Actual sleep was minimal and irregular for quite some time before adapting to this method of delivery, and needless to say there came about a total transformation of personal life relationships and activities.

In retrospect it comes as no great surprise that the apparent randomness and near chaos of this physically unorthodox method, would turn out in the long term to be so spiritually orthodox, well organized, and precise. By removing self-desire and then focusing upon spirit delivery, the mission then began to smoothly flow once pure faith took its rightful place at the lead.

Early on I understood as you also shall, that we are simply earthen vessels of a far greater power, and when our will is contrary to this master plan, there remains only conflict within and without our being, that only serves to stagnate proper soul growth and development. Enough said regarding personal circumstances and opinion. There is a spirit world at work within each of our individual worlds, that must keep both positive and negative energies in balance. If this were not true, we could not exist in the presence of our Living God, much less one another. Today is a good time to begin reuniting with our better half...(soul) by seeking inner truth.

Travel with this book beyond the physical comfort zones, to an area of inner being that is far more critical to universal conscience and soul understanding. When we venture beyond the temporal restrictions of our five earthbound senses, into the limitless full potential of our sixth sense born of spirit, a whole new world of wonder shall open up unto each willing and able human being, where forgiveness and not wrath awaits us.

Prayer, meditation, and good works, shall be our escort on this road back home to God. As we journey closer to understanding, we shall first pass the checkpoints of knowledge and secondly wisdom, as each station must be visited and cleared in their appropriate order.

Though the physical body may rebel, to fully comprehend "the word", we must fixate in spirit upon the source of its message as being directly spoken within us, to us, and for us. This channel shall first help improve our imperfections individually, and then collectively.

Look not toward doctrinally main line religious or secular correctness only, for they are lacking in terms of the far greater spiritual truths that we actively seek. The scriptures of each one God religion are divinely inspired words, that serve us well in spiritual lesson and are timeless in their guideline, but we must take those long ago directives to the next level of actual practice if we are to grow into the Oneness of God.

Reincarnation, or resurrection as it was once known, is referred to openly within each testament and religion, but we in the western world are called heretic if we dare believe. The return of souls is an indisputable fact of ongoing life experience, and an immutable law of the universe, which far exceeds any human law or religious order for that matter. I say to ye of little faith that do not believe, patiently test this spirit within true or false, for why else do you "think" Christ reappears; for His own spiritual good or for ours?

Each religion has failed miserably by its doctrinal effort in keeping us falsely grounded. Congregational worship within the human community is still our religious bond toward one another, but true spiritual edification must rise up and present itself, if we are to make this leap of true faith in God that is quite contrary to restrictive dogmatic beliefs. The biblical "miracles" are products of pure faith exemplified beyond historical reason, but since when does limited reason have jurisdiction over our limitless spirit soul. We are holding back our full human potential by allowing the finite mind its earthly control, while the spirit soul of truthful understanding lies subserviently dormant. Is it not time to shed our dead and decayed outer skins of age-old doctrines, and rebirth our souls divine spirit of truth, as we now depart Pisces for the new age Aquarius?

As the universe and its contents continue in motion so also must we, or be left far behind. Human corruption within our "higher" societal institutions has too long distorted pure Godly truth, and we can no longer tarry, by allowing mere mortal interference to shape false beliefs, thus barricading an otherwise clear and true path to our own God within. Whether we spirit adapt accordingly or are left far behind, is again a matter of free will. This journey will have its difficulties for each reader, but maintain strong faith and perseverance as the bends, bumps, and curves upon this most worthy road shall soon straighten, smooth, and then safely deliver each eternal life to its true heavenly home.

Spiritual truth can only come unto us within the avenue of soul and its pure Godly will, and although in bodily sin each of us is fallen, we may rise up once again upon grace!

THE ETERNAL DECLARATION OF INDEPENDENCE

Love is the greatest gift that our father bestows upon us, and true faith in return is a proper acknowledgement of this grace. It is those of an evil generation that require a sign in order to believe. Is not the evidence of life itself within humanity's knowledge of its limitlessness, coupled with the constant renewal of creation each day, more than ample testimony as to the power and continuing graces of a most merciful living God and king?

Belief which comes to light primarily through fear, lacks care and compassion as the essential elements of unrestricted love. The gift well received produces joy in abundance, while the enforcement of this gift is indeed contrary to its very nature. This loving and caring spirit which is God, comes freely to each, so freely give in return according to the measure of your faith. The source of perfection lies within the hearts of all who seek it, whereby this pursuit of understanding through free choice enables God's unlimited truths to supercede our limited vision.

This area of which I speak is the "kingdom of God," an indwelling territory often mentioned in scripture, representing the final destination that we must reach on earth to achieve life everlasting. Those who come forward in their own name are historically well received, but the souls who bring the word of God are continually rejected. This barrier to understanding must be removed at once. Humanity must cease its emphasis upon self centeredness and move on.

Many will tell you of earthly things, but I shall continue to echo the true sentiments of heaven to all ears willing to hear. Test this spirit true or false, but be subjected no longer to the dictates of false doctrines that persist in today's world. Each religion and sect has their own set of beliefs and virtues, but not a single human agency has achieved the purity of truth. Physical knowledge is simply temporary and of this world only. Spiritual wisdom is our pathway leading to eternal understanding. All three of these pursuits are attainable in the here and now, and to fully realize the whole we must add the sum of all parts. This must be accomplished in exact sequence.

One without the others is an incomplete formula toward His truth. His laws, His Christ, and His living word form this triumvirate. This spirit of understanding although other worldly in its origin, must be assimilated into our very being as an acknowledged gift. As we strive in unity toward God and then one another, His desire for our oneness through Christ's teachings shall not be in vain. "There is only one to call teacher and that is the Christ spirit."

Class is now in session as the teacher resumes His lesson plan. As the world begins to take on an unfamiliar and far different physical form, seek God's living word of truth before the time of great tribulation, fully realizing His spirit of love as an eternal part of our very being, quite capable of understanding and conveying this infinite beauty in the world soon to come. Those who pride themselves on the pursuit of physical knowledge based primarily on logic and reason, are shortchanging their total being on the weightier matters of eternal life through directive spirit.

All religions have somewhat failed in actual practice, due mainly to enforcement of human laws and doctrines which misrepresent God's eternal law of conduct and commandment to truly love one another. It is human beings that are unforgiving and unwisely still judge. People of today seek an inner church to attend, whereby faith may be given to God without interruption or human corruption. Faith is the best offering as our declaration of independence.

War is hereby declared upon all religions and belief systems which obstruct the natural pathway of God's living word to us! Doctrinal enforcement of self centered religion shall no longer be tolerated among people whose spirits call for true liberation. The historical confrontations between egotistical main line religions has accomplished nothing in terms of redemptive value. Our houses of worship are not near empty only because of human indifference or religious complacency, but rather the breach of trust that has occurred between bureaucratic religion and everyday people.

Any belief system which claims its doctrine superior to another, has dealt God himself a tremendous blow in His war for ecumenism. As we go forward in unity according to God's truth and not our own, the teacher stands before us at the podium once again, declaring to all ears willing to hear... His living word.

If anyone is wondering who authored *The Immaculate Conception,* it shall soon become quite clear that this work is not a human endeavor, but rather a heavenly one by divine commandment and covenant. The only human involvement is in recording and fulfilling this eternal promise.

At first, I was that frightened child in all of us, who stands alone at the edge of that infamous pool of water, while being told that everything will be fine when we finally jump in. As we carefully survey every danger in our immediate future and surroundings, there is the everpresent reality that this water is over our heads, but of no real threat to our receiver. Our hope is the parent whose assuring arms and confidence will serve as the safety net in this soul searching leap of faith. Encouragement is the key determining factor during this eternity in time, as we plunge head first into the great unknown. While submerged under water we wonder whatever happened to those seemingly firm and outstretched arms of our hope, when suddenly we are scooped out of the drink as if by some miraculous rescue. Unrelenting joy is the best description, and for the first time in our young lives we realize that victory is ours over fear. Let us leap forward in spirit today! God is our father who stands in that pool, waiting as long as it takes for us to take our leap of faith into His awaiting arms, this life's greatest reward and eternity's finest treasure.

Separation from one another is separation from God as well, and if we do not accept this truth as self evident, then we cannot begin the healing process that commences with repentance. Human divisions through race, color, creed, nation, culture, religion, etc. has so extended its boundaries as to now include community, neighbor, church, household, and even the territory of self. Where else can this cancerous enemy go before we defend our very souls? Never in our known history has a war been so devastating, and as the casualties mount we refuse to meet evil head on. In terms of survival, the human instinctually will act in partnership versus any invader if our existence is threatened. The only real battle, confrontation, and war in this lifetime must be fought and defeated within the framework of self. Evil as an excuse must be minimized and then eliminated, as we move toward the light of truth without it.

The call for this most critical unity among humanity is now! The final dividing line is drawn and soon all others shall be erased. Daily life upon earth is a series of victories and defeats, and in our quest for truth and unity, we should never give up the good fight along the well lit path that God has set before us. There are those of us who strive to open new doors, and also those of us that insist upon closing doors, as well as those who block the doorways of doors that are padlocked from truth. Let none of the above deter us from living God's truth, which far exceeds any individual concept of our own self truth, and may His light shine forth into the proper relationship He so desires to forge, both with and among us.

Our abuses of free choice have formed an insurmountable barrier throughout the course of our history, that only God Himself can remove when we ask Him to do so with unified prayer, good works, and a return to true faith which shares love in common. The time has now come for the great spiritual revolution, whose battlefield is located deep within each of our very souls. The obvious weapons of destruction are those free choice abuses, and the foothold evil has upon us must be commanded out at once. Although this war is invisible to the untrained eye, the results of its deathly destruction lies all around us in plain view. The victory of good depends upon our will to repulse, and then replace evil with that goodness of everlasting light.

The Immaculate Conception is forever our map and guide to spiritual freedom, which like every other freedom comes only with a price that we must be willing to pay. That premium can only be true faith, and its portion is to be paid up front. I have heard it said that freedom is never free, but I say to you that eternal spiritual freedom is far more expensive. There is no type of knowledge which exceeds pure kindness, nor a branch of wisdom that extends beyond care and compassion, and most important of all, there is absolutely no form of gifted understanding to serve any greater earthly purpose, than God's commandment of brotherly love in truthful and devout practice. Knowledge, wisdom, and understanding, are three distinctly separate and progressive earthly gifts, freely given and readily available to each of us without partiality according to grace, not through the human channels of logic, reason, or rationale.

When the aforementioned appropriate works accompany true faith, thus fulfilling our collective calling to unity and common destiny, whereby individualism is sacrificed in favor of God's true will towards oneness, only then shall we receive our spiritual gifts as divinely appointed and without expectation. Any service that we provide in this world on behalf of God, should be counted only as a repayment toward accumulated debt. If true understanding of God is that which we aspire to, then it must be precisely upon this road that we travel back to Him. As our world drifts ever further away from His core human principles of divine purpose, hold steadfast to good faith by not allowing any influence to take it from you nor from those that you love.

The solution to every dilemma is our faith toward God within. This inner faith surfaces as we continually pray with sincerity, and if it is straight from the heart He responds without delay. He may not always give us that which we want when we want it, or what we feel deserving or undeserving of, but He always provides us with that which we need according to His desire, regarding our soul's best interest.

Our limited perspective of God is due to our applications of free choice, which confines our otherwise unlimited potential. His viewpoint is the scope of all that exists both on this earth and beyond, and we must respect and confide in His judgements. As the clay to the potter, who are we to question our creator?

We sincerely hope this calling will best serve humanity by sharing with an open heart, *The Immaculate Conception* of our experience. Feel His living word speak...and the truth shall set you free!

There is a distance that we have created between God and also one another. *The Immaculate Conception* shall close this gap once again. The one who is greatest among us, falls far short of human doctrinal law perfection according to the letter of its nature, but it is the merciful spirit of God's truth and grace law in practice, that allows each of us a closer walk with He. Our vehicle for this journey is only pure faith, and the sacrifice of self will is its sustenance. With self will aside there is no deterrent to the energy that each soul must attain, as we reflect and not destroy the precious energy fields of one another, that welcomes our bonding light to God. The entire history of our earthly existence is predicated upon the conflict resulting between differing beliefs blocking light, and thus preserving darkness to our detriment. As light enters a dark room, even in small portion, it is defeated by that light.

A final word to each religious affiliation, sect, or individual belief system of this world in regards to God's truth: Pursue the pathway of truth through the channel of soul understanding, without forsaking our living God's ability to further teach each of us today and hopefully tomorrow in accordance to plan. Handle all truths with extreme caution, and remember always that human doctrines are derived from our nature of imperfection. Judgement is reserved for powers beyond humankind, and beliefs are nothing more than the carry forward of human conceptions. Traditions and cultures are suitable identities for proper physical world practices, but have no redeeming value in the spiritual. No religion of human origin is one hundred percent accurate in all of its claims, for in humanity there is no perfection. The very best that we can hope for in this lifetime is to strive towards that perfection which is God's love within our souls. This can only occur through first our own individual, and then our completely united spiritual transformation towards oneness. This is God's true formula for setting human unity in motion; first within and then without.

If indeed we understand that no human being is perfect, how much easier to understand is our compounded imperfections in tandem. The greatest challenge to unity is not in our belief systems and their differences regarding doctrines of truth, but rather in their enforcement upon others which displays a lack of intestinal fortitude, hindering forward progress and ultimately God's truth which lies beyond debate and scholastics. These poison fruits of free choice are the only obstacles to unity, centering upon our selfish instead of selfless nature. Bringing our total being into focus and balance will allow for God within to effectuate His plan for our greater good. He knows better than we what is needed toward improvement.

This requires a complete severance of the physical appetites we tirelessly feed, in favor of spiritual healing that we most desperately need. Putting our lives in their proper condition is not an easy task, but is essential to achieving life eternal. Individualism and self servitude are deterrents to the good fruits which God wishes for us to freely partake of and cherish. Let us sacrifice free will and this self servitude upon the altar of salvation and mercy.

These latter days of which the holy scriptures clearly speak are now upon us, and we must decisively answer our collective calling as a unity of one. It is good to believe that our universal faith is well founded, for in unbelief there is no avenue of hope. This special faith in God comes directly to each of us through the channel of His holy spirit, and is our only pathway to eternal life. We need to listen carefully to His inner voice of divine command, by awakening at once from our most dangerous spiritual slumber. If I could guarantee you that contained within these upcoming pages is the absolute cure for cancer, would you take the time and effort to not only read but to also understand them? If not for the sake of saving yourself if so inflicted, would you not at least extend yourself for another whom you care deeply about? If your answer is yes to either of these questions, then I ask you to please continue on. Our greatest battle is ourselves, and every earthly war is its compounded effects. When we defeat ourself, there is no other enemy to fight against, in this world or the world to come, as God's victory in us shall bring peace.

Far more critical than any physical cancer is the everpresent and all encompassing singlemost deadly spiritual disease, that imminently imperils the entire spectrum of earth life today! Beyond any natural force it is the greatest killer ever known to our world, and destroys not only the physical being but far more importantly displaces the spiritual. There is no easy way to present this but if allowed to continue flourishing, it shall very soon bring life as we know it to the brink of destruction. Is this not truly a just cause for our finally establishing a universal human unity versus the forces of our every self inflicted evil?

The compelling evidence is indisputable and surrounds us in plain view on a daily basis. As jurors in this case we must either convict or acquit the offender, but we can no longer stand by in the state of eternal deliberation. Temptation is its territory, and our only defense against this unwanted invader is that pure faith in God through our gifted free choice, combined with a keen spiritual focus found only contained within a truly repentant heart filled to overflowing with earnest and sincere prayer.

Self imposed evil and all of its poison fruits are the common enemies to our Godly nature, that have systematically consumed the very fabric of our human morality, thus placing collective humanity itself in critical condition upon the path of life on earth's once hopeful and peaceful continuity. The time is soon coming and already is, for each soul to choose the side that best determines its fate both individually and collectively, as divinely created products through God's most amazing grace. All are God's children with a birthright born of spirit, so let no influence stand in the way of your perseverance to His calling, a straight ahead and focused quest towards the imperishable crown. Make no mistake about it, the war to end all wars has already begun above in the form of spiritual revolution, that shall eventually culminate with the scriptural promise of our physical witness. The entire membership of humanity can no longer embrace spiritual neutrality, and believe me when I say that each and every vote is counted most dearly with God. Armageddon is the within battlefield upon each soul, that must stand and deliver for one side or the other. Choose for the soul, as the body has only a fleeting lifetime.

God has forever campaigned tirelessly on our behalf, asking only that we assertively and decisively exercise His gifts so graciously given, by aligning ourselves with Him both physically and spiritually. This display of intestinal fortitude requires an absolute commanding out of His adversary and ours that dwells deep within and all around our very essence of being (selfhood).

The very best that I can offer in words is to state emphatically: Do not remain stagnant in between these two distinct mind forces of power within the midst of this great and final battle. Stand clear but forever remain dear to God and one another. At this very moment in history, we as humanity are being brought to our collective knees both literally and figuratively, before the judge of our soon to be departing free choice. Which judge shall you opt for in this case of eternal consequence, lest one be appointed to you by any further transgression or hesitation? Choose for self or God, but tarry no longer indecisively.

Please join together in fervent prayer for the continuity of this most precious gift called life, that our ever merciful king may resurrect in each of us His blessed holy spirit. Let us echo a unified and resoundingly affirmative plea to He who answers prayer. This humble and sincere request of forgiveness must come straight from the soul with a sharp spiritual focus that will defeat any and all distractions to the contrary. Our Father's response to this earnest prayer shall be profound and clearly decisive, if our repentant heart opens truthfully to His will and not our own. Eternal salvation is the crown that each person seeks to wear, and through the very special light of our living and educating Christ, we may reach the mountaintop of God's everlasting kingdom in the world soon to come. His long awaited bride shall arrive in all her glory as our own New Jerusalem (wedding). Let us no longer subject ourselves to the other judge in question, lest we follow in self's most deceptive footsteps of physical appetites and temporary world gratifications, leading only to the eventual demise of our gifted eternal spirits. Selfhood must bow to Godhood within, once and for all!

May the words of King David to Gad (not God) some three thousand years ago, still remembered in the beginning of Tahanun prayer, be our constant guide and companion in these forthcoming days, "I am deeply distressed, let me fall into the hand of the Lord for His mercy is great, but let me not fall into the hand of man." This is the choice that each of us can still freely make if we recognize the seriousness of these critical latter days, clearly described by the prophets and well documented in the holy scriptures of most every belief system known to humanity.

I was asked to return to the poor in spirit there needs, by relaying the knowledge, wisdom, and understanding as gifted through this journal of spiritual experience. This special unity of life's oneness is accomplished within the context and testimony of "God's Living Word," (Part 2) and our pathway of right direction set on "The Road Back To Me" (Part 3).

Kindly ask for understanding through deep and focused prayer, that God Himself may speak with you in this book, as clearly and graciously as He has spoken with me. Let knowledge evolve into the gift of wisdom, that can only be given and not attained, that you may also bear the good fruits of His love and resurrection found deep within the words of... *The Immaculate Conception.*

* The only aspect of this experience that remains unwritten, is the voice of our Lord so graciously given.   Amen.

Part Two
God's Living Word

THE TERRITORY OF CHRIST AND SATAN
WITHIN GOD'S UNIVERSAL TRUTH

For this journal to fulfill its intended destiny there must be a true understanding regarding Christ, and our false belief in the actual existence of a Satan, Lucifer, the Devil, etc. Throughout human history, as in the recordings of most every culture and civilization to date, we have assigned this adversary as the reason for our human failures. In universal reality there is no such entity apart from our own free choice inventiveness. By continuing to believe in conflicting forces at work within this world, we have hindered the progress of our soul development, thus setting up a good versus evil, light versus dark battlefield, that allows us to await outcomes that cannot occur, without decisively changing our ways and thus acknowledging spiritual truth. Good versus evil is decided by free choice, and the removal of self will is the final victory. This endless cycle must be broken, if we are to move forward in our soul development.

As in the physical realm of life, we have now also distorted the spiritual, and thus continue to restrict proper soul growth that could otherwise be attained in the here and now. Why do we wait for the transition called death to hopefully ascertain God's will, when it is well within our gifted domain to bond our will to His truth while on earth? We have created evil and all of its poison fruits through the thoughts, actions, and inactions of human weakness and sentiment. Let us destroy these contrivings of the mind at once, and allow our soul its proper pathway home. We can no longer live within this misunderstood and empty cycle of soul entrapment, as denial only serves to delay the desired spiritual connectedness of each living soul its return to God.

Evil is the invention of our mindset, that is a map of wrong direction pure and simple, forever providing reasons for our failure to decisively seek the light. Let us no longer hinder the natural progression of any soul upon its journey home, and may we instill the positive universal energies within one another as God truly desires, whereby war and conflict shall cease without, when so commanded from within. When the supply line of evil (sin) is cut, it can no longer survive. Sin is the only sustenance (food) that evil can digest, and we become its energy source by continuing in adversarial behavior.

The only barrier to every universal truth is our very selfhood, and its removal leaves no further obstacle to our oneness, and limitless potential as total beings most pleasing to God. The Christ educator within is our guide and Satan, as evil (self) its antithesis, as upon this truth we may return home...beyond the end of days.

EVIL

Evil is the antithesis of good and serves no other master outside of itself. It is about our choices pure and simple, and can no longer erringly serve as the reason for our shortcomings and transgressions throughout earthly life. The very essence of evil is completely dependent upon the sin that "we" feed to sustain it. As we reduce sin in our lives each day, the territory of evil continually weakens and finally disappears altogether.

Throughout human history we have allowed the humanly created entity still known as evil, to persist within our beliefs and mindset as an external force to which we then become victimized. This is no different than a child's unfounded fear of creatures and tales that do not exist beyond the youthful and overactive imagination, thus producing more attention than it deserves or warrants. Evil does indeed exist in the human consciousness, and has been expressed worldwide by countless performances and episodes, but the truth is that we not only create it in thought, but have further developed it through actions. Now we must defeat it through disassociation and our total conviction of will power, as its reality is only relative to our perceptions.

Boredom with life's inherent goodness has been our downfall since departing God's oneness, as opposite and conflicting forces such as good versus evil has forever been our collective object of curiosity, and each well knows what that did to the proverbial cat.

The recognition that we assign to evil is the fuel that elevates its standing in the human psyche, making our mission of its removal increasingly difficult. That which is not love is not of God, therefore it is of the earth and is thus destined to remain earthly; while we as human beings must move forward; thereby ascending heavenly. In most every civilization and culture to date there has been a profound belief in evil. Where goodness abounds there is no room for evil, and it shall cease to exist in any form. As we return to God within our very being, soul focus becomes that which is pleasing to God and through prayer, meditation, and good deeds, we discover that simple mention, display, or thought of evil is repelling and discomforting to our proper life balance. The inherent beauty of this life is best reflected in God's unconditional love toward us, clearly evidenced by all of life's blessings in the daily renewal of creation's gifts. If you must insist that evil is a real force in our universe, and thus provides excuse for negative action and immoral behavior, understand that all force is under the constant supervision of our one God and Creator in this and every universe, whereby any life force is simply a mere function of God's master plan at best.

There is an immutable law within our universe that is not subject to beliefs or interpretations, yet still remains elusive to our western world doctrines: Souls forever return in order to perfect their pathway back to the Creator. Once is not enough for any soul.

This law of cause and effect, also known to us as karma, allows each soul a multitude of earthly lives in which to manifest a proper soul development, thereby qualifying return. When the barricades of temptation, deception, distraction, and the like are taken down by free choice, all that we categorize as evil simply vanishes in favor of universal righteousness. Extremism such as Fascism, Naziism, Socialism, Imperialism, Communism, Capitalism, and all other "isms", are real to the world until we freely choose to eliminate their source of greed for the one true source. These are much more difficult for it takes their revolutionary death to accomplish, whereas our personal enemy of truth can be defeated without weapon as a sole function of human will. By disregarding evil and all subsequent trappings and characters, we shall weaken its imaginary hold upon us, and as light replaces dark, good replaces evil whereby Messiah's path is thus cleared and made straight once again.

MESSIAH

Messiah is not simply a flesh and blood human being, but rather a spiritual import that patiently awaits our soul invitation of partnership through proper preparation, development, commitment, and expectancy found in true universal understanding. Messiah as the anticipated one of most every religion has never left us as humanity. This Christ is God's holy spirit of light that forever guides each soul upon its long journey home, as the only teacher and minister of universal truth upon this earth. This spirit influence dwells in bodily form throughout human history to help move humanity forward, and is lowly, modest, and humble in its physical form.

It is the combination of cooperation and coordination between each of our life cycle migrations, to thus assist in each soul development throughout the universe; culminating with the outgrowth of this individually serving messiah from within. Messiah in its earthly portion completeness is the full realization of body, mind, and soul, toward its intended purpose within the essence of God's unity of oneness. This is a divinely created educator that ministers personally to each soul according to the universal law of cause and effect, based on our free will associations and soul readiness. This within of which I speak is our lifeline to God, where He has forever agreed to meet and minister unto each soul eternally. There is no end to life when referring to the soul, and there is no soul within body that was not lovingly created from our beginning. The messiahship potential is present within each person and in each lifetime, while patiently awaiting our call to unified action. The doctrine of separation is its barrier to proper growth, as we must look beyond the confines of physical earthly appetite. Darkness cannot contain this light, when we fully commit our souls to its removal.

Each religious, national, ethnic, cultural, and limitless other human divisions shall very soon gravitate us toward unity, as high speed diversity must prostrate to truth.

Let no religion or government of this earth further corrupt and confuse our right to spiritual gifts of God, by the enforcement of their respective doctrines and beliefs. Where human council has replaced and thus failed spiritual counsel, we must now stand and resist. The only satisfying church to the human spirit is found deep within each soul, not in the judgmental outer sanctuary of today's impotently bureaucratic houses of worship. Faith and good deeds are requisites in this life, but they are not a form of business, nor showpiece for personal or group recognitions.

Mainly due to our continued failings through external influence, let us each go within ourselves to ask and then listen for the answers to our unending questions. Institutional religion is afraid of us learning these truths, for it renders their external mission unfruitful. Prayer is the only communication avenue to God, as meditation shall bring His response. The "shepherds" of the flocks have failed by esteeming themselves as such, when their true mission is to develop and then promote each sheep from flock to shepherd. We must at once take command of our soul and redirect it upon God's pathway well lit, so that spiritual freedom may echo soundly from each life, a resounding affirmation of return to the cherished oneness once departed, as self will is then sacrificed upon the within altar of truth and grace. Whoever, whatever, wherever, whenever, whyever, and however you are upon this earth; go home to God in peace. You shall find Him in your silence. Amen.

SATURDAY, AUGUST 23, 1997, 1:52 AM
A CALL TO MISSION

The time has arrived for America to become a missionary to all nations. In so doing, she will in turn be missioned to by the earthly poor she serves, who in reality are the eternally rich. By truly attempting to give, we shall assuredly receive a far greater reward, otherwise unobtainable in our current state of being. Loving God and neighbor with all our heart is life. Prepare a loving place in each earthly soul for the arrival of He that created this heavenly domain. Eternal comfort and security is achieved only through faith, while earthly appetite is merely the nourishment of insecurity.

Give freely and willingly whatever is asked of you without any expectation of return, knowing that your father in heaven has done likewise for you. What do we have that we did not receive from God our Father? Pure wisdom is to likewise give. If you truly desire to find the way upon the road back to Me, then follow the heaven lit path of *The Immaculate Conception*.

If salvation is sincerely sought after, please help to prepare the way through true repentance of sin, earnest prayer to Abba, Father, and begin to walk as Christ does in the laws sent by commandment. God chooses us out of this world, we do not choose Him, so kindly present yourself and others as holy, blameless, and devout in prayer, for He is most attuned to our heart and not our words. The silent soul is our true voice.

Always give thanks through times both thick and thin, for His love is everpresent as a trademark of this covenant, whereby patience and longsuffering are paramount in hopeful expectation of our safe return home through the gate of the good shepherd. Our spirits originate in heaven and are fire tested on earth. Believe in the Lord for He is our "full armor" versus the extreme temperatures of all temptations. By opening our hearts to a far better way we can help change the world; one soul at a time. (Pray Ephesians 6:10.)

WEDNESDAY, SEPTEMBER 3, 1997, 6:33 AM
THE CHALLENGE OF CHRIST

The standard that determines real intrinsic value, both in human endeavor and spirit, is the eye. If the eye is good then we can be assured that the light is everlasting. The academics of the teacher, Christ Jesus, must now progress beyond the earthly classroom into spiritual practice, whereupon successful graduation lies eternal life for all who believe. We must become that which is He, for as He once plainly stated: "You are Gods." The time of which He spoke has now fully arrived. Our world leaders so oftentimes appointed by men are far too infrequently chosen by God. Recognize each by the fruits that they bear, for true wisdom is found in attunement to the latter. Those that walk among us bearing witness of the Lord, seek heavenly rather than earthly reward; so also should our selected leadership. Test those spirits for this most critical truth.

How can any person acting in true representation of God, accept or acknowledge personal credit for the works of the Holy spirit? These two distinctly opposite influences are contrary in nature, and as we well know by now; God and mammon cannot both be served. The only membership to which Christ belongs is the Holy Trinity. The bridge that He continues to build today spans all religions known to humankind, each as a byproduct of His original oneness. Individualism is the end result of progressive dividing lines created by humanity, commencing with nations and concluding with self, to include all separations of the original church of God. No religious sect holds the true answers to God's eternal truths, for they are freely given to each soul when ready, and only then.

We have officially entered into the biblical period known as sorrows, and should thus prepare each soul accordingly for the upcoming journey. Spiritual preparation is most essential. The real challenge of Christ is to return all lost sheep to the awaiting good shepherd. While most are in plain view, we must actively seek the many that remain uncared for and hidden from sight, as well as those caught in life's various thickets. With tragic consequences, the Lord has begun to teach us through the errors of our ways by bringing forth the media, its performers, and performances to judgement.

SATURDAY, SEPTEMBER 6, 1997
OUR ONLY GIFT WORTH GIVING"

The scriptures are now speaking much louder than words,
to all ears that are willing to hear,
Sorrows is in full progress as the Gospel's have promised,
overcome each apprehension and fear.

"One shall be taken and one will remain,"
is the statement that I issued long ago,
The world shall soon witness all the errors of its ways,
with the departures of both good friend and foe.

As mentioned early on pay close attention to the speed,
that the world is increasingly spinning,
While the evil has grown so far out of control,
Self appears to be actually winning.

This trend shall continue for an extended period of time,
as the new multitudes choose the opposition's side,
The frontrunner is the bandwagon that so many climb upon,
through delusion a most dangerous ride.

Momentum is a phenomenon that entraps the bulk of individuals,
who no longer desire my living bread and water,
When mob psychology is the rule the herding instinct takes over,
and the most intelligent are easily led to their slaughter.

Throughout your extended history in evidence time and again,
most recently in the second world war,
Where lunatics amidst frenzy dragged millions to their grave,
and very nearly placed the end at our door.

Dividing lines are an element that humankind has created,
contrary to our wishes from above,
Clearly drawn in the sand between each and every nation,
fully developed when all question our love.

It is unity that we seek in a world riddled with separation,
the exception in these days not the rule,
If true faith is maintained in God's plan from the beginning,
remaining steadfast is your most precious jewel.

Now open all eyes before blindness sets in,
and I shall display wonders to those willing to see,
Repentance is the ticket to eternal life through salvation,
guaranteed safe passage home on the road back to Me.

So many fine works I have produced in your being,
and many more shall I graciously provide,
Before the actual second coming on that great and dreadful day,
a grand finale to precede one heavenly ride.

A final request is to search the fields over,
so that My lost sheep shall not stumble or falter,
The Immaculate Conception holds the key to life eternal,
a loving heart is the only gift worthy of My altar.

SUNDAY, SEPTEMBER 7, 1997
THE ADVENT OF SORROWS

This world wide weather pattern commonly known as El Nino, is in reality our formal introduction to the beginning of Sorrows. The "Christ Child" translation of this term is mystically appropriate; especially when considering the biblical prophecy concerning the end of days; as told by Jesus in the Gospels. "For nation will rise against nation, and there will be wars, famine, pestilence, earthquakes, floods, and other worldly troubles. These are the beginnings of sorrows." (MARK 13:8) The tremendous percentage increase of natural disasters in the past fifteen years, and the extreme fluctuations in climatic conditions throughout the world, are far more than remote coincidences or simply attributable to only global warming.

There are currently some one hundred and twenty conflicts, and thirty-six wars being monitored world wide. Judge for yourself.

MONDAY, SEPTEMBER 15, 1997
LAST CALL TO ALMS

Increase prayer, meditation, and begin to practice fasting, as this will elevate spiritual awareness and diminish physical desires that are contrary to each other on this earthly plane. While constantly attending to physical stimuli, a life that progressively spreads out by overloading itself in daily tasks, cannot give proper consideration in time or effort to the equally important requirements of the spiritual self. Instill discipline.

Over the course of time, whether by day, month, or year, this original balance at birth has been shifted far out of balance. At the conclusion of each physically tiring day, there is more often than not very little energy reserved for proper inner reflection or thanksgiving to God. As days turn to months and then years, we begin to spiritually starve due to a lack of essential nourishment necessary for our total beings survival.

The spiritual portion of our lives has suffered severe neglect in the majority of human beings, and as a result it will be very difficult for this weakened spirit to propel our total being into eternal life. If we do not energize and nurture this critical element of life, there is a distinct probability of self destruction and subsequent extinction. Before dismissing this statement as far fetched or unrealistic, take a good long look at the times all around you. Is this world, in its current state, the byproduct of a loving God's peaceful coexistence, or an embattled and separatist based greed filled individualism?

He is demanding unity now, because we have approached the point of no return, and His longsuffering shall not further tolerate the evil we have collectively adopted through our misused gift of free choice. This is humankind's last call to finally awaken. It is an understatement for me to say that prayer, sacrifice as deprivation of want, brotherly love, genuine care and compassion, charity, forgiveness, repentance, and faith are critically required demands upon us at this very late hour. Please do not leave for tomorrow that which is undone today, for as we well know... tomorrow is promised to no one.

SUNDAY, SEPTEMBER 21, 1997
A DAY FOR UNIFIED PRAYER

Throughout our entire history we, as humankind, have endlessly aspired to seek the mysteries of God and His world, through the brightest minds and greatest scholars ever born of flesh. By applying every conceivable technique devised to this day, our true understanding remains hopelessly unfulfilled.

I make you this pledge, that all truths which God chooses to provide shall soon manifest themselves through the most unlikely of sources, by the pure and simplistic form of unified prayer. Their basis of research is faith, and as God's elect, with a birthright born of spirit, those prayers will assuredly be answered. Feel free to test the spirit to confirm this claim.

Spiritual answers are unobtainable through a physical line of questioning. Spirit is spirit and flesh is flesh. The latter cannot explain the former even though it is contained within. In the gospel of John chapter three, Jesus is approached by a teacher of the Pharisaic Jews named Nicodemus. This religious mentor acknowledges that Jesus has truly come from God, for there is no other way to explain the wisdom through which He teaches, as he visits Jesus under the cover of darkness only. While questioning Jesus in regards to eternal life, the response was, and is, that you must be born again in order to reach the kingdom of God. Nicodemus did not understand then nor do most people today, because its understanding is reserved for those born of spirit. It behooves each of us to enter through the narrow gate where that which is born of spirit originates, avoiding the pitfalls of that wider entrance where flesh is undeniably fleeting. John the Baptist baptized with water at the river Jordan for the remission of sins, but only Christ can baptize with the holy spirit that provides eternal life. Jesus told Nicodemus that if he could not understand these earthly things, he would certainly not understand that which comes from heaven. *The Immaculate Conception* shows us the way to an eternal life of spiritual transformation, through faith in God and repentance of sin with sincerity of heart.

"GOD'S SIMPLE EQUATION" (WORKS + FAITH = SALVATION)

"Flesh and blood cannot inherit the kingdom of God," is a profound biblical quotation. It is our spiritual soul that goes forth.

We are all born of flesh and blood upon entering this world, and soon fall under the dictates of earth. God is our continuous overseer but, like any earthly father, will not fully determine our eternal destiny, that is partly based on freedom of choice.

Judgement is merely the formality that points the direction of the pathway we have already walked on earth. This portion is comprised of our words and works. The second requirement of God is that we believe in His only begotten Son, whom He sent to us in order that we may be saved through His sufferings on the cross. Remission of sin for all of mankind was the price of His sacrifice, and repentance is our individual responsibility in acknowledging the power of the life, death, and resurrection of Christ. This is our inner faith. (works + faith = salvation)

As you can now plainly see, works are the results of our physical being and faith is the product of our spiritual being. Now go back to the first sentence of this page and read it again.

The only part of our total being that can live eternally is our soul. Why would we allow physical criteria to sentence our soul? "As in Adam we all must die, but through Jesus Christ we all may live." If this statement is false, then our faith has no foundation and we remain in our sins. Can any of us afford to take the chance, and deny God's simple request for our salvation? The true believer knows the answer, while the unbeliever, or questionable believer, has nowhere to go whether they are right or wrong. There is no grace through doctrine.

I speak to each of you that has ears to hear and eyes to see, not in terms of audio and visual but of attentive spirit, that your wake up call is now being given. The time is at hand to put your houses in their proper order, and to settle all accounts with both your fellow human beings and God. I ask you to allow that portion of your heart which is God, to access my message which also comes from the heart, and grant the opportunity to listen carefully and truly feel. In this way the spirit of God can communicate from one to another without physical interferences that hinder spiritual progress. Our physical self must step aside, and allow the spiritual self an attempt to save the total self from its destruction. When self is met and conquered in total it may then be discarded.

Each part of the human body has a specific function that is unique, and critical to the proper coordination of the whole. No part is more or less important than any other in the eyes of God, for if any element fails then a need becomes evident.

When this occurs, the healthy members must assist in restoring the entity to normal by providing necessary aid. This condition must also be applied when it comes to individual members of our societal whole, each as part of the greater body of humanity and the even greater entities of the entire earth, universe, and beyond. As each bodily part belongs to our being, we belong to the church, and the church belongs to God. Therefore, all is God's, we in Him and He in us. Oneness through unity is our collective calling. It is time well spent to ask His forgiveness and believe in His Son Christ Jesus as our eternal teacher.

THE MESSAGE NOT THE MESSENGER

The importance of God's message is not the messenger. Focus upon the content of what He is saying and not through whom. Our physical nature is too easily sidetracked from the spiritual gift. Take it for what it is and nothing more. God has used earthen vessels throughout our history to relay critical information on a need to know basis. He is a living God who was, is, and will be forever involved in life. Human rationale has no relativity to our creator, for who will question that which made them? Recall the potter to the clay analogy. We are only a small segment of life and certainly not the whole show.

Solemn prayer is a critical element in achieving heavenly understanding. God knows our hearts and pays little attention to our words, especially if they are spoken without sincerity. When speaking with God, be found holy, righteous, and blameless without spot, utilizing true faith as an offering of love. If God judged upon our words, where would we be?

If you are to verbalize prayer, speak inwardly to your soul, for that is the location of His light everlasting. God is spirit. "Ask and it shall be given, knock and it will be opened, seek and you shall find," are directives aimed at the soul, whereby all the truths and mysteries that He wishes to reveal in His due time will be unveiled. Our time has little to do with it.

Most oftentimes when we pray, we are searching for the words to say through our mind, and we know not what to say. By praying from the heart, God speaks through us in spirit, using our voice to express the innermost heartfelt feelings. This form of prayer is genuine, true, and uniquely different on each occasion, easily accomplished for us and most importantly it is pleasing to God. This ability in prayer is attainable upon granted request for repentance, and far exceeds automatic prayer of memorization known as rote.

Pray in the spirit (soul) instead of the physical (mind) and you will be amazed at God's attentiveness. This is His residence where both faith and love abide, as truthful understanding and peace are His greatest gifted treasures in return for our sincerity. Pray Abba, Father many times with your soul and let this spirit overtake the physical. Strive for the spiritual gifts of God, and this "special" relationship shall flourish and be added unto you.

When the disciples asked Jesus what they should pray, He told them to say "The Lord's Prayer." Our Father who art in heaven, hallowed be thy name, etc... By omitting the remainder perhaps you will open to the New Testament Gospel and realize our aims.

Those of us that receive spiritual gifts, fully realize the responsibility which accompanies them. When you read Corinthians 1, they are accurately explained by St. Paul. There are varying gifts that are at work in our world, each as important daily contributors to the greater good of God's overall Master plan. Individually they appear to be trivial, but in tandem they become the main source of our eternal hope; in the form of unity. Each tile in God's mosaic is being precisely fitted for the most worthy purpose of His ultimate masterpiece. Unknown to the separate membership is the beauty that they comprise in unison. God handles all details regarding this cohesion. Diligently about their business they perform each task as required following the leadership of the holy spirit, often, totally unrelated to normal human endeavors and everyday routine. They operate strictly on faith, thus believing in the physically unseen but by no means unknown. This inner business of serving God is not a guessing game or a stab in the dark, but rather a service rendered from the soul where the light shines everlasting. Call upon Him in faith and He will answer. We may each become benefactors of this amazing grace, but must first bring our spiritual being back into its prominent role, as guardian of the total person which is then pleasing to God. Let the soul be reinstated to its rightful place.

We must authorize our souls to commandeer this eternal journey, that inevitably every developing person shall soon embark upon. Humanity cannot receive anything unless it is given by God. The evils and hardships that we witness daily are not of God, but rather of the earth, and the resulting human behaviors represent the byproducts of free choice gone astray. When we believe that the world's fate is left up to humanly weak determination and control, once again we display our lack of understanding concerning God's overall plan. Humanity does not discover anything, it merely uncovers that which already was given.

True wisdom is indeed a spiritual gift and not a physical attribute. God's plan, which is ongoing, shall only endure according to His timetable and not our own. Humankind's continued evolution is merely an allowed gift of our creator that may be revoked at any moment, and presented at judgement as witness to free choice gone astray if so desired.

Our excessive determination as a race to travel beyond the will of God, shall undoubtedly place us in difficult standing with He. My hope is that we are wise enough to discard the evil influences devised by the few but detrimental to the many, and remain steadfast to the principles of unity with God, established long ago as an everlasting covenant based on righteousness, truth, justice, faith, hope, brotherhood and unconditional love.

God is fair and shall judge us individually, but let us each make a valiant effort to assist one another in an attempt to achieve the oneness He has forever desired. We owe Him that and so much more, as our our souls continue on through grace and mercy.

THE WAR TO END ALL WARS

We speak only of that which is given, and nothing further, as these prayers center around a complete trust that we have in God, knowing full well the holy spirit shall keep us on course. We do not intend to be casualties of this war, but rather survivors who will be able to point our fellow beings in the proper direction. We are not preachers nor eloquent speakers, but rather good soldiers that can follow orders in a disciplined fashion, and thus relate these experiences in fact only truths. Feel free to draw your own conclusions from our testimony. We must become battle ready before the sands of life's hourglass run dry. This effort we make is not about fighting the windmills of Quixote and his elusive Impossible Dream, but an invisible foe that has left many visible casualties in its wake. This war is for real and the stakes have never been higher in our history of conflicts. God is warning us now to take up arms in the form of repentance and faith, then to march onward in unity toward the victory of our salvation, and everlasting life among His company of souls.

Bodies shall be lost but it is the spirit that we seek to save. If you choose not to join us, please pray for us as we for you. The true spirit at work in God is lowly, having little or no desire for public acceptance or human based elevation. There is absolutely no earthly appetite that requires being fed, for the nourishment of spirit is fully satisfied in the form of God given understanding. The difficulties that we have witnessed from certain cults, religions, and overzealous preachers, is not the message which perhaps is being received, but the lack of self control and discipline exhibited upon discerning that message in the light of physical influences and temptations.

Many well intended seeds or disciples of the word become lost by the wayside, as victims of selfish interjection when it spots a weakness to exploit. These people are to be pitied and not condemned. Their hearts were true but the word was seized. This example I give is only a slight indication of the craftiness and deceit to which the physical self subscribes. The Lord has prepared us throughout life for this confrontation, and we are ready to show others how to win this victory for God.

Consider yourselves as newly enlisted soldiers, and that your life depends upon preparations which you must make before going to the battlefront. We that are of the spirit have become well trained drill instructors, only taking our orders from the highest appointing authority. Find us quickly and incorporate God's will toward eternal life, by taking this critical stand. The time for action is now, so put on the full armor of God. Make no mistake about it... this is the war to end all wars.

The only way to collectively survive this coming collision of forces, is to unite in prayer for each other through God our Father, and remain steadfast to His commandments, in hopeful anticipation of the second coming and reunification with He. We must voluntarily turn from the errors of our ways, as individuals first and as a brotherhood next. Earnestly ask God to save each of us from the path of eternal destruction, and make a commitment that you will love Him with all your soul and strength. Do it not with lipservice but rather with faith. It is God's will that no soul shall perish, and that saving power shall sustain us.

Those that receive spiritual gifts are chosen for various tasks which coincide with each other, although we are unaware of how. That is not for us to know, because we would at some point incorporate a physically related cure for a spiritually oriented symptom, simply due to the fact that we are human.

God has placed His elect under the laws of grace, supplanting the former hold of self evil that is predicated on sin, of which we were all born into and once charter members. When you become born again, the old you has died so that the new spiritual you may live. There is no human intermediary needed in spiritual grace, although many church doctrines would have you believe it so. Our God is not about confusion but rather precise organization, and as long as we follow the voice in command, He shall deliver us into eternal life. Through His gift of grace, we may each become the benefactors of this special eternal life that forever goes on living.

Divide and conquer is the strategy of our nemesis, selfhood and evil appears to be winning in this world of separation. From nations versus nations, to the inner sanctum of the family, it has succeeded in distancing the new multitudes from our Godly commands. We must tear away from this deathly grip, and see through to the light everlasting, that can only be realized by asserting our gift of free will. Refuse to let evil pass sentence on your soul, by beginning to make right each choice from the heart.

People that depart suddenly from their otherwise happy and content life will explain the change as a calling, and inevitably become involved in some type of religious mission that harkens from God. Our particular calling does not seem to follow along a normal line of intervention, mainly due to a complete lack of prior religious interest or education in this life. Our particular call to battle has deep and imminent characteristics that center around an emphasis on unity, repentance, faith in Christ, map of salvation, brotherly love, advent of sorrows, preparation for spiritual war, wake up call to all who are sleeping, end of days, etc. which are probably common to many, but the word that comes through most emphatically is: a mission to serve the poorest of the poor, and by this we are directly referring to the earthly rich.

This message is a collective calling that is all inclusive to each who is willing to partake at this most critical juncture, and an open invitation to become born again through a drastic spiritual reformation experience, as provided for in *The Immaculate Conception* on a step by step basis of revelation. We are passing from the Pisces to Aquarius sign, which is water to air. This spiritual age is the propulsion and recognition of soul development over the physical properties of earth. As a rocket ship must shed its excess weight upon entering orbit with greater thrust, so also must our souls rise up to the source of each origin.

WEDNESDAY SEPTEMBER 24, 1997
WHERE IS GOD LOCATED?
(Look no further than within.)

Most of us, even after thousands of years in our evolution, do not understand where God is actually located. We believe that He exists but are unsure of His whereabouts, and pray toward heaven which we believe is upward. God is not only an external entity that is separate from our being, but more importantly, He is an internal spirit that lives in each of us at all times. God is not disconnected from us at any time, and awaits patiently our calling upon Him, at moments of thanks as well as of need.

We have placed Him at distance from us, not He from us. We are oftentimes involved in choices that are disapproving to God, and it is much easier if we pretend He is not there. As we continue to separate from our creator, due mainly to our abuses of free choice, we lose touch with His power of love that fortifies our soul versus the forces of evil (body), and we tend to develop in a manner that is contrary to unity and His desire for oneness.

If you truly are seeking God, then you must look inwardly with pure faith requiring absolute sincerity of heart. The kingdom of God is love, not located millions of miles away but buried deep within our hearts and souls as the essence of each life.

The temptations of this physical world are such that we do not grant proper attention to our spiritual self, which in fact is the only recourse we have for eternal life. This is a critical error that can cost us our souls development. By rejecting the dictates and temptations of earthly sin, we move closer to the spiritual priorities which are of God, and thus present ourselves in a more worthy condition, whereby His message may be received. We must bring into balance our total being, if in fact we desire to be judged blameless upon the coming day of the Lord.

Make a simple list for yourself using any period of duration that you wish, and put one category in each of two columns. The first is daily physical activities and the second is daily spiritual activities. Is the time and effort spent per day a balanced ratio? Please take a moment of most serious thought. Do you attune to the needs of your permanent spirit, the same energies that are granted to earthly appetites which in fact are only temporary? For any number of reasons or excuses given, the fact is we are perishing because of allowing the physical beings complete dominance over the spiritual through choice.

Modern day alibis do not hold water with God. We must be of little faith to think that God would not supply our basic needs. Does He not grant the most helpless of life forms a means of survival and sustenance? What we fail to recognize is the stark difference between need and want, and that shall be our downfall unless quickly reversed.

Once need is exceeded, imbalance among the entire membership is born, and subsequent greed becomes the dividing lines that polarize the brotherhood in a hopeless and endless despair. Blind and fools are we who do not see and then halt this pathway of eternal stagnation, by correcting the errors of our ways, so as to resume proper growth.

Speak to me of humankind's genious and I shall display to you our stupidity. How far along in real progress have we come? The forms of life including human beings that have gone without what we would term basic necessity, are the ones which draw closest to God and He to them. When your physical life's survival is challenged on a day to day basis, the spiritual part of your being rises to the occasion. That is why the chosen of God relinquish excessive comfort in favor of poverty, knowing full well that the spiritual will emerge as the physical decreases. The curse of our excesses is what convicts our soul, and regardless of which religion or belief system we subscribe, it is difficult to disagree that this earthly life is temporary.

These people of whom I speak realize the necessity for balance. Spiritual life is eternal, but we must enter into that life incorruptible if it is to be with God and His chosen. Pay homage to your spirit and give your total being a fighting chance at survival, by entering into earnest and frequent prayer, that the greater good be served.

Fasting sounds too demanding to us of the western world, but in recognition of those who are fasting unwillingly throughout the world, by cutting back on excess we may become consciously aware of their plight and decide to make a real effort at mercy. Challenge yourself to go without food or drink for just a couple of days, and I assure you that your spirit will surface and teach your body what it should already know. Perhaps a small degree of real human compassion will be born. Good luck.

We are the poor in God's eyes, for although well to do in terms of material possessions, we are destitute in true spirit. Our reward is already given in the physical, and what we do with this advantage has eternal consequences with God. All of these answers can only be found by looking into our mirrors with total honesty and frankness. Our mission is to sound this alert.

By limiting our over abundance, we can satisfy real needs that exist in abundance, and contribute to a healing process that must precede salvation. Volunteerism and missionary work are born of this precious spirit, and needed in every community that one may live. The need may not always be visible but is nonetheless everpresent, and if not in the physical, most certainly in the spiritual. Expect nothing in return from people when performing God's work without acknowledgement or praise, knowing that your charity and prayer in secret shall be rewarded by our Father openly. Amen.

FRIDAY, OCTOBER 10, 1997 – PUT ASIDE ALL RELIGIOUS AFFILIATIONS. GOD WITH US IS ENOUGH... IMMANUEL

In this past year I have attended, on several occasions, five distinctly different houses of worship, to compare and contrast their varying doctrines of belief, and to better determine how and why we drift further apart from each other through the course of our religious and human history. In each faith that I continue to observe, my heart and mind remain open and attentive toward a more accurate and truthful understanding of our living God.

If we took the time and effort to put aside personal beliefs for a brief moment, you would be very surprised to discover how similar we are in spirit. Our differences in life, for the most part, are physically based, which means that over the course of thousands of years many doctrines, inherited beliefs, translations, theories, etc. are partly erroneous and impure. If we can somehow come to terms with this basic truth, then we may finally realize the answers that each of us seek are found within, through spirit and not through body. God is the source of this gift, and we must prove our worthiness to Him in order to receive it. The answer is found in solemn, earnest, and heartfelt prayer. This is where He agrees to meet us, and is where we must be directed to for our holy communion.

We need to tear down the dividing walls of belief based on tradition only, and completely rebuild our collective faith upon unity with God and one another toward universal truth. As Judaism bridged Christianity two thousand years ago and then Islam, 600 years later, we must bridge humanity now! Each individual human soul is a church within itself, and if we relate to one another through this vessel of understanding, God will rise to the occasion and act upon it. If we slide any further on this continuum of self individuality and separation, God will recede from overriding our free choice, and we shall be left with only our own devises.

Each religious church organization could start this process by removing all of their signs that proclaim individuality. God with us (Immanuel) is far more than enough in itself. Let us commence proper dialogue with common ground principles, and allow the Lord to protect us from our self proclaimed path of destruction; otherwise we are sadly on our own once again.

God is an infinite spiritual entity that is incomprehensible to us as finite human beings. If this was not so we would have a completely clear understanding of His being. Our spirits may know God, but He did not intend for us to relate to Him in the physical realm that we exist on earth. We must find Him through faith, and that path is only found in each caregiving soul. If we can reroute our misconceptions of the importance in serving physical appetites, and channel those energies toward that which we know is righteous in spirit, then we stand a fair chance at eternal life and liberty. God knows each of our needs, and will fulfill them according to the measure of faith that we exhibit in truth. The further we pursue avenues where we do not belong, the more difficult it becomes for us to attain His true understanding.

We now journey toward Saturn, one billion miles away, with the power of scientific minds that would better serve humanity by assuring each on earth be properly housed, clothed, and fed. These are the abilities we have been gifted by God, that through misuse leave our world dangerously lacking in essential love. The price of this blatant mistake will be devastating in judgement, as one way or another we are all accomplices to that which we turn a blind eye or deaf ear to. We must discontinue our loyalties in serving that which imperils the essence of our existence, as the few are putting the many in serious jeopardy, not only on this planet but in our lives to come.

If individuality is such an important part of our being, then stand up and be counted in the sight of God, so that our lifeworks and faith can be fire tested in the flame of truth. If you think that the physical wars in evidence throughout our history, where the enemy was visible and known, have been devastating according to witness, take heed that this spiritual war now blazing and mainly invisible, has begun to show physical signs where the unseen enemy is far more perilous than we could ever imagine. The new multitudes have been mentally drafted though unknowingly on the side of evil, and must desert those ranks at once to again be labeled as friend instead of foe. Self must be at once separated from soul!

MONDAY, OCTOBER 13, 1997, 1:35AM – RED ALERT!

You are My voice in the wilderness proclaiming to all,
come forward each and every good nation.
For your final saving grace in these days soon ending,
choose repentance as the ticket to salvation.

The flag that we fly is one of great caution,
therefore the color is mainly decorated in yellow,
The beast from the east is the antichrist soon rising,
your history's most dangerous fellow.

This plan of great magnitude is a direct threat to the west,
that ultimately becomes the book of Revelation,
Heed the news in their world and examine it carefully,
when peace is announced war soon commences for the duration.

Both have been battle ready more years than you know,
preparing each boy from the tender age of five,
This attack is a joint effort, of "The Reds" past and present,
as the yellow jackets are abuzz in their hive.

The nest has been stirred and they fly all about,
many neighbors shall first suffer their sting,
Weaker nations succumb quickly as if deathly allergic,
where immunization is not possible to bring.

As their momentum increases they become insatiable for power,
with combined technology no country is out of reach,
For these most dangerous bees will satisfy their needs,
to survive they must practice what they preach.

Capitalism is contrary to these doctrines of belief,
and for a time they were isolated from this path,
But with economic invasion as an attack by free enterprise,
war is declared in self defense of this wrath.

Understand the ideology of a systems breaking down,
where the populace calls for a freedom type revival,
The powers that be have decided to slug it out,
rather than relinquish their control for survival.

They are the final frontier of communistic authority,
and their population is bursting at the seams,
with nowhere to go and a substandard style of living,
the realities for most is of nightmare and not dreams.

The picture that has been painted over thousands of years,
is the only portrait they understood life to be,
but when those blind eyes were opened to the conditions of the western world,
they desired to learn more about the free.

When the younger generation became educated abroad,
they returned with more than military information,
It was easy to now confirm through modern communications,
and intelligence blocked by each government station.

The multitudes are still sheltered but the panic button has been pushed,
their power source can no longer sit back,
for their exposure is forthcoming and the Great Wall is crumbling,
their only option is to give in or attack.

It is the latter they choose after witnessing the results,
that the Soviets still are suffering in transition,
to avoid the embarrassment of truth mobilization is their only answer,
to create diversion thus accomplishing their mission.

When you cannot provide the right response to the questions of your people,
it is then only a matter of time,
Before the pyramid of power comes tumbling on down,
and you will be hung for this capital crime.

Do not ever underestimate the power in numbers,
and their ability to partner with that which they lack,
for one supplies the weaponry and the other the foot soldiers,
a simple formula engraved in many a plaque.

Your country will defend but as I stated November last,
trouble from within is their treasured moment to seize,
your military is spread too thin while policing the world,
a paper tiger falls from grace in this breeze.

Remember our lesson plan on the topic of intestinal fortitude,
a rare quality that the eagle had once,
it is hard to disagree that those days have long since passed,
where the hunter is now the prey evil hunts.

Make straight the paths for each spiritually lost soul,
which is life eternal not the physical that you see,
and upon My return to this infamous battlefield,
become good fruits to bear on the branches of life's tree.

Come each territory and nation as I remind you once again,
from the foothills and summits of every mountain,
to partake of this wisdom which is My heartfelt donation,
living water flows freely through My fountain.

Ingest this knowledge and wisdom thus preserving eternal life,
and then I may do what it is I do best,
as the good shepherd of all sheep My promise is thus complete,
returning each soul to the safety of My nest.

JEREMIAH (23:20)

The anger of the Lord will not turn back until He has executed and performed the thoughts of His heart. In the latter days you will understand it perfectly.

JEREMIAH (23:28-29)

The prophet who has a dream, let him tell a dream, and he who has My word, let him speak My word faithfully. What is the chaff to the wheat? Says the Lord. Is not My word like fire? Says the Lord. And like a hammer that breaks the rock in pieces?

QUOTES FROM CHRIST - EACH AS A PART OF AN EXPLICIT WRITING CONTAINED IN THE BOOK.

* The poor are not in terms of economic means, but rather in lack of knowledge, wisdom, and understanding. Return to them their needs.

* If you truly desire to learn, I am He who teaches, etc.

* Speak with your friend who is the pastor, for as it is in the story you know of two cats, so it also is with he.

* Lucky is he who may sit in this class,
a select few at best but none of the brass.
My students are chosen by a process unknown,
it pleases me well to see how you've grown.

* Remember the dream that you witnessed this night.....(11/16/96)

* These two books I grant to you as gifts of the season,
understand them both well for this critical reason.
All truths are contained in the pages you read,
to fulfill any religiously philosophical need.

(both black leatherbound in gold script, New Testament in right hand, The Immaculate Conception in left) - Dec. 21, 1996 - Vision

- I realize for the first time that a book is being titled, no longer just a journal of divine messages and lessons. It is now very clear that this particular book has already been written, while I continue with the formality of recording it.

* I am the one who is to prepare the way for He that is to come.

(Explicitly emphasized (3) consecutive times in this vision.)

- The following (3) messages came in the month of May, 1997:

* Concern yourself not with the importance of selling this property, but rather encourage the prospect of reconciliation (Final day of work as a real estate broker - May 17, 1997).

* This book is the most difficult summons you shall ever serve (reference to constable position).

* Heaven's little drummer boy, await patiently your drum, let it be is still the advice I proclaim, with the latter days approaching in this merry month of May, our agenda regarding graduation day is the same. – Pentecost Sunday May 18, 1997 – My final day of work after 15 years, with 5yrs. to retirement cut short.

* Whosoever abideth in Me, I abideth in also.

* Research the Dead Sea scrolls and discover My true path. (French Connection to the Essenes is correct.)

* Welcome Elivien.

* When you asked Me quite frankly how to recognize these powers,
I informed you that they were predicated on heat.
Remember that which you witnessed as those fragments from the sky,
came to earth while I sat next to you in My seat. (vision)

* Rely upon your kindred spirit to guide you through your physical beings confusions.

* The only real significant difference in forthcoming evaluations of your testimony, as to whether it is born of prophecy or delusion, lies truthfully within each heart upon which it falls.

* Jesus at 34...the Firmament.

* If you truly seek the answers to life's most difficult questions, look no further than the simplicity of earnest prayer through the purity of your heart...My direction is inward.

* Remember always our covenant of holy communion, consecrated with the blood of my human sacrifice, now renewed by the promise of faith in My living word. (November 23, 1997)

* In earthly things be children, but in My Word be adults. My word is truth and its path is understanding. The word is Mavaqh.
* The media prepares the food for the public to eat,
and is well aware that the populace will consume whatever it is served.
May your menu be limited to choice health foods only,
especially when it comes to the delicacies of My living word.

* You shall soon come to know who I am through the acceptance of true inner wisdom and the eternal understanding of total self.

* Take this bread and eat for it is my body that I break for you. Do this in remembrance of Me that I may be with you always. (Last Supper words.)

* True care and compassion in this life travels beyond the confines of humanistic love into the eternal realm of Godly love. Within the House of Israel I have forever faithfully observed the fasts...but rarely the feasts. (Mar.5,2000)

* To each religion or individual belief system with intent to convert, I hereby issue this challenge: Have you sincerely lived in and among those that you intend to proselytize for an extended period of mission? Brotherhood is best established without the interference of our contradictory human doctrines.

* Jesus is Koriath. (Vision in dream as written in chalk upon sidewalk.)

* You ask Me through prayer to show you the way and most assuredly I shall continue to do so. My way is very simple. Observe the direction that the world is currently traveling and walk contrary each day.

* If you care to witness my ministry firsthand, you must first possess a most durable pair of shoes, for the road is long and my words are few. (Mar. 6, 2000)

* Now return to the House of Israel and remind all of My children, what is truly required in becoming a Jew. Remembering always that you travel by divine command only, on "The Road Back To Me" they have you. (Day One of David) Final words.

Q: Please explain to us *The Immaculate Conception*?

A: Not only was Jeshua immaculately conceived within the virgin Miriam, so also was Miriam conceived immaculately to Anna of Machaerus (Explicit vision - December 21, 2001).

* Gather together the sick and the well,
for this mission of mercy you need to foretell.

THURSDAY, OCTOBER 23, 1997
ON A WING AND A PRAYER

It matters not how old we are in terms of earth years, for that figure is only representative to length of time concerning our physical experience on this plane of life.

Many people have lived what we would term as a full life, but in reality may not have ever grown beyond infancy in their spirit. When we speak with one another, regardless of age, it should be with respect to the true spirit of that individual not the age, condition, or experience level of their physical being. In each human being lies the spirit of God which is timeless, therefore in His eyes we are equal parts of His oneness through the grace we are gifted called love.

If we conduct our lives within this grace as it was given, and not fall victim to our sensory appetites, then we shall grow, flourish, and endure as eternal souls with our Creator. If we continue to strive with physically oriented behaviors and aspirations, then what we seek in this regard shall indeed be found. We must collectively set our ideal towards that which is eternal, and humanity in general will be the benefactor both then and now. This is the path that must be followed to achieve salvation, as proper dialogue among each spirit is the essential first ingredient toward eternal life within the unity of God.

Keep in mind that any limitations a person may have in the physical state, is most likely compensated for in the spiritual. God well knows how to balance our being, so is it not time in this evolution to do the same with our free choice as gifted?

Our priorities must begin to shift from the physical to the spiritual in appropriate preparation of His day forthcoming. This realization is to educate us in spiritual understanding, thus replacing our apprehensions and fears that presently persist. When we bring our spirit into balance and the mind to compliance, fear and death no longer have dominion over us, and we shall be able to stand steadfast in the presence of God.

In our current state of physical dominance, the spiritual life has been severely oppressed and must be at once rescued, or suffer the inevitable demise associated with earthly dictates. Our spirit must assume the leadership of total being that it once had, in order to save itself from the dust of earthly ruin. That which is born of flesh is temporary, while that born of spirit is everlasting. The choice is a simple one. All that we have to do is accept this, and then make it happen.

What is not born of love is not of God but of the earth, and must therefore remain on the earth. God is spirit and that spirit is love, totally uninhibited by the confines of our finite capabilities as human beings. There are no physical dimensions to this grace, nor is it contained within time or space from universal perspective. Each of us is a part of our living

God, most evident in those that have called upon Him, and as a result have come to direct their lives according to His true will. All souls are equal. Qualities such as care, compassion, righteousness, truth, faith, hope, loyalty, etc. are byproducts of this special love that the world in general is literally starving for. Charity is the resultant action of these good fruits in motion. Those that are truly of God reflect these heavenly gifted characteristics at all times, and you will easily recognize them as not of the ordinary. Each person has equal access. The balance in life's boat has shifted to the rear, and has taken on excessive water. Each of us as passengers on this same vessel, must bail out the excesses in a cooperative and interdependent manner in order to collectively survive. The means for saving our lives from this threat to sink and subsequently drown, is our soul and its abilities God given.

Eternal wisdom is only attainable through the channel of soul produced understanding that encompasses the mystery of spirit, prayer, and love. The mind can only teach from its sensory experiences and recordings thereof, which limits total understanding to physical stimulus of earthly experiences. The most intelligent people ever born as human beings, cannot acquire the gifts from the spirit of God, if they in fact are not given to that person. Spiritual gifts are gifted plain and simple, and are thus unattainable through the physical accomplishment of any person. Grace is the result of faith.

This is a dividing line between God and man that God prefers to discontinue, if humankind acknowledges His will for unity. God is reaching toward us out of His love for creation, and His covenant from our beginnings in true honor of that love.

God has made wise the foolish, and shall make foolish the wise, in the form of His word soon to be in evidence for our witness. Only in God can love be perfected, and only in the person of Jesus Christ was this perfection made manifest to humankind. He taught us how to overcome the physical world (death) while in the flesh, and to prepare for life eternal in the spirit. He completed the cycle of Adam (humanity), and of the Torah (law).

Through God our father in the name of His son, we are invited to become born again as a collective unity, no longer as isolated individuals and spiritually lost sheep. We must become Godlike. Please take some time to reflect upon these words in solitude, and come to understand, that to which your heart is capable of accomplishing toward the preservation of eternal life. Give God's true love a fighting chance, through consistent prayer and our continually developing faith.

God is our sail and eventual wings. The rudder of direction is His gift of free choice. The vessel afloat is our total being.(spiritual and physical) The waters are our earthly life. The sky is life eternal. The wind is evil and dry ground hell. When the wind begins to blow, the fate of the craft becomes endangered in unknown waters, and must rely upon the stability of its sail and constitution of the boat's structure. If one side or the other becomes too heavily loaded, the vessel will first sway, tip, and eventually sink. If the waters recede and the ship becomes grounded, that fate is equally dangerous to the structure. The rudder must be handled with care at all times. Our boat must then adapt to flight as the sail becomes wings, thus lifting the spiritual away from the physical abyss. This separation is necessary in order to preserve the survival of the vessel's main component, which may now safely travel onward and upward.

We must always make certain to be spiritually prepared for whatever conditions prevail on this unchartered journey, knowing full well the dangers of both wind and water, as well as dry ground toward the fate of this precious ship. When life's waters are too deep and a wind storm appears, there is the presence of anxiety and fear. The sail and rudder form a codependence, while the boat's fate rests solely upon their abilities to righten and also navigate. When the water recedes (earthly life) and the wind dies down, we must save the spiritual vessel through our faithful and true soul...on a wing and a prayer.

THURSDAY, OCTOBER 30, 1997, 6:37 AM
LET THERE BE LIGHT

The essence of God has never been a mystery,
since day one of His miracle called Creation,
Through myriads of years we seek the answer to life's question,
simply stated in His very first quotation.

Curiosity is an element that has hindered us since Adam,
as our focus sways constantly left and right,
The only real direction is our true inward perception,
of the source who said, "Let there be light."

God is our spirit and that spirit is love,
anything else is a byproduct of this earth,
For only through love and the perfection of its nature,
shall we travel with this power that grants birth.

Wisdom is a spiritual gift which concerns life eternal,
accomplished not through the abilities of our mind,
It is only God given at the appropriate moments, to bear
fruit of a far different kind.

We must follow the leader in this one final parade,
understand clearly I speak only of the heart,
Unity of life is now critical as we pass by the judgement stand,
display righteously this greatest gift He could impart.

In love there lies hope when all else seems lost,
we knew eventually He would confront us with this choice,
The errors of our ways shall be presented as evidence,
ask for God through earnest prayer not your voice.

Faith is the answer to that light simple and pure,
in a world that features complexity and much pollution,
Humankind is not progressing but rather chasing its tail,
overlooking love as the only solution.

We seem to enjoy making life difficult with power, ego,
and self pride, that encourages superiority in the realm of confusion,
These are dangerous crimes which carry stiff life sentences,
while imprisoning our spirits through physical delusion.

The freedom we cling to on earth concerns the law of sin,
as increased temptations and opportunities lead us astray,
From the essence of God whose truth is the law of grace,
life eternal is slavery to the way.

He is the answer to every question well explained in His opening statement,
how foolish are the wise that have sat,
upon their thrones of indignation throughout the course of human history,
why did we ever look further than that?

FRIDAY, OCTOBER 31, 1997
TERRITORIES WHERE WE DO NOT BELONG

As the world itself and humankind age collectively, we must understand that all real increase in terms of growth is a natural progression, not unlike the development of any life form individually within this cycle of life. This is the essence of God's master plan whereby each living organism fulfills as a part of the many, the ultimate destiny of the whole which is one. The world aside from humanity has indeed grown in that perfect harmony, despite the countless numbers of contrary types of beings that exist, be it plant, animal, insect, etc. The primary reason that instability in life's delicate balance is so prominent today, is the basic fact that humankind has overstepped its bounds. In this manner I am directly referring to our God given grace, where free choice has invaded territories of life where we do not belong. In essence we are destroying the very essence of our creator.

In our overzealousness to surpass another's accomplishments, we no longer play within the framework of rules, not only God's but humanity's as well. We seek to arrive at ends without conscientious regard to the means. This is the formula for disaster and the path we currently walk. If we analyze and not ignore our world today, these facts are strikingly obvious to the most casual observer, regardless of age or experience level.

This statement is not strictly relegated to human beings, as many other life forms sense these dangers in a very real way. So many have directly suffered an early demise through abuses, decimation, and extinction, in large part due to very little conscience on the part of humankind. For a species that was gifted the responsibility for so many, through the lack of intestinal fortitude, we have cowardly abused this gift, thus betraying each covenant with our Creator.

The reason for this breakdown is our blind obedience to greed. This trend of self-centeredness must be discontinued at once. Our gifts from God were designed to enhance the process of life, with a peaceful coexistence among all beings great and small. Needless to say, we do not even coexist properly within our own species, and as a result through the course of history have failed to develop into the spiritual entities that we are.

In reality we have stagnated in the physical state, when our eternal essence is spiritual in nature. Although our senses are dictated by the physical, which is temporary and of the earth, we must allow the light of truth born of spirit to shine forth. This area of our being is the soul whose fruits are faith, hope, charity, kindness, and all the byproducts of love. We have prematurely hastened the aging of our physical habitat called earth, and now seek life support from God, where we always and forever turn when our backs are up against the wall.

When will we learn to acknowledge His grace through the pure thanksgiving of prayer and good deeds, in both good times and bad? God must be asking himself after thousands of years of longsuffering and patience, is humankind really worth saving?

If proof is necessary to convict us of our crimes, the evidence mounting within nature itself is extremely compelling testimony. Instilling artificial remedies to counteract natural events, is a mistake humankind began implementing to the detriment of the circle of life, now expanded to an uncontrollable degree. We have attempted to play God, and that is an unforgivable error in judgement. Through free choice we have sacrificed all of life's inherent beauty, to prolong our own existence as selfish beings, not the selfless being that God created with unconditional love and great joy.

Humanity has never sufficiently obeyed the critically important commandment of loving thy neighbor as thyself, therefore it has also failed in a proper relationship with God and nature. We become so enraptured in self accomplishment, that we are blind to the source of every gift which can only be given. All so called achievement is only defined in terms of grace. We are selling our souls to delay an inevitable physical aging process, that in reality we have hastened. Let us pray.

SATURDAY, NOVEMBER 1, 1997
IS GOD'S MESSAGE GOING RIGHT OVER OUR HEADS?

Please allow me to attempt an illustration of the process by which God teaches us. If we can come to realize through prayer and understanding that God is an all loving and encompassing spirit, and not think in terms of His being as strictly a separate and external divine entity, then we are on the right track. God is everpresent within our total being, faithfully abiding in us as we may also freely choose to abide in Him.

God is not only our teacher but a teaching process as well, reaching out to all of life by providing instinct, insight, intuition, knowledge, wisdom, and most importantly love. From these gifts we may arrive at an overall understanding of our creator, thus enabling each life form to properly coexist with one another, in the harmony of God's original master plan.

Our methods of physical learning must be redirected to spiritual. God fully understands that we are one, and there is no partiality with Him when it comes to spiritual gifts requested righteously. We as humankind, in general, have not truly learned how to ask Him properly, even though the sum total of this human ability was presented to us two thousand years ago in the being of Jesus.

At this point in our history we should be walking as He did, preparing all souls for their inevitable eternal journey. Instead, we remain in the same physically based sins, and even more so, that has plagued us as a species from the very beginning. Any form of greed and separation from the oneness of God is man made. It is physical and temporary in nature, contrary to the spiritual and eternal love that, God so desires for each of us to attain and maintain in common. When will we become wise enough to see this simple unseen truth?

We must utilize and develop the under achieving sixth sense born of spirit, rather than catering to our five physical senses born of this earth only, and someday fleeting with the body which they direct. Please give careful consideration to these words, for they may very well be your ticket needed for safe passage home on the road back to me.

I am no different than anyone else, and experience the same fears and frustrations of each day that come with being human. One thing that I know, and wish to share, is that God is now speaking loud and clear, as my heart and mind stays attuned. May you also receive this blessing through His saving grace. Our only hope for real progress and spiritual survival as a collectivity, must be born from the complete understanding of this most critical eternal truth. The Lord our God is one, and from this oneness comes all!

When the spirit of God intends to inform us, He sends a message which passes freely through our conceived physical world of earthly dimension. This message arrives as a crystal clear spiritual mist, enveloping us amidst the confusions of everyday life, only conceivable and interpretive to our spirit, and passing by if we are too physically preoccupied. Spiritual focus will allow for this educating spirit to be received by our total being.

We have oftentimes heard the cliche: "That went right over your head." This is a direct reference to missing out on a point made, where the speaker realizes their listener(s) did not understand the true meaning of the message sent. God is not only external but more importantly internal, and that area of our being is the one essential part which constantly reminds us of our true origin. This bothers most people, because they are not comfortable with His spiritual presence, in such close proximity to their physical behaviors. God understands this, for He is all knowing, and nothing is hidden from His sight, including our innermost thoughts and feelings. This inner conflict can be resolved only through earnest and heartfelt prayer, where the spiritual realization of faith, hope, charity, love, and all other good fruits, are collectively birthed in each human soul.

When you pray to God, try praying inwardly to your soul instead of outwardly and above, for in this manner you are acknowledging God's presence as a part of your being. This is pleasing to Him, and will subsequently be a tremendous lift to you, as you begin to feel that special inner comfort which accompanies truthfulness as the product of grace.

Our minds do not always know what to say or pray for that matter, but our souls speak volumes to God. The wisest among us is foolishness to God, when techniques of craftiness or deceit are employed to somehow divert His attention. We must face the facts of who and what we really are, and in that way alone shall true understanding be granted.

It is because of our human selfishness, and believe me that no one is exempt from this truth to some degree, that we are kept from the selflessness required by God, to move forward as a unity toward His eternal desire of love through oneness. We must put aside all previously held doctrines, and concentrate on God only if we are to fulfill His commandment and thus unite. Common ground, not higher ground, must be our collective aim, and the ideal of every religious movement.

Love and unity are bonds with God, separation is a product of man. In the reality of our oneness ideal, this mission is too greatly under developed, and as a result we continue to separate further, both physically and spiritually to our most dangerous detriment. The time is long past due for this most critical element, required of our total eternal being to be served and then elevated. The abilities of our human heart (soul) is the inborn entity of which I speak, and our only connection to God's true will. This must be utilized in each individual by free choice, so that God may then interconnect all parts of His master work.

In the same manner that we constantly miscommunicate, not only as nations but individuals as well, it is not possible to be at one with God while enslaved in this declining physical realm. Our physical being continues to dominate the spiritual because we have allowed for the servitude to our five physical senses. They consistently rule over the one eternal (sixth) sense, thus diminishing its proper development for the benefit of total being. The five we are all familiar with: (sight, sound, touch, taste, and smell) serve the temporary and physical aspects of our being, as navigational aids in relation to earthly matter. The sixth sense is born of spirit not of earth, and is the one connection we must rely upon for true universal understanding. Once acknowledged and put into proper practice, it becomes our guide and companion, as that unbounded link to the other side. The main component of our inability as humans to adapt from physical to spiritual beings, is strictly a lack of focus and concentration toward that innermost important realm of spirit. We generally give up on ourselves far too easily in this regard, and can only regain our likeness to God, by asking Him directly through prayerful meditation, to forgive and forget our iniquities.

That which we spiritually lack, is mainly due to distractions born of physical origin. We have allowed our physical world to become so overly involving in the essence of our being, that our true eternal being of spirit is shut out from the education it should be receiving. It is essential that we redirect the energies produced in our minds, to meet the needs of our spirit. Proper balance is obtainable if, instead of remaining as slaves to the temporary, physical, and fleeting dictates of the mind, we actively seek the eternal, spiritual, and everlasting fruits of our hearts, with the soul development ideal as paramount. There is no substitute plan for this critical eternal truth. Only because of inactivity, not inability, to collectively pursue this path, do we grow apart by denying and then defying the very existence of God within us. Accordingly, our earthly fate shall thus be determined.

In the Lord's garden where the wheat and tares do indeed grow together, the harvest shall certainly provide a separation as we are biblically informed. The wheat represents continued life and will be stored in His barn, while the tares shall inevitably become bundled and burned. Evil has no place in God's kingdom. This new field of our being is seeded with perfection, and can only germinate with the proper application of living bread and water, otherwise known as God's pure love and tender mercy for each soul.

Although bodily, we may soon share a similar fate, it does not have to be so in regards to spirit, where free choice long ago gifted can place us safely back upon the path of righteousness, through God's everlasting truth and grace. This is the mission of the Christ spirit as our teacher throughout the ages, that has been with us without fail for untold generations of support. All that we need to do is ask, that the door of truth be opened.

STAND UP AND BE COUNTED BY THE LORD

That which is helpful is not always welcomed, but is it not better to be forewarned than to be unpleasantly surprised? God has forever maintained His covenant of love with humanity, despite our severe betrayal of that faith, as evidenced in His enduring patience and longsuffering throughout human history. There are no guarantees in this life, and we never know when our number is to be called, so it behooves each of us to take stock in our collective soul today. Tomorrow is promised to no one, and in that regard, the kingdom of God is always at hand. Is your life currently in its best condition, and are you prepared to face the judgement with head held high, in glorious anticipation of the Lord's return? If so, please step forward and help others to understand, who for whatever reason do not. It is not good enough to satisfy only the individual spirit, when there is a critical need that exists in our body at large.

The world we live in today is literally starving for spiritual guidance. Those of you that have been gifted in spirit, must come forth and share this treasure so that each may choose life. All previously held secrets are to be revealed to the brotherhood of humankind, so that none shall say they were uninformed. The hour is late and although you may stand in a righteous place, do not think for a moment that by standing still you cannot be overrun. There is no forgiveness for understanding not revealed, as all treasures are to be stored in heaven and not earth. I make this demand, not as one who speaks on my own behalf, but rather the holy spirit which states its command through me. If you are an unbeliever, feel free to test this spirit of truth. Believers know the true word from God when they hear His voice.

Humanity must now be trained for battle, and those of whom I speak in regards to spiritual leadership, are to come forth and be counted as instructors and trainers. There is no comfort in being a soldier of salvation, nor was there ever meant to be. Put away all books as scholars of the word, and your faith shall soon be fire tested in the practical application of spiritual war. The softness must now be shed in preparation of battle. We must soon depart the security of this life and our temporary assignment, to answer the call that we knew in our hearts would eventually be echoed. If you are truly a man or woman of God, then you will rejoice in this invitation, for such are the ones that the Lord needs to rely upon in these days.

He asks that all prior protocol to traditions of silence, secrecy, solitude, retreat, etc. be abandoned in favor of pure hands on missionary action. Those who have long understood the words I now speak, please emerge as shepherds into this battlefield of lost sheep. It is no longer adequate to be only students and scholars of the word, or to be individually attuned to God, for the time has now come to open the eyes of the blind, so that they may clearly see the true light up on the road back to me.

Kindly come out from behind the veil of all monasteries, abbeys, and retreats. The word is now forward and no longer retreat. From the pulpits of each church, temple, mosque, etc. you must come forth in the spirit of courage, so that your followers will be unafraid in your hand, and lead them confidently forward to the awaiting good shepherd. If we are Christ's, then we must become Christlike by carrying His cross, not through daily and weekly reaffirmation of true believers, but rather by truly searching out the fields for the multitudes that are lost. I challenge each of you to accept the real challenge of Christ, and that requires outright sacrifice in comparison to our existing comfortable, safe, and secure nests. With God as our witness and ongoing strength, let us meet this new challenge head on, with enthusiasm and great vigor! The Lord is indeed our shepherd and in Him we need not fear.

The word, which is God's and not anyone else's, can no longer be preserved as a depositor's investment, cleverly hidden where the world cannot see. This design of intended security breeds insecurity in the masses, and is contrary to the true desires of He from whom all business stems. It is now time to furnish His complete account, in the shining light of plain truth. This is not a condemnation of the good fruits you may bear, but rather a note of demand to collect with interest, the account so long ago established with each bank of religion that He chose to do business. For thousands of years this account has been entrusted without checks and balances, and it is only fitting that performance is required upon request.

The payout requested by God is unity, and that will require the closure of each bank (religion) which fails to comply with these guidelines. The interest those religions have spent to further their status in wealth, will be heavy laden in tax. God is also the eternal accountant, fully aware of each deposit and withdrawal transaction that has ever taken place. With the war and poverty that exists today in so many parts of our world, and the gross imbalances in wealth distribution, I tend to believe that the Lord has several questions regarding the wisdom applied in our usage of His overall contributions.

If you believe these words, that oneness through unity is God's command, then step forward today and serve that ideal to which you were originally called. If people cannot find you, or the doors of open communication and dialogue are locked or even slightly closed, how is the greater good being served from person to person and church to church? A pure church is not a building structure, it is God within. Does it fulfill God's essence of oneness if the parts of His machine most able, are not willing to operate at peak performance?

Closed doors have become an acceptable part of the bureaucracy in many religious affiliations, and access to clergy is limited at best. This policy must cease immediately. Keep in mind that no religion is one hundred percent accurate in all claims of its faith, therefore let none be judged by another. Come down from those ivory towers, and please minister to a world in critical need. It no longer suffices to only providing holy book answers of complex questions that require assertive actions. We must now physically perform that to which we spiritually attest, by rolling up our sleeves and dirtying our hands, as Christ forever comes to serve and not be served... let us also do likewise.

OUR TEACHER IS NOW A WARRIOR

The word of God can no longer be safehoused when He says it is now time to spend. A proper nurturing is only possible through complete and uninhibited freedom of divine wisdom. Do not coddle or control it any longer. If you are too comfortable with your current position in the world, and these words are upsetting or unsettling to you, then I am indeed serving you well, without injustice or prejudice. All degrees of earthly comfort are physically and not spiritually based, and in this regard I do you no harm with a simple but poignant reminder of our true mission and origin of purpose.

Physical dictates cannot commingle with spiritual directives, for it clouds the purity of God's message sent to us, that we sometimes tend to relax and lose focus upon. The ship called earth has begun to take on water that imminently imperils the lives of all on board, and regardless of rank or title, each member of the crew must now go below deck and bail. It is best for each of us to go voluntarily and to serve the greater good, before it is too late and that unity is commanded.

Is the effort you put forth daily giving it everything you've got, or is it just good enough for what this world deserves? Only the mirror of your soul holds the answer to this question, and only in God is that reflection revealed. We must collectively elevate to the next level of our beings potential, in meeting this new challenge I speak of from God. The days are upon us that the scriptures proclaim, and if we are well prepared in practice, the main event will be glorious. Pep talks are temporary motivators, but biblically sound doctrine stands the test of time. This is not to say that every word contained within the scripture of each religion's text is accurate. People need to hear from God in a way that is pleasing to them, whereby the written word may speak the volume so desired. Whether loud, soft, or somewhere in between, God's word will shine through with all its appropriateness of understanding.

Remember always that our God is the same for everyone, and that He is a living God, free to move as He sees fit, in and among us. The great battle has begun and our teacher is now a warrior.

WEDNESDAY, NOVEMBER 12, 1997
GOD'S EDUCATING SPIRIT IS THE WORD

Jesus as Christ was and is, the educating spirit of which I speak. At the appointed time in our history the Word became flesh, as God felt the necessity for a profound divine intervention. This statement issued to mankind was manifested in a presentation of spiritual reality, to a lost world of sheep gone astray, and a civilization unable to move forward as a unity. The advent of Christianity was the enlightened result of this human display of love, sacrifice, and truth of resurrection. His mission was not only to Israel, but also to unite the entire known world under a common belief in the oneness of God. The eternal truths that He brought to us two thousand years ago, have still not settled into our human understanding as a whole to this day. How do we account for this spiritual lapse?

This is primarily due to our continuing reluctance to search the heights of human spirit through heart, as opposed to the depths of flesh through coercion of the influential mind. I speak not only of mind over matter, but more importantly heart and soul over both mind and matter. Herein lies the true answer to every religious question. Contrary to this unity is all subsequent separatism in life, not only in religion, but in each human institution and individual soul. Divide and conquer is a timeless strategy, implemented by every evil intentioned source to gain power over another. It logically follows that if we choose this path, it shall inevitably become our epitaph. Use the Word to live by instead.

May I suggest that a focus on the Gospel of John, where the teachings and parables of Jesus mystically live, could bring to light a new found spiritual experience and pure understanding. The other three synoptic Gospels of Matthew, Mark, and Luke are good in story, but are built upon each other chronologically. This will give you a good start on learning about spirituality. John's gospel seems to speak directly to each person. in spirit

Corinthians 1 is also an excellent resource in terms of spirit, while many of the psalms, proverbs, and prophets provide additional insight, the real key to scriptural understanding is prayer's inner focus. The greatest biblical scholars that have ever lived, could not fully grasp the true meaning of Christ's entire message, through physical study of the words alone. They realize that there is always a missing element which prevents solving this mystical puzzle, no matter how many times it is analyzed, scoped, or probed. Those seeking His truths should understand by now, that they can only be obtained as gifts of the Lord pure and simple.

The long held mysteries and secrets of the world, are now being revealed to students of the Lord. The process of selection is unknown, but lucky indeed is he who may sit in this class. Jesus was a man who came not to be worshiped, but rather to teach us how to worship God as the Father He knows, and to show us who and what we really are in regards to eternal spirituality. Jesus is the living testimony to heaven sent doctrine and love, which enables each of us to gain citizenship with our creator. Attunement to our spirit and its abilities to perpetuate life, is as far as we should be looking while seeking inner answers concerning God. Infinite truths are unattainable by finite means, for even a computer in all its brilliance can only produce from that which it is given. Humankind's combined experience is still finite. Spiritual aptitude is infinite because our spirit is also infinite, unconfined by time, space, or matter. It is easy to now see where our true full potential lies in life. Our spirits are not lost, but they have been simply misplaced and somewhat forgotten, sort of "out of sight out of mind." How many times have we misplaced an item and then frantically searched everywhere but where we left it, right under our nose? The same is true with our faith and spirit. We just seem to look past the most obvious of places. I sincerely hope that each of you find these treasures of the heart and cherish them. In terms of direction, take the heavenly avenue of earnest prayer. The true essence of Christ is a spiritual gift which cannot be accomplished through physical criteria. Please search your heart for this spiritual reality in God and His universe, and then shed each apprehension and fear in favor of universal truth.

May the Lord bless and protect each of you in pursuit of His righteous path.

MONDAY NOVEMBER 17, 1997
A CALL FOR SPIRITUAL REVOLUTION

I come before you today with an open heart and a most caring soul, not only as a person of flesh and blood, but far more importantly in the spirit of God. I speak not on my own behalf but rather by the holy spirit that dwells within us, and which now determines a need to express its sentiments to our collective conscience. The world in which we currently exist is faltering swiftly, and our general tendency is to helplessly observe while going about our routine daily business. The enormity of this complex problem appears insurmountable, and is in fact impossible for humankind alone to address. This feeling of despair that we share in common as human beings is not shared by God, and as we well know, that which is impossible for us is not so for He.

The time has come for a unified stand versus the momentum charged drive of evil, in and among us, that persists from nation to nation, house to house, person to person, and realm to realm. This constantly gaining newfound support, is contrary to the wishes of God, and subsequently presents an imminent danger. I speak not of a debatable or segregated issue that only surrounds a particular belief, but rather a terminal cancer that is destroying the entire inner and outer body of humanity. If we continue to separate ourselves in doctrine through self seeking, then this cancer will thrive and thus cause indeterminable numbers of spiritual deaths. The only means available to us in producing remission, and successfully combating this common enemy, is through the oneness of our God, and a responsiveness to His beckoning call for unity.

By traveling further along the path that we currently walk, many innocent lost sheep shall be overrun, that otherwise should have been saved by us, as brethren and caretakers of fellow souls. We must become aligned with the source of righteousness as children of the true light, overlooking differences of culture, tradition, and opinion, in favor of collective spiritual survival.

This attack we are under poses a direct threat to our total being, and must be acted upon responsibly and immediately. It is no longer enough to say that we are doing the best we can under the circumstances, as each of us must reach down deep inside for that gifted intestinal fortitude, which can feed the hunger of the greater good. We must fill the void that is widening amongst our brethren, by overthrowing the dominant powers of separation and confusion, that forever hinders and barricades the truth.

Most revolutions are based on the removal of the existing power structure, in favor of the people's choice. The only difference in this revolution, from all others known to humanity, is that the enemy entrenches within, and must be fought on that turf and defeated individually before being conquered collectively. We are losing many battles but the war is yet undecided, for each soul still possesses the most lethal weapon of destiny in the form of free choice. The order is to use it or lose it. God will stand with those who are loyal to His commands, and we pray for those that are not.

Ever since Adam, the curiosity of mindpower has led humankind further away from God, and continues to carry us ever closer toward the excessive vulnerabilities of physical temptations, and their resultant corruption that forms spiritual isolation. This is a great strategic blunder with negative eternal consequences. Only through our souls can we alter this treacherous course, and place all lost sheep safely back upon the true path of God. Each of us must eventually die an earthly death, but not a spiritual one, and I say let us go down fighting the good fight versus the forces of evil and all its subsequent trappings.

The heart of the flame is the place to be, while actively rescuing the multitudes in danger of the Lord's coming day. Make yourself this pledge, that we shall not be neutral bystanders on the temporarily safe outer edges, which inevitably become engulfed in a smoke, thereby producing an unnnecessary succumbing to inhalation.

Take on the challenge of active duty, only found in God's blazing fire, to which we were originally called, thereby trimming the excess fat while training our spirit to its full potential. A battle ready mode for deployment in His majesty's service. Return if you wish to the safety and comforts of the mission from whence you came, or stand and be counted as true frontline soldiers of salvation. The options are clearly before you. The study period of our history has now concluded, and the Lord's test is scheduled to be taken. Please put away all study material of scholarly research and analysis, and I will show you a far superior method of obtaining understanding. Becoming a soldier in any righteous war, is a truly courageous act of spiritual valor, and this is the war to end all wars, whereby voluntary enlistment is held in higher esteem then an unwarranted draft command. When this conflict of spirit, already in progress, spills over onto our physical realm of being biblically known as Armageddon, it will be too late to join forces with the Lord, now risen from His throne and departed for the battlefront. Remember that which you hear and see today, and although you may disagree in principle, I assure you that all of us will be changed in a brief moment. Bear in mind that our God is a living God, as capable of teaching us now as at any previous time in our history. New scriptures are being written today, that work to make straight the pathway of the Lord once again.

Never has the need for divine intervention been so critical as we face the most intimidating, formidable, and challenging opponent ever known to humanity in a showdown of free choice. We can no longer look the other way as this cancerous evil (self) grows in and around us, to the point of infecting our very souls. Call him forth and look straight into his eyes now, then order his influence away from your life once and for all, remaining steadfast to the principles of unity within our Godly covenant. In self we discover this enemy from within, as our partner shall deliver us from the enemy without, and together we may share in the Lord's ultimate and undeniable victory of eternal life.

WEDNESDAY NOVEMBER 19, 1997
A CALL FOR SPIRITUAL REVOLUTION (CONTINUED)

The words that I issue may not always gain favor, or even be those that you wish to hear, but nonetheless they are spoken by the spirit of truth, and thus by that authority they are deserving to be heard, and need to be said. I congratulate each for your tireless, unselfish, and continuing dedication to this heavenly cause, and now ask you to further challenge your spirit, in achieving true understanding through an elevated degree of courage and perseverance. The hour is now quite late and our time is very short.

That which is known of the holy spirit can no longer be suppressed or concealed, but instead must be revealed to all people for edification and shared experience. No one is frightened if our spoken and written words are born of personal misconceptions, for there are simple societal solutions to that particular type of behavior. Real apprehension and fear is birthed by the potential possibility and subsequent probability that we are correct, and thus say to you, that together as a unity we shall replace each of those many apprehensions and fears with true understanding. This is accomplished through prayer, repentance, faith, and brotherly love within the hearts and souls, that we were gifted.

Please do not confuse confidence in the Lord's directive, with a lack of personal humility or modesty. I assure you that I remain completely humble and attentive at all times, fully aware of the everpresent deceitfulness of temptation and pride that the evil self features. As anyone else is, I am also physically exposed to this temporal delusion, but my focus upon spiritual teachings at this point in time is accurate and precise.

I have come to know the difference between both educators, (self and soul), through the process and gift of discernment, and that each person must utilize this in daily life, by trial and error to overcome evil. When I found out after my death like experience that I was born again in spirit, I did not even know what the terminology meant. Without any prior formal religious education or church membership in my life, including never having read any part of the bible, I thought that "born agains" were a religious affiliation, not unlike any other church group or doctrinal organization.

On September 22, 1996 I received my first active spiritual message following that September fifteenth spiritual baptism. The week in between was seven days of total disorientation. After deriving the content of this message, I delivered it to the home of a Jewish rabbi that I did not even know, much less the fact it was just prior to Kol Nidre prayer and the religious high holyday of Yom Kippur. In retrospect, the message was extremely profound at that time, although I was unaware of its power or its purpose. I sat in this man's living room singing the praises of Jesus Christ, and described in detail the context of these special words spoken to me, while assuming he being a Jew was an adherent of Christ. This was a prime example of my total biblical illiteracy and spiritual infancy, but far more importantly it was an awakening of faith that later develops into loyalty and understanding.

The Lord has a way of penetrating the shell of unbelievers, and does not hesitate to send His soldiers into that battle. The lesson learned was that I was too young spiritually to take action so early on, but it also showed a willingness to actively participate in the Lord's master plan on faith alone. Faith must be the prime motivator toward truth.

To this day I do not belong, nor have I any intention of joining a specific religious group or one particular human belief system. Anything that I have come to know or relate to in terms of spirit religion, has directly been derived from the teachings of the holy spirit on a regular basis, and not by any human being. I remain in a type of solitary spiritual confinement, which does not require the constraints of physical solitude, as long as focus on the teacher is paramount. The Lord is well aware of the importance of peace and tranquility toward our spiritual learning, but He calls His shepherds to search harder for those sheep which are lost or even caught in various life thickets. The Lord has placed his confidence in each of us, to take a leadership role in bringing about His desired harmony.

Spiritual confinement can be more accurately defined as freedom. While remaining devout in prayer, words, and lifeworks, we may continue to receive the Lord's good fruits through the purity of His love, and upon the receipt of understanding, to then share openly this blessing with our fellow beings in all walks of life.

Death upon this earth is only death to sin, and I for one have already experienced the death through Jesus Christ. I have also not had the opportunity to gain any excess comfort or regimen in my mission, nor do I believe in receiving any such comfort.

Another rule to which I adhere, is the Lord as my only master in answering to upon this earth, and in that way a discipleship develops swiftly. Putting your money where your mouth is brings a fresh, blue collar approach of Christ to the white collar trend of today, where real sacrifice and loyalty to His calling, has generally given way to the excessive comforts of this western world, and its physically oriented temptations and dictates. The realization of spiritual rebirth is what each of us need to acquire today, in order to travel homeward as a unity in peace.

The most commonly asked question that I receive in regards to this quest, is centered around the idea of where I find the time to produce these writings or gather such ideals. My response is simply that I make the time, and if I am not performing to the best of my spiritual ability, then another previously acquired physical commitment must be dropped cold. One at a time the stages of the rocket must release, if the mother ship is to gain the necessary faith propulsion in reaching its destination of spirit. I look at my life on earth no differently. I am fully prepared to receive and relay all that the Lord is willing to reveal, not for myself but for the brotherhood. Some of us must be tuned in to God in these critical days, so I have since volunteered and been graciously accepted. I have never been one to wait for another when it comes time to converting thought into action, and do recognize those moments very clearly.

As we return our free will and self to God, there is only light without darkness. Dependency on this world only, is to lose sight of the spiritualness of our being, that holds the real key to life eternal, and our soul development upon this plane of existence. We must become the Christ by which we are taught and believe in, and rise confidently out of the cradle of spiritual infancy. We have preferred to remain nestled within the security of spiritual childhood, as opposed to walking upright with the cross He still must bear, because His teachings remain unlearned. There is no rest or fulfillment for the teacher whose lessons go generally unheeded. We have crawled far too long and by now should have been up and running, but at the very least we must stand together and walk forward hand in hand. If unity is to be attainable in this world of separation, it will occur to us only through the grace of our almighty God and father. Let us do our collective part as humanity by meeting His peace. Christ does not appear on earth to bring the distinctive separateness of His being to light, but rather to show us the way in which we are capable of walking as well. For the past two thousand years we have been unable to move forward as one in this regard, because we continually serve the temporary and not the eternal.

In terms of my lack in human qualifications to speak from a religious pulpit, the gift of the spirit qualifies my speech. Jesus is the cornerstone of the pure church of God, and St. Paul was a pillar of early Christianity, and neither would be considered today as having proper or formalized enough religious credentials. Their human based diplomas are indeed nonexistent. I do not claim to be in that company, but it is the same spirit which instructs our pathways, and that spirit is given without partiality to whomever and whenever our God so chooses. Although spiritual gifts differ from one to another, it is the same spiritual teaching source which works all in all.

Throughout human history the Lord has utilized earthen vessels for the purpose of bringing forth His Word, and my experience is no different in this regard. Obviously, He has found a need to communicate with us at this point in our development.

If anyone has questions as to the accuracy of my claims, please feel free to test this holy spirit true or false. It would be wise to at least remain open minded to your heart, while seeking your choice of scientific or spiritual proofing. Make good use with your gift of free choice, by asking inwardly that same spirit of truth which I speak of and you also possess. You may be very surprised at the outcome of that prayer if it is requested in earnest, as the spirit speaks volumes to ears willing to hear and eyes to see.

While testing this spirit of love, may you not be foolish in seeking extraordinary physical evidence for a spiritual gift that is born of prayer and commitment. Flesh is flesh and spirit is spirit, and any testing should acknowledge this truth. I have traveled and continue to travel the Lord's path heaven lit, and through spiritual rebirth would be honored to show each person the way "upon the road back to Me."

Join with me in becoming born again in preparation of the Lord's next coming. This is His invitation and not simply my own. In my hand you may confide your fears, and we shall overcome them together, with the guidance and love of the holy spirit. This lesson was taught two thousand years ago, and as a unity we have not fully complied to this day to any great degree.

Do you not agree that the time is near at hand to realize the truth of our eternal spirit, and to put that understanding to its best overall use? I offer my life as a living sacrifice to this end, by answering the call of discipleship to the best of my ability, with a warm welcome to each of you who is willing to do likewise. The spirit of God is among us today, and there has never been a better opportunity on this earth to make a real difference. If any claim that I make is not the truth of God's intent, then I would ask Him to remove the gifts He has bestowed upon me, in favor of another that may better achieve His true desires.

SUNDAY, NOVEMBER 23, 1997, 6:42AM
ARISE FROM THE CRADLE OF SPIRITUAL INFANCY

In the most absolute silence amidst the dead of night, comes a crystal clear voice profoundly proclaiming righteousness. It is the voice and figure of the Lord. "Remember always our covenant of holy communion, consecrated with the blood of My human sacrifice, now renewed by the promise of faith in My living word".

For the first forty years of my life I have consciously withheld my heart from any total commitment, be it toward others or self. I have awaited patiently the uncertain and unpredictable calling of total being, that has now indeed surfaced and presented itself clearly before me. This revelation is a call to spiritual action. It is not something that you can make happen, it simply does. Regardless of personal thoughts, words, and aspirations that guide our physical lives, it is our spiritual voice which answers the true calling of God, and is in fact the essence of each mission. Prayers from the heart are the echoes of spirit, and to those who ask with faithful sincerity, they are heard and then answered by a gracious and abundant love that is God. Only through He that can reach the heights and depths of our inner spirit, is understanding and eternal life to be found. By applying physical remedies to spiritual problems, we are mistakingly overlooking the only real solution. God is spirit and that spirit is eternal love and life. Anything else falls short of the mark, and is not of God but rather of the earth, and thus shall remain forever as such.

We know that flesh is flesh and spirit is spirit, and therefore must elevate in unity to meet that which is God, by actually performing His will and not simply realizing that it exists. Each individual being must come to understand their importance as to the overall plan which God has devised for our benefit. I tell you the truth in that every vote is counted by the Lord. When our will becomes as one with His, there is a unified peace.

From the dimension beyond we are formed by the thought of God. We are created from one spirit and, although many in number, God is well attuned to each part of Himself that produces either positive or negative energy, and will shed all elements that detract from the well being of His greater good known as love. It is absolute foolishness to be a deterrent of this mission.

This calling of mine is not an individual one, but rather a collective calling to include the majority of people that are no different than I, as seen through the loving eyes of God. If individually we can share a common belief in the almighty, then His desire for unity in truth stands a fighting chance. We shall respond to Him in unison through the power of prayer. Each of us must come to realize in this lifetime our own true destiny. The confusion we encounter is that we believe our individual destiny is somehow distinctly separate from all others in this world, and that we have no effect on the outcome. This could be no further from the truth, in that by God's design we should travel together as one in eternal peace and harmony.

Our collective destiny is intended to be held in common. Separateness is contrary to oneness, and therefore all that we do which involves any self fulfilling individualism is also contrary to God. This also includes the division of religions. Any dividing line installed in this life, be it of nation or individual soul, is a man made product of free choice misguided.

Throughout our early lives we are cultured and trained to desire being something, and are often asked to respond as to what that would be. To this day, I have not desired to be anything but who I am at any given point in time, and in that way can be open to whatever God deems necessary in His appointed time. I am very particular when it comes to an earthly career vow. Our responses to this question tend to vary according to age and gender, but the pattern is formed nonetheless as we supply the standard line of answers namely doctors, nurses, lawyers, athletes, police and fire, singers, movie stars, etc.

These responses tend to change as we grow older and our world opens ever wider. As the complexities of life increase so also do our options, and we stop dreaming of what we could have been. The once simple and safe life of childhood becomes a maze of confusion and indecision, no longer the pure and simple as previously envisioned, where we become not only confronted but more dangerously swallowed up by ever increasing, consuming, and progressive physical delusions. Do not ever stop dreaming. I say to each of you who has fallen victim to this earthly curse, go back and become born again, because we still, to this day, have not got it right. The kingdom of heaven is designed most expressly for this purpose, as we must now back up and correct our errors and omissions of the past, if we intend to move forward in truth. This is not a popular method of transformation but is indeed required. "In earthly things be children, but in My word be adults, my word is truth and its path understanding... the word is Mavaqh." Strive for righteousness in body and spirit and the Lord shall in turn serve us well, for this is our true earthly destiny and mission.

The importance of physical safety is taught to us repeatedly throughout life, and in due time we in turn teach others the same. Especially when teaching our own children, we take a more critical interest in the extreme necessity of a crystal clear understanding on their part. There is no room for error. Love, care, and compassion are always the driving forces in preserving this collective well being, are they not? As children of God, He as our Father has all of these same concerns and even more, for when it comes to our well being, we have oftentimes chosen a most dangerous and threatening path.

Think for a moment of how He must feel ,being unable to protect us because of our abuses to His gift of free choice, and the pain which comes when your children refuse to heed good advice. In this way you shall come to truly understand God's pure intentions.

The importance of spiritual safety is what each of us need to learn, understand, and then apply in this gifted blessing. The same energy and concern that goes into teaching physical safety must be utilized toward the spiritual, for that is the vehicle that must carry our total being on its eternal journey. This under utilized natural ability is also a gifted trait that produces an instinct when fully developed, no different than our animal instinct for physical safety. In other words, we have tremendous untapped spiritual potential that very few people have focused upon in this lifetime, and as a result grow old in earthly years, without proper parallel growth in spirit. As a result of this gross negligence we cannot achieve balance.

The here and now outlook on life, is a distorted and extremely narrow view of the overall picture. Our true spiritualness of being has been for the most part neglected, as the new multitudes have shifted the wide majority to the side of physical and temporary gratification. Our physical world is spinning out of control, and has thus become a safety hazard, by far exceeding both our physical and spiritual safety limits. Although speed is seen by many as exciting, it also kills. Increasing involvements and commitments to physical stimulus, only further distracts us from feeding our spirits with the proper nourishment most essential for survival. We are being starved to death spiritually without realizing the imminent dangers. Blind and fools is what we have allowed ourselves to be, despite the forewarning of Christ some two thousand years ago. We remain in this downward spiraling tailspin because of our inability to pull out through mutual cooperation and understanding, which is a primary prerequisite of God's unity. The end result is the same as any other downward moving object.

This inevitable crash is a product of pilot error, where the poor training of these flyers is evidenced by a basic fuel shortage, that leaves them far shy of their destination. Spiritual infancy carries a price tag we cannot afford to pay. The few that understand this truth and practice indifference towards the spiritually immature majority, have been historically held down and persecuted through pure fear and ignorance. The blindly obedient to greed have always been able to sell the label of blasphemy and troublemakers, in societies unable to cope with truth. I would like to think we, as a society today, can move above and beyond those judgements of self centeredness and spiritual naïveté.

The sad commentary here is that we know the truth but are afraid to face it. I sincerely wish that these words can bring about a positive change in our world through the hearts of each and every individual, bound and determined to learn the realities of God, and willing to work at it for the hope of tomorrow. We must grow up spiritually before soon succumbing to the dictates of earth only priorities, that all of us clearly see as the proverbial writing on the wall. If I had learned this lesson through physical means, you would have learned it also, and this book I write would be unnecessary to share unless the spirit of God determined a need for reminder. If spiritual safety was a well drilled and recognizable constant of human acceptance and practice, this message would not pass through me from the Lord as profoundly and directly as it has. We consistently refresh, rehearse, and remind ourselves of physical safety precautions, but why not spiritual?

Throughout our history the Lord has used earthen vessels or messengers to convey His directives. This ability of His did not cease with the biblical personalities thousands of years ago, for as we well know, our God is a living God unconfined by time or space. The main reason that those who have truly borne His messages are persecuted, is that fear which forever grips the guilty. They must act upon this intrusion, by greeting the gift of righteousness head on with much contempt and aggression.

None of us wish to be reminded of our faults, but if it bears the fruits of positive change, this effect can move the world forward one spiritual soul at a time. A wise person will take the medicine of advice and criticism together whether they like it or not, if presented to them with the proper elements of care and compassionate cure. This is how we learn to receive the spiritual gifts of divine knowledge, wisdom, and finally understanding.

Those who speak a true message from God belong to this world, for it is only the message itself that is otherworldly. When we learn to accept this gift of grace for what it really is, only then can we move forward together as a unity.

For those that have mistaken or misinterpreted receiving God's message, inevitably we recognize that fact and dismiss their testimony through various methods. Others that have truly received a message but cannot cope with the sensitive handling of this mission, consequently fall by the wayside through no fault of their own, and the living word is thus seized.

Again there are others who receive the Word with great joy, but because of earthly priorities and commitment cannot produce. The ones to watch are those that turn this world on its head, by flying up into the face of societal expectations and disease. Those of whom I speak are the ones Jesus referred to as seeds planted in solid ground, where they shall produce up to a hundredfold, and thus carry the hope of humanity on their backs.

Accept or reject but do not sit still when it comes to standing with God, or His adversary in these most critical latter days. Apply the knowledge, wisdom, and understanding abilities you were gifted, and discern the truth through your heart and not your head. This takes time, effort, dedication, and focus, but I assure you that it is well worth the price of admission. As an automobile begins to rust with age from the inside on out, the same can be said of our spiritual soul. If the external support system is not properly preserved, then deterioration will take down the internal with it as well. I speak of our physical bodies and their subsequent behaviors, which oftentimes jeopardize the precious abilities of our internal soul being. The physical power structure becomes so domineering that we cannot hear the cries from within, a most terrible gift to waste. The evil ones haunts is the territory of our mind, where self strives to adversely influence the decision making process. This existence is merely the folly of accumulated negative energy.

This corrosive and most dangerous cancer can only be uncovered and removed, through spiritual vision and a departing command. To our greatest detriment and the most casual observer, it should be obvious that we must at once locate, define, and destroy this entity which prevents true understanding from shining forth. No physical human enemy in our history has been allowed this kind of latitude, and neither should this most serious threat to our eternal spirit, be able to continue functioning adversely. Prayer, faith, and repentance of sin, shall conquer this evil as we achieve a unified perspective on spiritual focus, and therby return to a oneness departed.

Attention span disorder may be a recognized physical ailment, but we can ill afford to allow our spiritual attention span to waver any longer. The prognosis of that plague is death. We must get beyond the doubt of divine intervention, that persists only because our mind and body disallows our heart and soul, from expressing the ever presence and welcoming truth about God.

If asked today what I would like to be when grown up, I can honestly say that the best job in the world is being a servant of God, now actively seeking to change the world through truth. I pledge to continue to do so until His return, always assured that my uncommitted heart was reserved for a higher purpose.

I have always known that this day would come, but I just did not know when. This strong desire to accomplish unity among all religions and peoples, is a human based impossibility, but I say once again that with God in charge, all things are indeed possible. Until the Lord is reinstated to His proper and rightful place within each of our daily lives, front and center heart and soul, I shall not rest and neither should you.

THURSDAY, NOVEMBER 27, 1997
THANKSGIVING DAY IS ALWAYS TODAY

Ever since the very first moment that man was created, the spirit of the Lord has been our good shepherd and guide. For those sheep that have become lost throughout the course of our history, the steady hand of the almighty has forever remained within reach of our return grasp.

The Lord's holy spirit has always maintained its established true path for all to follow in this lifetime. The essence of God is the perfection of truth and grace, born from the timeless fruits of patience and love toward His everlasting creations, gifted to humanity in the person of Jesus.

The temporary ruler of the earth (self), has nothing in God, and we oftentimes confuse his misdirectives with the actual directives of our Lord. The former is physical while the latter is spiritual, where never the two shall meet eternally. If we are to become properly balanced in this physical state, we must understand the critical importance of serving our spirit, unless it is only the temporary for which we strive.

On this Thanksgiving Day and every day, let us look beyond the temporary satisfactions of earthly food and temporal life. Giving thanks to God should be an ongoing process in our relationship with Him on a day to day basis. All that we have has been freely given, and what we do with that advantaged dominion is subjected to careful scrutiny. The best way to acknowledge our gratitude is with heartfelt prayer, directed inwardly where His spirit forever meets ours.

Saying grace for the food we are about to eat, is a proper and well received verbal gesture of conscience that serves a physical function, although this type of food we shall hunger for again. God sincerely wishes for us to desire, His nourishment sent from heaven that feeds our spirit. In this regard I am referring to the living bread and water of which Jesus often spoke, known as spiritual understanding, and which only He can provide. It is biblically stated that Jews seek a sign and Greeks wisdom, but humanity is best served in pursuit of understanding.

SATURDAY, NOVEMBER 29, 1997
BE THE BEST YOU CAN BE

An expedition is nothing more or less than the initial exploratory pathway set before us by God, be it in terms of earthly or heavenly travel. I have been fortunate to experience traveling upon this heavenly path of spiritual freedom, that can only be accomplished through the will of our Father, at His designation and appointed time. The day has come for each of us to awaken from our spiritual slumber, by realizing and developing this potential we possess. Although we are outwardly and obviously physical beings, more importantly we are spiritual beings, that can recognize these two separate but equal entities while existing on this earthly plane. Being somewhat restricted in the physical sense of bodily form, our spirits are free to travel beyond the body and to return as well. This is best accomplished through prayerful faith in a state of solitude and peace, whereby earthly distractions can be minimized. The only reason that we as humanity in common have been unable to receive this gift, is mainly due to spiritual negligence, and a lack of soul focus which has deterred our overall growth.

This gift is being withheld because of our constant preoccupation with earthly appetites. An exchange or redistribution of energy from the physical to spiritual, will allow for a proper shift in our balance of power, thus providing our total being with the necessary fuel to travel eternally. In essence we can supply a natural resource to our being, that has always existed but was simply not fully discovered, extracted, and then formulated.

If you think for example in terms of crude oil, which has always been physically present beneath the earth's surface, but only in recent times discovered and utilized by humanity to its greatest capacity, it is easy to see how spiritual enhancement could be overlooked and under developed as well. In other words, there are yet many finite entities that remain undiscovered and unfulfilled in our world, not to mention our infinite abilities, that to most still remain invisible and unknown.

It is the spirit we must now serve which contains the key to our eternal potential, and therefore deserves our completely abiding faith and collective best efforts. Being the best you can be is a performance requirement often heard in western society, but the real meaning of this statement to mission, comes with the inclusion of meeting the spiritual challenge now before us as a civilization of divided brethren, to stand and unite.

MONDAY, DECEMBER 1, 1997
RETURN TO THE FAITH THAT SHARES LOVE IN COMMON

Gather together the sick and the well, that all may partake of this conventional wisdom. The end of the age that the prophets proclaimed is upon us now, no longer a topic of speculation or anticipation, but indeed a fact of life to this generation. The branches of the fig tree are tender, it is true, and the fields are white for harvest. Arise and repent your sins to God today, for tomorrow is promised to no one. You need no other personage for His church is within. His door still remains ajar but shall be very soon closing, as we must turn back to the faith that shares love in common.

The Ten Commandments and The Golden Rule are survival guides to each of our lives, as is the belief in God's only begotten. Over the course of history nothing has changed in the eyes of God. What was good for us then is also good for us today, and will be good for us again tomorrow. This is how the Lord works. Our God is unchanging, and all that we term as change is in reality only part of a cycle. All that is of God returns and repeats with clarity and consistency, as in the case of each returning season and soul. Improvisations of earth's natural gifts are strictly inventions and contrived fantasies of mankind. Human adaptations and so called progress are merely gifts of enlightenment that only God can provide. Do not confuse spiritual gifts with human achievement, because this misconception places distance between each other, and more importantly our creator. Separation is of the earth only and cannot share the spotlight of life eternal with the oneness of our creator.

TUESDAY, DECEMBER 9, 1997
GENTILES OR JEWS?

With Christ we are both, without Him we are neither.

Are we Gentiles or are we Jews, or is it not that clearcut? Individually we are neither completely, but collectively we can become both. Allow me to better explain this dilemma. Being born a Jew is not a birthright or prerequisite for salvation in physical or spiritual terms. It is true that God's original covenant was with the Jews as His chosen people, and we have also learned through Christ that each of us regardless of ethnicity, may become a part of eternal life as God's elect. What constitutes a Jew in God's eyes is the important meaning.

The kingdom of God is attainable for all who believe in the spirit of God, and thereby obey His commandments in life. Becoming a Jew is something that each must earn, not a right that is guaranteed by natural heritage as a given. Israel is written upon our souls by God the eternal author, and not so clearly visible by our varied outward appearances. We are all of the same creator and thus qualified to become children of God as He has so determined through His Son. Spiritual awareness of truth provides us with that passport. What we then do with that privilege in this life, determines our eternal destiny as true seekers of God's will or our own.

The most costly mistake that we as humankind continually make, is to worship any human being as if they were a deity. That is a critical human flaw that creates separation, and as we well know by now, separation is not of God but of the earth. There is only one God, and although we must heed the message of those He truly passes through, we in no way should elevate these earthen vessels beyond their human status.

Several people in our history have borne legitimate messages from God, at critical points where a need was determined for divine intervention. Any other way would be too much of a shock. Today is no different in this regard, and in fact our need has never been greater. God does not always give us what we want when we want it, or what we think we deserve, but He provides us consistently with that which we need as a whole to survive. Do you worship or condemn the courier who brings you a much anticipated letter or package from a loved one near or afar? The courier is only a means of delivery thereby doing the job. The importance of that which you treasure is found within. It is of the sender and not the messenger. Their joy is in the glory of happiness that they were able to help provide you with, well knowing the content of the gift and its origin. This is how God works through us without earth shattering force.

Jesus the man brought the spirit of Christ to us from God our Father. The educator found a worthy body from which to teach. He never asked that we believe in or worship Jesus Verona the human being. He only asked us to realize the loving spirit He possessed. Without ample humanly based training or religious qualifications, He conveyed the message as the spirit of God determined to a world gone astray from pure faith. His life was a reinstatement of God's eternal truths that have forever remained the same.

The fear of truth is what motivates persecution, and that is what placed him physically upon the cross. The death of Jesus the man was determined not by Jews and Romans, but rather by His Father as a sacrifice without equal, that made possible the life of Christ as the everlasting spirit of truth through resurrection, and the advent of the holy spirit helper. This was the evidence displayed to humanity as death now knowing rebirth, and thus became the mission of our witness to that holy spirit helper, which He sends us to this day. Jesus as Christ lives in each of us, and will answer all who ask of Him in truth. Only then may you consider yourself a child of God in reality.

As Jesus was clearly undeserving of death, for He had no sin, His sacrifice was for each of us through our sin, to realize spiritual life that goes beyond earthly death. Without this belief that death has no grip upon us, our faith is unfounded and we will indeed die as unbelievers. What benefit does this road provide for anyone? Through free choice you may take it, but the road less traveled points home.

God offered His son as a human sacrifice to make a critical change in human development, that had prematurely brought itself to the brink of destruction. Jesus possessed this spirit within. He speaks to us not as a scholar, but rather as a teacher with the authority bestowed upon Him concerning heaven sent doctrine. This messenger is indeed unique for He not only brings to us the wishes of God at a particular time, but far more importantly is the living testimony of God's eternal being at all times.

Jesus the man lived and died as do each of us in the physical. Christ was His spirit which continues to live and teach, so that we may come to clearly understand our own human potential through His life, death, and resurrection. It is precisely this pure understanding which allows for the gift of eternal spiritual life, readily available to all souls willing to perceive.

Jesus Christ combined both physically and spiritually, is our eternal standard bearer. God fully realizes that each of us cannot live up to Christ or His teachings at all times, but He also does not expect us to turn away from His truths in self defeat. Unlike Christ, we are only human, but as in Jesus the same spirit of God is everpresent in our soul, and forgiveness is thus obtainable upon request. We cannot continue to bury our spiritual heads in the sand. In God's holy spirit we may fully rely upon this everlasting advocate of hope. (Christ). This is the spiritual love He blesses us with through His law of grace, which overrides any contrary beliefs regarding earthly laws. Human laws are made for law breakers, not for those who abide in the law. True faith in God and its application to life, is the only law we need to live by. This was our most important lesson in human history. How well have we actually learned it?

For the past two thousand years, humankind as a unity has not adequately appreciated the sacrifice of our creator and Son. How much further longsuffering and disappointment could anyone endure as to the state of sinful affairs on earth, that are allowed to not only continue but to persist and actually thrive? That man who died on the cross for our sins was part God Himself in spirit. He has never asked us to sacrifice anything as a show of faith in the equal partnership we casually enjoy.

As dead weight in this partnership, we have become overly burdensome, and must be shed in favor of the greater good. The original bond between God and humanity is a one way street where our free ride is about to end. We have miserably failed in upholding any semblance of our end to the covenant, and who among us would dare to deny this glaring and despicable truth of non-support. His only request is that we properly acknowledge His sacrifice, through prayer and repentance of sin toward salvation. Is that request really too much to ask of anyone in good faith?

When a relative, friend, or even an acquaintance passes away, we offer our proper condolences with respect to the family from our heart. Does God's loss of His only Son, and of whom we are eternally a spiritual part, not deserve at least the same recognition and compassion? The time has come to face our demons. If we feel no spiritual loss to what God has suffered and continues to suffer, then we cannot expect to be a part of that spirit of love which shall live eternally. How could we ever?

A non decision or a planned decision to separate from God, is a decision to accept the temporary fate of the earth only. The burden of proof is on each individual to self disassociate from the powers that be, by simply exercising free choice today. If we stand still and fail to act it is as dangerous as acting wrongly, for even the well intentioned and innocent can be hit by this runaway train known as self.

A decision for Christ and His living word, is a decision for eternal peace to be shared with God. People that did not understand His words then or even now, are failing to see the spirit shining forth, and are too preoccupied with judging the physical man, instead of receiving and most graciously cherishing the spiritual gift. His mission on this earth was to help us realize and then utilize the spiritual abilities we do in fact possess. He was not then and is not now speaking over our heads about that which we are incapable of grasping. He is simply educating us to an underdeveloped and under utilized area of our total being known as spirit. This was and is, absolutely necessary for humanity to further progress in gaining overall understanding of who we are and where we are going, at the most critical point of human stagnation in spirit and brotherhood. We began to develop religiously and spiritually for an extended period of time following that earthly life of Christ, but have never truly maintained the lessons of our teacher as a unity to this day.

The errors of the "church" that led to reformation caused a split. Is it not commonly heard throughout our developmental life, that we should strive to get the best out of our God given gifts? Christ was simply saying that it is not only the physical development of being that counts, but more importantly the spiritual, of which to this day we remain as a species caught in early infancy through transgression. A pastor once told me that I may be transgressing, and that I was going back to another time period. Perhaps he was correct and that is what the Lord has been teaching me these past fourteen months, so that I would find that road we missed so long ago. It would be hard to disagree with the fact that humanity is lost in confusion. We must rise and begin to walk or else continue to lie in the spiritual cradle and die, along with the most powerfully adverse influences at work in this aging and corrupt physical world. Please remind yourself today that when my time is up, I am going to be counted as a walker toward God, and not as a crawler away from Him. Through faith we may stand and also speak to the Lord.

In the past two thousand years we should have fully developed both physically and spiritually into well balanced harmony. The lesson was clearly provided and is still being provided, but we have not paid close enough attention to the teacher then and now.

Failure is the end result if the required work is incomplete. I do not care how old anyone is in terms of earth years, for those are but fleeting moments on the eternal calendar. Our true age and growth period in God's view, is measured by spiritual maturity not physical, and in that regard the human race is a child about to die of old age, without ever growing in a proper balance of total being that coincides with universal habitat. We must catch up to our spirits, but without the intervention of God it is impossible for us as human beings to accomplish. Go straight to your heart and ask Him faithfully to perform this miracle. He shall answer in truth as He has always promised and delivered.

God would like us as humanity to now remove the man Jesus from the cross, and to give Him an appropriate human burial. We have seen and understood that He died as a man for our sins in this physical world. The holy communion is rightly kept for this remembrance, as faith in His living word moves us forward. Let us now enter into the glory of His resurrection which is Christ, the living spirit of God, without forgetting the man. We must also die to sin so that our spirit may eternally live. This death that occurs is not physical, but rather a spiritual death where we become born again as Christ has promised, during both His life as Jesus and the holy spirit helper ever since. In this way we continue to live in the physical world through His resurrection, minus the sin we are born into and develop. We can now become Christlike without experiencing the actual death of total being. Jesus is our prototype of full potential, and our shepherd to God.

Once born again, the spirit of Christ will bless you with the gift of the holy spirit, in a spiritual baptism that only He can provide. The laying on of hands by a person who has received the holy spirit, was a formality for this exchange during Pisces. In essence we may become Christlike in spirit and are then able to transform human law, thereby becoming Jesus like in the flesh, and shifting our balance of power from the physical back to the spiritual where it has always belonged. Without gaining His spirit first we cannot hope to live up to His teachings. Let us now move faithfully into Aquarius.

We are now prepared to truly become citizens of heaven, and may conduct our lives accordingly on this earth under the laws of grace, no longer bound by the laws of sin with its physical and temporary dictates. We die through Jesus the man, and are reborn with Christ the Lord. Jesus once said that with His help, we will perform far greater things than He. This process of transformation is exactly what He meant. We can accomplish this exchange without suffering the same earthly death that He freely gave to us for our eternal edification. All that we have to do is to put His lesson into motion. We now must graduate from His classroom and into the real world, with the fruits He did bear, that His life, death, and resurrection were not, are not, and shall not be in vain.

THURSDAY, DECEMBER 11, 1997
LOVE IS ALL

If you listen closely to your voice within, there is a knocking upon the door of each and every heart. For untold years through the distractions, deceit, and confusions of the evil one, that distinct knock has been generally unheeded, ignored, or unheard due to self. The time has come for each of us to bravely walk towards that door, and then answer our call with great joy and happiness, by greeting the spirit of Christ with a warm, loving, and heartfelt welcoming embrace. Invite Him into your life and eternal truth shall be yours, as in that truth He will set you forever free. For all of the doors that we have mistakenly opened in our lives, never have we been as fortunate to receive a guest such as He. The Lord will guide us into the everlasting peace of His being, by replacing the apprehensions and fears of this physically temporary world, with the love and true understanding of His spiritually eternal one.

In these days of increasing physical dangers which pose a direct threat to our total beings security, a far reaching evil has taken hold upon humankind. We must willingly and assertively step back and take account of the damages suffered thus far, and begin repairing, rectifying, rebuilding, and then reversing the general misuse of free choice. The only solution, is to individually tear away and then stay away from the vice like grips of self, and to defeat this devastating enemy within, that has too long masqueraded as the prince of our best interests. Assuredly this is a prince, but of self interests and not God's, which is why it is appropriately known as the prince of darkness.

Make good each choice with a spiritual focus, by allowing the light to shine forth in your life, and in this way only, you may achieve the inner peace that comes by walking with the Lord on His heaven lit path.

Somewhere in our storied past, we as humankind simply took a wrong turn on the road to heaven, which has since misguided us into a lost world of critical proportion and imminent danger. We must now go back spiritually and rediscover the proper route of travel on the road back to God, which can only be found on the map in each soul known as the Lord Jesus Christ.

Hope is required, faith is essential, charity is necessary, prayer is commanded, and only then may truth and understanding be founded upon His everlasting grace and eternal love.

Accompanying each of these good fruits must be this true vine and Godly root, to support us as branches on the tree of life. Although it is too late for consoling the man Jesus, who has sacrificed himself for our sins, and thus suffered unbearable pains upon the cross, it is not too late to help ease the far greater pains that His spirit of Christ has been enduring ever since. His earthly sufferings at least had an ending, but because of our reluctance to collectively abide in His spirit, those spiritual sufferings shall continue on until His next coming. It is our calling and pure duty to acknowledge His sacrifice for us, not only upon the cross but more importantly in each and every day since. Never once has He turned His back on us when in spiritual need, or wavered from His original covenant to humankind. Where are we as His equal partners? Would any of us honestly participate in such a one sided partnership based on neglect and self servitude?

I have now fully awakened to help inform those still sleeping, that the Lord has officially declared His final request of us. We should clearly understand His wishes by now...love is all.

DECEMBER, 14, 1997
OUR KINGDOM OF GOD IS ALWAYS AT HAND

Throughout biblical scripture, the Old Testament books of Prophets has quite accurately foretold the coming of important people and events in our history. The New Testament gospels concerning Christ and the Book of Revelation, are also sources of scholarly analysis in predicting future occurrences.

The epistles of Paul which comprise about one third of the New Testament, are mainly accounts of his efforts in preaching Christ to the Gentiles, and also contain his inaccurate prediction of Christ's second coming during that generation. The original Apostles also felt the impending anxieties in their lifetime, as to His return and the subsequent end of the world. Their human sense of prediction was not based on an actual promise of Jesus, but rather a hopeful anticipation of His coming. Although their timing was inaccurate as to an imminent Armageddon, they were not incorrect in preaching the kingdom of God near at hand. The fact is that Christ did indeed return as promised in the form of the holy spirit, which was presented to each Apostle at Pentecost, to Paul (Saul) on the road to Damascus, and then untold multitudes continuing to this day.

When He told His Apostles that it was better for them if He went away then to remain on the earth, He was referring to the unconfined abilities that He knew the holy spirit would provide. Those that have received the gift of this spirit feel the same anxieties as those men did, because the source of our teachings is timeless and unchanging. The word indeed had become flesh. The kingdom of God is always at hand and it is not for us to know our own end time, but to always be prepared for that day. In light of this fact there is no better time then now for that preparation. Our world may be confusing but free choice is clear.

The rationale of the holy spirit shares nothing in common with human rationale, because the former is born of spirit while the latter is a product of earth. The impending war to end all wars, is the battle that each of us must wage within our own spirits and for our own souls, in this lifetime and very soon. Although Armageddon is biblically described as a devastating physical battlefield, it is this spiritual battlefield I speak of which determines our ultimate victory or defeat within. No one except God knows the exact time that judgement day occurs. The same rule applies as to the movement of the holy spirit.

Jesus clearly stated in John chapter three, that the holy spirit is much like the wind. We hear it all around us, but know not where it came from or where it is going. As mere human beings we cannot know the will of He that created us, unless He so chooses to appoint us those truths. Who are we to question that power which breathed life itself into us?

The holy spirit is a gifted communication line between the Godhead and humankind pure and simple. Religious truths are not able to be developed by humanity because they already were in place before creation itself occurred. What God desires for us to know will be given as He sees fit.

These truths of which I speak are eternal in nature, and can only be provided through God's grace, thus unachievable to human ability or our futile perseverance without holy spirit directive. Any human analysis of our living God's intent that goes beyond the day to day marching orders and echoes of His spirit, is ill conceived and an absolutely total waste of time and effort. Becoming a good and God fearing human being is the beginning of heavenly truth through knowledge, wisdom, and understanding, regardless of our religious affiliation or doctrinal beliefs. This requires the spiritual focus of dedication toward our heart, mind, body, and soul, and all other strength we can muster. Salvation was never designed as a birthright or an easy task, but nevertheless remains a most pleasing invitation to life eternal with God and Son.

As children of God, we are each eligible to share in His kingdom, but must earn that designation each and every day. At the times when we cannot fulfill the standards of God and fall short of His expectations, remember always that we have an eternal advocate in Christ, where forgiveness is everpresent and understanding continually dwells.

To become truly born again requires the systematic termination of all the poisonous earthly fruits from deep within our souls. The elements of greed, hate, prejudice, lust, envy, deceit, contempt, and all other offspring of sin must be removed. Upon proper request, God will step in to your life and remove these evils immediately. He forever maintains that this is true, as daily creation renewal is that attestation.

The elimination of these sins allows for the good fruits born of spiritual love to be seeded, rooted, grown, and then nurtured. This separation of our tares from the good wheat can occur in this lifetime, making the Lord's work that much easier upon His arrival. This process is a painless and eternal comfort. In accomplishing this otherwise impossible mission, we must direct our heartfelt prayer with a keen emphasis on spiritual focus towards God. A complete transformation of our total being takes time, patience, and determination, but is well worth the eternal reward of continued life in this very special realm.

All of us are sinners, all of us make mistakes, and all of us fall short of the mark, but all of us can make amends with God by limiting our mistakes, and removing our sins in a way that draws us closer to Him instead of creating greater distance. Each of us must stand up and believe in ourselves and one another, enough to declare and then act upon a willingness to meet God with a statement: that I shall not allow Satan as self to achieve victory through me or my brother. This requires the intestinal fortitude that we each possess by gift, possibly misplaced but not missing. Looking deep inside allows His light to shine forth righteously. As you begin to prioritize your life through choices pertaining to God, He will move you in such a way that brings balance to your total being. This critical accomplishment is most essential in eventually fully pleasing ourselves, fellow, and our maker. In order to receive the help we truly need, each person must take their own initiative to sincerely ask and then commit. This soul realization shall set you free.

As each spring season brings the hope and joy of renewed life, so also must we command our old spirits away from "the winter of our discontent", and into this new age and eternal paradise. Let us move forever forward together at a slow and steady pace. Plant the seeds of spiritual life that they may blossom as fine perennials, and not merely temporary annuals in the Lord's garden.

The fact of the matter is that we have each been purchased as slaves to this earth. Our only saving grace is that we possess the ability through free choice in becoming either slaves to sin, or slaves to righteousness; a clear but often difficult choice.

The physical world laws for each of us to follow came through God's servant Moses, while the spiritual laws of truth and grace could only come through Jesus Christ.(letter and spirit of law) It is these intangible qualities born of spirit that brings out the best in each of us, and supercedes any humanistic law. As we consistently fail to live as we believe God so desires, perseverance to the standard of Christ should not be abandoned.

Rather then easily giving up and continuing a downward slide, utilize His forgiveness as a springboard for self improvement. In this manner, although many temporary setbacks of personal expectation are sustained, we achieve a higher overall level of being by learning the errors of our ways, then correcting instead of repeating them. This produces a smooth stepping stone of hope for our newfound bright and eternal collective future.

The growth process of becoming Christlike in these graduating spiritual developmental stages, is no different then the methods we employ in our physical growth stages between childhood and adulthood. If the critical lessons of life go unlearned, then some particular deficiencies will result. Patience, love, care, compassion, and perseverance will produce a fine spiritual adult offspring that avoids those pitfalls through a proper upbringing. It is the direct responsibility of each person that has received spiritual gifts from God, to step forward and share this light. We are not teachers, but are chosen as earthen vessels of the teaching process which originates in heaven with Christ Jesus. This is the equality and the oneness that our father in heaven, and every other parent strongly desires for all their children. Only a firm belief and commitment in the Lord can deliver us to the next stage of spiritual evolution. The Lord is the mirror of our soul, and in that mirror is our true reflection.

THURSDAY, JANUARY 1, 1998
TIME IS NOT AS WE KNOW IT

Our lives upon this earth are but a brief moment, amidst the eternity of our Lord's pre-established sequence of events. Time, as we have come to develop and understand it, has been measured from sands and sundials, to the more modern digital technologies and calendars of today and a soon to be tomorrow. Throughout the course of human history, and despite the changes we as humankind have instituted, the Lord's purpose remains timeless and unchanging. Although free choice is a gift of our essential being, we oftentimes believe that with this gift comes control of the world's destiny, when in reality it is the true will of God which shall prevail in standing the test of time. The maker always holds the authority over that which He makes, unlike the dissensions of humanity that persist with poor choice. The only watch that we should be concerned with is the one that we were told to be keeping in expectation of Christ's return, as our Messiah within.

This time of which I speak is to us yet undated, but its process has already begun. Being well prepared spiritually, is the wisdom and knowledge of critical prerequisite to eternal understanding.

The earthly end of days will not be an occurrence established by humanity or its designs, but rather an inevitable cosmic event, in direct response to our sinful nature's progressive failings. Forgiveness must be requested and then obtained, to avoid the coming wrath of God and the pitfalls associated with judgement. Remaining as bystanders and thus accessories in this trial, would be an ill conceived notion and most improper judgement.

We must separate from the force which created separation itself, and stand distinctly apart of all evil association and influence. As we teach our children to avoid adverse influences throughout their lives, our Father is now asking each of us to do likewise.

Seeking our future through the means of ungodly channels, is a most dangerous venture into territory where we do not belong. For a future to be seen, it must have already occurred in time on a spiritual plane. Through spiritual gifts and abiding love, God freely provides all that we need, and discourages our wants that center on self.

MONDAY, JANUARY 5, 1998
ACTIVELY SEEK THE IMPERISHABLE CROWN

Contrary to the trend of popular belief, the true desires of the Godhead are not centered around bureaucratic Christianity. We live in a world filled with non-practicing and self proclaimed true believers, as well as the lost sheep known primarily as questionable or outright unbelievers. The real shepherds of Christ are far too few in number, amidst the many ravenous wolves in this heavenly sent field of dreams. Those that proclaim loyalty with their lips but denial by their works, stand on far shakier ground than they could ever imagine.

The seeds that were planted in the fields long ago, have been nourished and nurtured long enough and their time has now come. Abilities to sow and then to reap must emerge at the harvest, for that which is to live eternally must first die an earthly death in this cycle of salvation. Christ was and is the way. Those that are Christ's in the true spirit of His word, must firmly move all potential shepherds forward to now mission in His calling.

Please discontinue the practice of tilling barren ground, and begin seeking new and fertile territory of more abundant harvest. The religious leadership must now call for this expanded mission, whereby each congregation more assertively and systematically soon graduates its members from students to instructors in the field. By continually reaffirming and coddling the daily desires of true believers, the more critical needs of many lost sheep go forever unfulfilled. If we have done our job well as servants of God, then all to whom we have ministered, should now have Christ as their teacher. With that being the case, each must go forward in Christ and minister to those that know Him not. That prior dependent relationship shall cease to exist, but a much stronger bond of equal partnership in Christ is birthed.

There was an old saying that I recall very similar to this point. "Mother's are not to lean upon, but to make leaning unnecessary." The same holds true for those who represent God in abiding faith. This is the necessary lesson of leaving the nest, whereby flying with God on those gifted wings, builds new nests for the needy. When you come to truly know Christ, you will find it is He that was created to bear our burdens, not our fellow human beings.

If this special love has become a part of your life, then kindly help others to discover His path. In sharing this gift, you shall achieve no greater sense of personal satisfaction in this life. By branching out in God's mission and offering our lives as a living sacrifice, we better our world one soul at a time, and in the process God will attend to every need along the way.

From the standpoint of the bureaucratic church, it is better business to keep their members in the nest, but the Lord is well aware of their potential ability to fly, and the subsequent responsibility of church leaders is to encourage that to happen. Do not be so assured through human rationale, that as leaders perpetuating passive spiritual infancy, your mission is as highly regarded as you have come to perceive. The Lord well knows the difference between genuine Christianity, and its marketing presentation for commercial use only. Is the product that your church is putting forth a true representation of the spirit which was, and still is Christ?

The Laws of God came through His servant Moses, while truth and grace arrives to humanity in the being of Jesus Christ. If we truly understand that God is unchanging, and that His word is evidenced in scripture, then we must also realize that He is a living God, and as active today as ever before. To truly feel His presence is to embrace the holy spirit of truth He sends, and abide in the living word as well as the written. In this way we shall grow ever closer to God, and one another once again.

After giving some thought as to the policies of each church, remember always the cornerstone upon which every church is built, and the feelings of His heart in creating that covenant. If the conditions of this world today are not as they should be, then let us each do our part in making the necessary changes.

With the help of the Lord, through a commitment to unified prayer, we can persevere in faith to the end of our days, and thus share in His eternal glory of peace everlasting. We must rise in unity to the next level of being, by championing the cause of our Christ within.

Describe it as you will, but God does not subscribe to fancy window dressing, or showings of faith that lack real substance. This may be sufficient enough for public consumption, but does not hold water with the Lord. What is similar to us in appearance may be glaringly different to God, as the eye and the soul can provide quite opposite viewpoints. He well knows the truth concerning the intentions of our hearts. In talking the talk, be also well prepared to walk the walk. If we are to step up to that higher level of human performance, we must do so in a humble and dignified manner, and not with the pride that has forever hindered our spiritual potential. Preaching is done with the feet.

The gate to God's kingdom is narrow indeed, and to walk this path we must truly give it our all, as a unity built on the premise of teamwork whereby true champions are founded, not by the exclusive individualism of selfishness and separation that hinders us.

As long as there are lost sheep that remain in the fields, do not ever stop striving toward the true will of God each day. Real satisfaction and contentment are eternal awards, not earthly rewards that can be achieved or presented in this lifetime. Only through our quest for the truth in God's spirit of love, lies the real treasured prize of His imperishable crown.

WEDNESDAY, JANUARY 7, 1998
ALL FOR ONE AND ONE FOR ALL

Imagine, if you will, that the world in which we live is a large country farm, and throughout this farm are various types of life forms daily existing within their respective habitats. Although every seemingly separate grouping is distinctly different in nature, each share a common bond with one another that they may or may not be aware of, namely their survival based on a codependence that only the farmer fully realizes.

On this farm, as well as every other, there is a farmer in charge. The farmer in this case as in all cases of life is the Lord. His main objective is to coordinate all the separate but equal entities which inhabit His farm, and to successfully develop the entirety as a unified sum total of the individual parts. If only certain groups are operating sufficiently while others tend to under perform in their mission, then the farm itself as a whole cannot prosper, and in due time may not even survive.

Life as we know it today has become a strikingly similar analogy. Although each individual person or group of people may tend to view themselves as an insignificant portion of the human entirety, (around six billion and rising) in reality this false assumption could be no further from the truth. Each of us originates from the oneness of our Creator, and in this form He is an integral part of every human being He creates. Located deep in our heart is God's everlasting spirit of love, whereby we are never alone or insignificant in any sense of the word to Him. It is in this spirit we must now look at life. Many of us are oftentimes guilty of giving in or giving up too easily during life's daily trials and tribulations, where more often than not our guard comes down, and we begin losing those everyday battles versus the adverse influences of evil self servitude.

To win this war for the heavenly cause, we must keep our guard continually up, and fight the good fight until the final bell. Every round that we lose along the way separates us further from God, but He forever remains in our corner promoting victory.

As St. Paul alluded to in his first epistle to the Corinthians, each member of the body performs a unique and important task in the overall development and well being of the body itself. If one member suffers, all the members suffer with it, or if one member is honored, all the members rejoice with it. Individually we are members in the body of Christ, while collectively in His spirit we must become that unity of oneness which He requires, of those who seek salvation and eternal life. Although we shall indeed be judged individually, it is the well being of all our members that should concern us as God's elect. Paul was referring to then as I am reiterating now, that each of us plays a critical role in determining our collective earthly fate, whereby taking heed of only our own lives is unacceptable to unity's ideal.

As Christ came to earth in the being of Jesus, to serve rather then be served and offer salvation not condemnation, does it not follow that we should abide in each other as He has in us? Peaceful coexistence on earth is no longer a utopian concept, but rather a gift that God is still willing to give us in spirit. Perfect harmony fully realized is a free and individual choice for His spirit of love, manifested to all in the Book of Life.

To approach any level of being thus acceptable to God, we must now begin to climb that stairway to heaven one step at a time. Faith, virtue, knowledge, self-control, charity, perseverance, Godliness, kindness, and love, will take you to where you want to be. One way or the other, we shall become reunited however briefly, and judged according to our good faith and works... or lack thereof. May each soul be blessed upon its journey.

When various passages in the New Testament compare Christ's return or second coming to a wedding ceremony, He is forever the bridegroom and New Jerusalem His bride. The guest list of open invitation refers to our individual faith and worthiness to attend. In the world to come (New Jerusalem) all doors will be closed upon the arrival of invited guests. Jesus directly refers to the critical importance in several parables, of our keeping a constant watch in hopeful expectation of His return. *The Immaculate Conception* is written for the heavenly purpose of extending to all, this gifted invitation to each New Jerusalem within.

SUNDAY, JANUARY 18, 1998
KNOWLEDGE + WISDOM = UNDERSTANDING

In this life there is one binding and most essential element which humankind shares in common, and that is a portion of God. We know that God is spirit and His spirit is eternal love.

If reconciliation with our maker is the desire of each human being, proper dialogue must first be established between all of His children, through a formula born of His true everlasting love. Knowledge + wisdom = understanding is that simple equation. We cannot fully attain life's eternal reality without graduating to this level of truth, which includes applying it to our lives. Knowledge (the physical learning process of our minds) must precede wisdom, (the spiritual learning process of our hearts) and then be combined together to equal overall understanding. (the eternal learning process of our spiritual soul)

Two thousand years ago we were graciously gifted this formula, when the word became flesh in the being of Jesus Christ. As of this writing, we as humankind are no closer to this truth and its application than that long ago time of His earthly life. We must now shift our fixated and limited human perspectives of worshiping Jesus the man only, by redirecting those same energies into the resurrection of His spirit which is the Christ. The movement and direction of Christ is straight ahead only, where our focus must remain if eternal life is to become each reality.

The confusions and deceits of the evil presence among us, is forever occupied with the encouragement of our continued misdirection, to divert that spiritual focus of which I speak.

The physical pain and sufferings of Jesus upon the cross of our sins, was intensely cruel and humiliating but nonetheless came to a merciful end. It is the ongoing spiritual pain of the Christ spirit resurrected, that we continue to crucify by failing to raise ourselves up in recognition of His sacrifice. Those are the tears that have yet to be dried, as our resurrection of humanity remains hopelessly stagnant in a world of separation.

This educating spirit known as our living God, did not cease to exist with the physical burial of Jesus Verona in Jerusalem. His spirit lives among us today at our most critical juncture in history, as we must collectively strive to become that which He taught us, through His loving gift of truth and grace. By actively seeking truth we shall assuredly receive His grace, and may then proceed in our proper soul development.

No teacher can achieve fulfillment or a sense of gratification, until those whom they have spent their lifetime teaching, equal and then exceed all expectations of their pure curriculum thus taught. In His life by example He informed us that we are Gods, and as we follow His path, greater things than these we shall do.

Jesus Christ is not only a Jew of the original covenant, but also a Gentile of the new covenant in whom every being may hope. He is the first fruit of the resurrection but by no means the only one, if we follow in step with each lesson of our teacher toward home.

In these past two thousand years we have failed miserably in the lesson plan presented to us, and as a result are totally unprepared for the transition from a physical to spiritual state. All of us shall be moved regardless of our achievement level towards eternal life, but it will be a much smoother ride if we prepare our total being accordingly for the upcoming journey. This will require the unconditional release of our deathly grip upon the materialistic madness, that encumbers and then consumes the very essence of our being, thus suppressing the will of God. Our spirits must be rescued immediately, if they are to avoid the demise to which our physical beings have been sentenced. This is not an illustration or preparation for death, but rather a divine call to life through His eternally unwavering love for creation.

God gave of Himself to humankind, the spirit of Christ in the being of Jesus, and now offers us the same spiritual gift through His living word. Knowledge + wisdom = understanding. We cannot arrive there without the one that has already gone.

The first stage is achievable through our words and our works, while the second stage is conceivable with true faith and prayer. The third and final stage is only receivable through the divine revelation of His oneness, realization of this eternal truth, and the proper acknowledgement (repentance) of His loving grace. To be Christlike requires the connection of all three entities, and this is our spiritual gift of salvation.

THURSDAY, JANUARY 22, 1998
THE FINAL COVENANT: FAITH IN HIS LIVING WORD

The following were the words spoken to me through revelation on November 23, 1997 upon awakening at 6:42AM: "Remember always our covenant of Holy communion, consecrated with the blood of My human sacrifice, now renewed by the promise of faith in My living word."

The very first revelation on November 3, 1996 was as follows: "Assuredly I say to you, the poor are not in terms of economic means but rather in lack of knowledge, wisdom, and understanding... Return to them their needs".

Our third and final covenant is true faith in His living word. This original message that was sent to me in spirit, shall soon travel full circle, thus becoming our collective understanding. What greater gift could our loving God impart in this lifetime? I have a strong sense about me that this mission to complete *The Immaculate Conception* is now upon the immediate horizon, but what do I really know of the master plan?

If the Lord so chooses to speak through us again, I wish for Him to know that we shall always be listening and keeping watch. I have come to know God as a caring friend, in waiting for each of our spirits to come forth with eternal love and brotherhood. If this were not true I would have certainly told everyone so. For these past sixteen months, and for each forthcoming day that I am allowed to live through grace upon this earth, I shall give praise to the Lord almighty toward His heavenly abode, within and above.

I pray that each person may find inner peace through these words, and I assure you that the Lord will attend to your heart's every spiritual need throughout life. Be patient and simply ask Him. The only way that I am able to complete this mission, is by using the only formula required for all missions to thus be completed. Through focus, perseverance, prayer, and living one day at a time we shall achieve, conceive, and then receive that essential element of eternal life, found only within faith of His living word.

From every religious branch grows fruit of a far different kind. Take something from each but never it all, and understanding shall be yours. The answers to life lie in the root unseen.

MONDAY, JANUARY 26, 1998
THROUGH MY LIVING WORD YOUR HEARTS WILL GO ON

The journey that we are soon to embark upon transcends both time and space. This is not a passage to be measured across the miles, but rather a heavenly mode of travel through human degrees of spiritual faith. The third and final covenant of faith in His living word, is the last commandment by which our vehicle may travel back home.

The gift of free choice was granted upon creation for the express purpose of ensuring our total being, its safety through all experiences in this lifetime. The first of the three eternal gifts presented to Israel, is the deliverance of the Torah through Moses at Mt. Horeb, (oral and written law) also known by its peak called Mount Sinai.

This gift contains all physical laws pertaining to earthly life. It requires no additions or subtractions at any point in time. The precepts of the Torah (613) include the Ten Commandments and are eternal in nature. There are seven additional rabbinical precepts for a total of 620. To live by the Torah is to love God with all our heart and soul, and our fellow human beings as ourselves, where daily application soon converts into instinct, and faith becomes our life guide and mission as with all other developing religions as well.

In order to understand the true meaning of its directive, the Torah must be renewed in worship on a regular basis in spirit. As it becomes an integral part of our daily being through that innermost reflection, the Torah forever serves as a reminder of our enduring and everlasting covenant with God and His love for creation. It is the spirit of the law, not the letter, which points us toward salvation. To become the law is to be greater than its words. In Jesus, it was accomplished, and through His spirit is our Christ eternal.

Our God is an unchanging and timeless spirit of love, that provides His world with that which is needed, when it is needed, and through whomever He so chooses to send His word. It has come to all religions at the time of their origin, and remains in spirit for the continuity of one God belief. Jesus became the living Torah through truth and grace, thus opening our pathway to God, one and all.

The second gift of eternal consequence is the spirit of Christ.

This spirit again came to earth two thousand years ago, and dwelt exclusively within the human beingness of Jesus Verona. The Christ is God's educating spirit which continually provides humanity with a standard bearer of eternal truth and grace. Simply stated: Jesus as the Christ is the teacher and the teaching process that must be followed into the kingdom of God. His physical life is the pathway in which we must pattern our lives, for all through sin fall short of His spiritual example. Through God's teachings, sacrifice, and resurrection of Christ, He clearly displays to us the true meaning of everlasting love. In Christ the gift comes eternal forgiveness upon repentance, and an advocate for our shortcomings that can deprive salvation. In His spirit of truth, we have an ongoing hope based on faith. "Love one another as I also love you"...is our eternal covenant. As we bear our own cross, the fruits of total being shall appear in the form of Christ, and be made manifest upon His tree of life eternal.

The third and final eternal gift from God to humankind, comes to us as the product of faith in His living word through Christ. Within our collective calling by *The Immaculate Conception,* I am confident that God's purpose will be served in these words to each soul upon its journey home, as another life cycle thus concludes.

We must pierce through the physical shield of this life's trials and tribulations, by cutting away the main distractions which prevent clear and concise spiritual true understanding, namely the temptations and confusions through the application of delusion. Our weapon of choice in this momentous battle for freedom, is unified prayer toward a universal spiritual focus. By penetrating and then exposing the existing power structure of today's world, we can begin to see the light of spirit breaking through that guides our pathway to everlasting peace.

Once we establish the connection to God's true spirit, it is imperative that we remain committed to this open line of communication and education. This requires a complete spiritual rededication of our lives for the greater good to life eternal. As the evil presence among us forever stimulates our five physically corruptible senses, we must reroute these same energies into best serving our sixth sense born of spirit. It is in this vision that we shall realize a far better world, through the choice separation of adverse influence.

Instead of continuously adapting and complying to a world on the downslide, we must now stand apart from the errors of our ways, and avoid the forthcoming sentence of guilty by association. We must first individually and then collectively, reject the earthly dictates which not only surround us, but more critically have become internalized and overwhelming to our very spirits. God is once again providing us with a comprehensive life care system of love.

DANCES WITH WOLVES

It is you I have chosen to come dance with the wolves,
take good care in these fields of great danger,
though alone you must shepherd I am never far removed,
at every turn awaits the safety of My manger.

As promised time and again, I shall inform you only in parts,
for your protection in and outside the ranks,
keep your attention strictly focused on My direction straight ahead,
as I provide the eternal guardian for your flanks.

In regards to such concerns as the sands in My hourglass,
stay the course upon your heaven lit path,
you are neither behind nor too far ahead of schedule,
in accordance with My coming day of wrath.

As I hand over the wheel navigate safely through these waters,
your destiny is to come forward and take the helm,
there will be many more passengers than you could ever imagine,
this Titanic is bound for a new eternal realm.

As you stop in each port kindly welcome all aboard,
each one's fare must be received and paid in full,
there shall be no stowaways on this great and final voyage,
dress My lost sheep warmly in the finest coats of wool.

The key to your success in thus completing this mission,
is to make certain that enough life boats are onboard,
so that each may have a seat when the main vessel fails,
the distress call shall be answered by your Lord.

For the inspirational music to thus captivate each soul,
hereby written for this new days coming dawn,
while directing the multitudes to safety sing our psalms still unknown,
through My living word your hearts will go on.

The most important factor is that no one becomes lost,
each spirit an essential piece of My puzzle,
I assured you months ago that when in fact you were ready,
I would gently remove both chain and muzzle.

Through your dreams of recent days you have rightly assumed,
that the time to step forth has begun,
this marathon race which began sixteen months ago,
has lost many along the road you still run.

The Imperishable Crown is an award without equal,
maintain the perseverance we have taught you since birth,
for this ever elusive and most precious of jewels,
through My living word lies your discovery of great worth.

This is My final commandment as you prepare to set sail,
toward the freedom of My wide open sea,
I salute you when completing *The Immaculate Conception* for all,
safe passage home on the road back to Me.

Although many are called very few in fact are chosen,
it pleases Me well to see how you have grown,
fear no one but your Lord and you shall never be steered wrong,
take this hand as I now rise from My throne.

To he who has My word speak it faithfully to the world,
in the latter days it shall become crystal clear,
as you endure until the end My new name shall thus be written,
upon your drum for all ears willing to hear.

This is My one final gift held patiently from the beginning,
with all its mystery very soon to be revealed,
not to presidents or kings nor the greatest religious scholars,
but to a simple heart that keeps Me carefully concealed.

The Torah with truth and grace are the only real companions,
take My gifts and climb aboard this unsinkable ship,
no human constitution is involved in its construction,
but pure faith determines each destiny on this trip.

Let no one deceive you from the covenant we established,
taking nothing for granted along the way,
as the parade line begins forming only one drummer can lead,
play well My friend as you pass by judgement day!

Our destiny is dependent upon the determination of human willpower, the spirit of brotherly love, and the grace of God. We must take a unified stand versus the forces of evil today, or suffer the fate of a sleeping world amidst this roaring fire.

If this wake up call is disruptive to your comfortable position in life, then our mission of mercy will be termed a fine success. May the Lord bless you in this world and in the world to come, and as always let faith be your guide.

FEBRUARY 2, 1998 "THE CHURCH WITH NO NAME" All are welcome.

If you are wondering why our church has no name, it is simply because names create separations and boundaries, and with God leading this church there are to be no separations or boundaries. A church is the place in each of our hearts which connects us with God, and then to each other through our common bond of love and spirit. God is spirit and that spirit is love. It is in this light that we are given a church born of spirit.

There are untold thousands of human religious beliefs and faiths that span the globe, and not one is free of their imperfections. This church is without human doctrine or beliefs, and in no way separates or distinguishes itself from anyone or anything.

The only aim of this church is human unity through God's oneness, to achieve knowledge, conceive wisdom, and receive understanding. If we agree to keep only God as our teacher, then we shall soon come to realize that these spiritual gifts can only be given.

Human accomplishments are limited to the physical world in which God has placed us, and are merely the byproducts of free choice. When we invite God into our lives, an unlimited new potential of our total being emerges, where wisdom and understanding become a part of us, through a spirit no longer restricted by knowledge. This is our pathway to eternal life, love, truth, and happiness.

The mission of God's holy spirit is to guide us through life. The spirit of Christ is that educating gift of our living God. Jesus Verona was the man to first receive this educating spirit, and upon his earthly death the spirit lived on in resurrection. This very same spirit lives among us today, and if we come to understand God through these teachings of His spirit, the narrow gate leading to His kingdom shall soon be graciously widened.

I have no religious affiliation or education, nor have I ever officially belonged to any congregation of worship. I am only an earthen vessel through whom God has chosen to bring this one message. Please respect my desire for anonymity and share in this gift. Our mission is to fulfill this collective calling for unity, by sharing His spirit with all that wish to walk in His kingdom.

If perfect love and everlasting life in peaceful harmony with God, is your aim in this world and in the world to come, then this church shall be able to provide you with proper direction. This is not a cult or new religion, but rather a born again experience which is destined to be openly shared with all.

We were placed upon this earth to live as one with God and nature. Through the influence of evil came the many sins born of separation and individualism, as we have become lost sheep from our shepherd, mainly due to the abuses of our gifted free choice. Separation is contrary to unity, as God is the spirit of oneness. His gift to humankind of brotherly love is the tie which binds us together in common, thus providing our strength to overcome any adverse influence that may threaten the essence of our collective being.

Our history of war is an ongoing testament to both the evils of human selfishness, and the righteousness of human selflessness in response to unwarranted persecutions and oppressions. Each entity that goes to war has lived on both sides of choice.

Today we are faced with an enemy that is far more destructive than any other in history, and imminently threatens our life on this planet. This once outside invader has now moved inside, as the war that we cannot see in progress is now being waged for our very souls, and choices will thus determine each loyalty. The fallout of this great battle, is clearly evidenced in the rapidly declining moral structure of our decaying everyday world. As you follow along this path of understanding, your spiritual awareness and focus will increase to a battle ready proportion.

Our first task at hand is to alert each person now sleeping, with a wake up call that will be unsettling in the beginning. Please do not make the mistake of ignoring this critical alarm. Through an organized system of daily preparation and revelation, we will then bring each lost sheep to the awaiting good shepherd. This war will be fought and won while still living in this world. It is our collective souls that must rise to meet this enemy. We must begin our battle from within, by making good today our long ago established covenant with our creator and friend. Once acceptable to God again, each soul may surface triumphant, and walk confidently but not proudly back home.

"THE MISSION OF OUR CHURCH IS UNDERSTANDING"

The fulfillment of perfect love can only be reached through the process of understanding God. This must occur through spirit. It is this love of which I speak that dwells within each soul. Unlike the everchanging physical loves that exist in our world today, God's love comes to us in the completeness of a perfection and eternal peace through His unchanging spiritual essence. Although we live daily in a physical state upon this earth, it is our spirit contained within that shall produce the understanding, to which our physical bodies and senses are incapable of transmitting or even receiving universally. Our daily preoccupation with various physical challenges and routines, leaves little time or energy if any, for the spiritual challenges and essential needs that too often become neglected. There are a thousand other examples, that we can relate to underutilization.

We do not hesitate in response to the call of our physical body, whether its need is critical or not. How much more important is the well being of our spirit, when we come to perceive its tremendous responsibility for our collective eternal survival? It does not make any sense to overly feed our physical being even when it is not hungry, and at the same time starve our spiritual self which requires proper nourishment as well.

I sincerely hope and pray that this church can provide for your every need. In order to reach our ideal of understanding as a collective unity, this system must be followed, whereby all of us may move forward in harmony with each other and with God.

Each person is at a different stage of spiritual development, so it best serves our purpose if we begin very deliberately. Please do not ever lose faith in your ability to understand, as prayer is our most vital weapon in this battle for life. Call upon God through your heart and He shall keep you going. It is not possible for any of us as human beings to unite one another worldwide, but remember with God all things are possible. The only system of unity in this world that stands a fighting chance, is understanding our spiritual gifts born of God's grace. His unconfined spirit beyond time and space shows no partiality. The most important aspect of this entire process is to find your unobstructed pathway to God through spiritual prayer, and to this He shall answer.

The words of these forthcoming revelations will provide each person with that necessary map of proper spiritual direction. Please join with me in this spiritual experience of brotherhood. With the advent of modern day communication technology, this message is free to travel throughout the world if we so choose, and as God so allows.

Remember always that our focus is set on God and His teachings, and that anything we have in this life has to first be given. We that are made must recognize the reality of our divine maker. All that I ask is for you to allow me to share these revelations. My covenant to each of you is that I shall not speak personally. Our mission is spiritual in nature and must remain as such. Unless a spiritual directive is given there will be no other message.

To this point in time I have recorded several pages of holy spirit testimony, to include prose, poetry, prayer verse, proverbs, parables, and other spiritual directives of revelation. If you ever feel a need to confirm any elements of testimony as to its validity, simply ask the holy spirit through the solitude of deep and earnest prayer within your heart where He still resides. When asked anything in sincerity He will answer you most graciously.

The holy spirit helper did not cease from teaching us in those long ago biblical days. Our God is a living God who is the same today as He was yesterday, and shall be tomorrow and forever. Fear nothing except Him and be well on your way to life's understanding.

Throughout today's world, the main line religions that have been historical fixtures in society, are now on the brink of total collapse. They shall never recover from this devastating truth until confessing their mistakes (sins) to both God and humanity. Somewhere along the way each religion has compromised its faith. The focus upon God was shifted from the foundation to the frame. Unity can only become a reality when all differences of belief are placed aside, in favor of God's voice being clearly heard by all!

His ecumenical master plan will be heeded one way or another. It is certainly best for all of us if we receive Him willingly, by stepping forward today with the offering of a repentant soul. If a person or group in any capacity stands over another, they are in direct violation of His commandment to love one another as He also has loved us. Laws are made for law breakers not for those who abide within life's spiritual and physical laws.

"Whosoever abideth in Me, I abideth in also". - Jesus Christ.

The first step that we must take is to become solemn and aware. Allow your sixth sense which is born of spirit, the opportunity to receive God's pure revelation born of eternal truth and grace. For thousands of years we have pushed this gift aside, in favor of serving only our five physical senses that are temporary. Where has this method of timeless spirit ignorance actually taken us? Is it not time to repair our mistakes that hinder soul elevation?

We must now convert our energies from temporary physical dictates into eternal spiritual understanding that may enable us to walk. Our church not only lacks a name, but human leadership as well. We must rise from the cradle of spiritual infancy through God, as our time has come to focus an inward only worship in truth. For the many religious institutions still unrepenting of their sins, it is wisdom for each of us to seek understanding without them. It is unwise taking the risk of being held guilty by association any longer.

When we gather in church with family and friends, it is intended for the express purpose of community with God and one another. It fulfills the need for that essential spiritual bond of love. Let us return to our houses of worship and bring this church, for without the physical connection to each other through worship and prayer, we soon drift dangerously apart in spirit as well. The major fault of church hierarchy, is blindness to us and God, but overall moral decay in today's society is the primary killer. We shall provide in our church the understanding for safe return. When a church becomes bureaucratic and worldly in nature, it begins to lose the primary focus of its original spiritual calling.

There is no financial obligations assessed to the pure church, nor has the Christ ever suggested payment beyond personal will. For church coffers filled by greed, and salvation sold through guilt, how great shall be the cost to the veiled church of truth?

Let us listen to what God is saying in regards to this crisis, and then act accordingly.

FEBRUARY 14, 1998 - OUR BEACON OF HOPE
*DAILY PRAYER BOOK REFERENCES.

*Let His living word be heard from this day forward, that the Lord is King, the Lord was King, and the Lord shall be King forever and ever. To His oneness and glory we entrust our soul.

His Torah (Law) is our trust, His spirit our everlasting teacher, and His living word our constant guide in understanding truth. We must now take a final vow in defense of this faith, by truly acknowledging His endless love for each of us, through the power of unified prayer within the entire brotherhood of humankind, as evidenced in Jesus Christ.

As holy beings of God we shall praise thee daily, and seek our salvation through repentance and the performance of good deeds. *It is only because of thy great compassion that we are able to stand before thee and offer our prayers and supplications.

May the Lord grant us peace and protection in our pursuit of true understanding, and may our thanksgivings be well received in His heavenly realm. *The Lord is our God, the Lord is one. To all who proclaim thy holiness please grant us truth and grace, and may His great name be blessed forever and to all eternity. May we enjoy life and ample sustenance with abundant peace from above, and may His tender mercies follow us all the days of our lives. To He who creates life itself from His heavenly abode, look kindly upon those that seek rebirth within your spirit.

Let us be counted as believers, for in unbelief there is no hope. To those whose faith still rests upon materialistic foundation, help to redirect their focus toward your eternal spiritual gifts. May this loving understanding the Lord still provides, embrace the entire brotherhood of humankind, producing a ray of hope in the earthly rich as well, otherwise destined to become the eternally poor. Although offering quite little through His living word may we obtain much, for in this simple truth lies all heavenly law. Eternal life is not determined by birthright or affiliation, but rather is gifted to all children who love God and each other. Every soul upon this earthly plane is God in part.

No religion has all the true answers for tomorrow is not yet, so keep faith as our beacon of hope while seeking His true light. May the Lord forever bless you and yours, and let us say Amen.

FEBRUARY 15, 1998
THE GREATEST MYSTERY OF ALL

It is not for us to know the full extent of spiritual gifts, only the human limits of their otherwise unlimited potential. Understanding is the earthly end result of human knowledge and wisdom, while love is the eternally full potential of all gifts from God to humankind, both in this world and the world to come.

Love cannot reach total fulfillment in our physical state, but through spiritual understanding we can perceive a greater level of truth. The human mind cannot achieve nor the heart conceive, of this immaculate territory where our spirits conception may be chosen to receive. God is forever willing to provide us with this gift. When properly prepared we shall receive this special vision of love, opening a new path of hope upon the road back to Me.

Our love for God and one another is a prerequisite to this gift, but it is His unique love returned that becomes our fulfillment. With His living word now explained through this experience of *The Immaculate Conception*, we may share together in this collective calling of unity towards His desire for our oneness.

Many shall question why as to this particular title, which has captivated two millennia of mysticism while awaiting to emerge. The only truthful response is in reality quite simplistic. *The Immaculate Conception* is a gift of God to all who choose to believe.

In and of itself there is a certain uneasiness that accompanies these words, which was purposely intended for everyone to feel. Regardless of our belief system or religious affiliation, *The Immaculate Conception* is a direct challenge to our faith. This message that He brings is not one of physical comfort but rather a teaching process of truth while discovering our inner peace.

Love is our only common bond in a world riddled with separation. Humankind is forever fascinated with the idea of unsolved mystery, and the *Immaculate Conception* was the greatest mystery of all! The power of Christ's spirit divided His old world in two, and that very same spirit shall unite His new world as one. With a force unlike any other He will gather all in judgement, and whether we arrive as believers depends solely upon free choice.

We must persevere the truth of understanding down the avenues of knowledge and wisdom, and upon the spiritual vehicles of earnest prayer and good faith we shall find our way home. The imperishable crown is the finest award that one can receive in this lifetime, and is the ultimate goal of all who truly live in the spirit of God. To be an entrant in this race, you must qualify in accordance with the rules of spiritual focus.

As our capabilities to further develop communication technologies increase, we bring the world ever closer to a real sensory and physical connection, that shall result in spiritual bonding. Our eyes and ears begin to open toward a vision of hope, that provides many cultures in need with the exposure once lacking within the framework of their world.

If we reach out and touch someone with brotherly love, then we begin to close the gap on self serving individualism. In this way we may offer charity as opposed to seizing opportunity, and begin to love one another as God so requires.

As we daily witness the gross injustices and imbalances in our world, we can geographically pinpoint these critical areas of need. What we then do with our gifted advantaged dominion, shall have distinct eternal consequences for all interconnected souls. Through prayer and faith we begin to participate in spiritual healing, that extends our involvement beyond passive concern.

As we pray for the betterment of the less fortunate and destitute, our own sense of being becomes greatly improved,whereby this elevated understanding produces a genuine care and compassion that inevitably leads to an action based love.

The times when we feel separated and even isolated from God do not exist in reality. The only distance between us and God is the distance we think that we have placed Him. By continuing to prioritize our busy lives away from God and not toward Him, creates a high speed lifestyle which is extremely detrimental to our overall safety and well being.

Please give strong consideration toward the proper balancing of total being, and that includes making time for giving thanks. This is an individual decision based on each conscience and heart.

WEDNESDAY MARCH 11, 1998
A TIME FOR US TO ACT

Strive to become a living branch upon the tree of life, by extending support to those precious fruits of His living Word, which can only be grown from the pure root of our living God. If we become branches that develop in a contrary manner to the purity of the source of our origin, then eventually we shall be broken off in any number of ways and for any number of reasons concerning that spirit of contrariness. I speak of religious groups that have lost their original focus of mission, by compromising the doctrines upon which they were founded, and to which the other human institutions have succumbed.

In following dead end paths to accommodate societal changes rather then staying the course upon God's unchanging route, we now travel together down a most dangerous and destructive road. Humankind must adapt to God's commandments and the precepts of His law, and not in any way expect for Him to adapt to ours.

The Judaeo-Christian Era is now coming to an abrupt conclusion, as the Lord begins to speak through us with His living word. This call is for unity among all peoples and nations, and in no way allows for compromise concerning human rationales, or a multitude of varying belief systems that promote distraction. The oneness of His spiritual being is the voice in command, and there can be no one else. Through the faith that comes with earnest prayer, we may elevate our spiritual gifts to the acceptable level of divine reception. In God's kingdom, we are "all" only equal subjects of grace.

This Judaeo-Christian bridge that Jesus Verona began constructing two thousand years ago, must now be completed with perfection as the bridge of humanity in its final phase of souldevelopment. The separateness of our main line religions is contrary to God's oneness, as their lack of proper dialogue among one another based on common ground faith, has egotistically held back this inevitable bridge's completion for untold centuries. At the time when each religion lost touch with the person in the street, they also lost touch with the pure Christ spirit itself. Community is based on a direct connection to God and each other. As a result of these betrayals, we shall witness the systematic dismantling of all incompatible aspects to His master work.

Biblical scriptures in both testaments have proclaimed through the prophets that we will be gathered in judgement as a unity, despite our ongoing resistances to the oneness God so desires. I would like to believe that we may acquire wisdom in this light.

All denominations have been weakened by their misconceived notion of righteousness, and by further distancing themselves from each other, they have failed God in His primary commandment of brotherly love. To love thy neighbor as thyself is most critical to any belief system, and without this covenant in action there cannot be a true holy communion.

Can you honestly say that you believe each religion and belief system, stands beside one another as opposed to over one another, even from within?

This commandment is second only to our abiding love in God, and has been neglectfully cast into the wind in reality, as though not ever having been presented or received as a commandment at all. The failings that we are confronted with today both in the religious and the secular, are byproducts of truth gone astray. Upon the quagmire of human greed and self servitude, sits the unstable foundation of uncertainty, that now includes most every religious membership. There is no longer a place of refuge for the untarnished heart, as our Godly ideals have been sold out to the highest bidder.

The focus has shifted from God to mammon as religion embraces both business and politics, by conducting its business in like manner and form within the corruptive framework of human society.

Unless the leadership in each branch of worship displays the courage and conviction of their calling, by properly and publicly confessing their respective sins and shortcomings, we shall continue to falter swiftly until no church is left standing. Denial of any self wrongdoing is an unpardonable sin, that people and religions have committed since the early days of creation. How does one confess to an entity that itself needs repentance?

Our faith must be placed directly in God's hands through prayer, until humility replaces pride in the religious order of priority. Our trust must be earned before it becomes reinstated, and we have the right to religious expectations beyond societal norms.

We live in a time of severe moral decay, and must actively seek refuge within our living God in whom we find comfort and trust. On this pathway of hope and through His living word now revealed, we shall discover a new understanding that He is willing to share, with all who may call upon His name sincerely.

Churches are dying off for many different reasons, not the least of which has to do with a general consensus of lost confidence. We have come to expect disappointment from the irresponsibility of government, business, and media in providing us with truth, but we cannot bear to witness our faith in God become a questionable entity through the tactics of compromise, that lowers religious self esteem to the dangerous level of our political and social elite. We cannot and should not accept these failings that deter pure faith.

Churches are not only physical structures, but far more importantly they are the place in our soul where God resides. The community we share with God is an inner religion, that we must worship on a consistent basis if a covenant is to thrive. From this special kind of community grows the fruits of love and understanding, unlike the forbidden fruits of separation that progressively poison the essence of our very souls.

This inner church of which I speak, is the source of hope that we carry with us wherever we go, and provides community to everyone with whom we have contact in our travels day by day. Each of us is a branch on the Lord's tree of life, and whether we thrive or are cut down, depends strictly upon free choice. Concern yourself not with what other branches are producing, but rather consider the root and how it supports all that grows above it. If not for the Godly root there would be no tree at all.

The importance of faith lies in this truth unseen, and many become lost for only believing in their physical senses, and not enough in that very special sense born of spirit. Our living God is that root which provides all the sustenance we require, and His living word is the nourishment that feeds. Through this eternal peace and comfort that accompanies His grace, let us not only survive, but flourish and thrive with fine growth.

As the harvest draws near... this is truly a time for us to act

WHEN RIGHT CONQUERS EVERY WRONG

The only way to change a persons wrong into a right, is to
feed them loving kindness through our everyday and night.
One step at a time without ever looking back, is the proper
pathway heaven lit to keep each precious soul on track.

Patience as our greatest virtue always easier said than done,
but when achieved upon this earth is every victory won.
When you think that all is lost and nothing more be gained,
is the point that I take over as your energy is being drained.

I am the source of your fullest strength a back up generator if you will,
and as doubt and despair try to enter in, your tank I shall forever fill.
Some fade far too quickly because they "think" they stand alone,
but those of true faith then and now walk each dog to its bone.

Lead a horse to water but you cannot make it drink,
is a cliche' in your world that stops well short of heavens brink.
The door by which I stand is that narrow gateway to every soul,
we are closer than you realize so choose ideal instead of goal.

An inner partnership is only disturbing when you "think" your team is one,
but nobody flies on solo missions while understanding is begun.
The kingdom of heaven forever dwells so calmly within thy chest,
simply awaiting a most proper invitation to be woken from its rest.

All that you now question shall be answered by this truth,
in so many ways you remind me of my younger sister Ruth.
Today is the very first day of your season known as Fall,
but you shall rise up swiftly then begin to heed our call.

So happy birthday forty-six in just one year you'll see,
I'll wait right here at forty-seven until you catch up to me.
The many barriers of daily life seem insurmountable and strong,
but together we move mountains... when right conquers every wrong.

NO GREATER LOVE SHALL ANYONE FIND

She has been sent to you with love as our gift from above,
in sin she no longer shall dwell,
but she does not wish to share the dark secrets of her past,
like the stories I did force you to tell.

For in you nothing is hidden and your punishments beyond firm,
please remember always that My true love is fair,
the responsibility you carry goes far beyond any human comprehension,
and your trials life to life who could bear.

Remain steadfast to our vow as that awaited moment soon approaches,
when darkness shall become subject to great light,
for this is where you are strongest and why you are forever chosen,
as the one who must lead heavens fight.

Inform her as you must that temptations are always poised,
to thus challenge for the essence of total being,
this is not to cause fear but to make fear most unnecessary,
as our pure faith is the only visual worth seeing.

If she does not believe you or can agree to take heed,
then display to her that which I have shown,
in a calm manner of speech understanding shall step forth,
so the seeds that I have planted may be sown.

One step at a time she shall come forward to our truth,
as she grows into the gifted passion you possess,
for the physical she so treasured presents danger and deceit,
a far cry from the spiritual beauty that we bless.

Our crown is divine Providence that takes a step beyond Cayce,
for these are the days of first string,
now the practice season has concluded and the substitutes take their place,
for to thee the "World Series" I shall bring.

As both of you do attain to the "true" desires of your hearts,
and not simply serve the mere reflections of your mind,
our simple math for you two is one plus one equals ONE where...
"No Greater Love Shall Anyone Find."   Amen.

WITH GOD ALL THINGS ARE POSSIBLE

When the religious educational system and process within the synagogues, temples, churches, and all other houses of worship began to disappear first in name and then reality, so also did "the spirit" of faithful and sustainable worship take its leave. The supply line of spiritual teaching has been cut, and the writing has now gone from the desks to "The Wall". Societal decay is the direct result of quality family and educational decay, that has also been destroyed within the public system as well as private school systems today!When people lose "The Will" to learn and practice morality as normal human decency, so also does the will to teach suffer an untimely death. The end result is the vast uneducated masses with and without "degrees", leading to lethargic and detrimental behavior within self, that grows steadily into rebellion.

This pattern of destruction births through its ignorance the chaos, confusion, greed, envy, and selfishness that we now witness in daily life through the medias insatiably evil lens.

A revolution versus the existing bureaucratic institutions that maintain control is the violent and inevitable outcome, that more often than not represents the eventual demise of each. In a world that operates on fast food take-out news on the run, the media will create for you its meal of choice.

The "disconnect" from the younger generations to the older destroys continuity of values which were taught, ones that each generation prior had learned and treasured, but not necessarily practiced in truth. This hypocrisy is glaring to a society overexposed to media hype, and a cheapened value system of "success".

As a result you are raising children that prefer non participating observation and entertainment, to directly active hands on personal involvement. You have become a crippled society living as spectators and analysts in the game of life very few know how to honestly play.

The acceptance of "total" media education as the one primary source of human knowledge, shall be your final undoing as progressively balanced body and soul creations of God. The whole (total being) is no longer able to function properly when the individual parts of being (body, mind, and soul) cease to work in complete cooperation and coordination with each other. Separation and divisiveness waits around every corner in your world of false beliefs.

The broken chain that begins with the displacement of true faith in the home, community, and daily life "educational" sources, sadly concludes with the testimony, witnesses, and subsequent judgment for this horrendously heinous and criminal activity. Only a truly repentant return to absolute faith in God, can bring about a reversal of misfortune. "With humanity this task is impossible, but...

"With God all things are possible."

Part Three
The Road Back to Me

The Immaculate Conception is written for the sole purpose of conveying God's urgent message to all that will hear. My only hope as its co-author, is that I have properly served both God and humanity by successfully completing this work toward His imperishable crown, which is the spiritual goal that we seek in this lifetime. My only request is to remain anonymous, and that all shall benefit through the understanding of salvation that we are being gifted, and that you receive the same blessing through the loving grace of God, located deep within each soul. The Word and its source is all that truly matters.

This pathway is heavenly lit for all that wish to travel upon the road back to Me, our innermost adventure toward truth. You will soon come to realize while sharing in this journey, the true spirit of love that is God. His only request of us is a most reasonable one: that as individuals, families, religions, nations, or any group, we shall walk together in peace and cooperation, thus displaying the unity of human fellowship that is most proper while inhabiting His earth.

This must be nurtured through a process that involves the actual seeking out of common rather than higher grounded principles, that can only occur with the sincere commencement of proper dialogue, and the will to attain an ecumenical level of existence. Individualism must be sacrificed, in order to achieve the fulfillment of basic needs in our fellow human beings with whom we co-exist in this imbalanced world, if in fact the greater good is to be truly served.

This book is presented straight from the heart, thus providing all lost sheep with a spiritually safe route home, by way of the good Shepherd. You shall find these pages to be vibrantly alive, as is our Lord who sent them. These words are not meant to instill fear, but rather to replace all fear with a clear understanding. Be ever so mindful while reading, that these works are not based upon any physical learning experience or religion, but are a product of the gifts that the holy spirit is free to grant.

I have lived my entire life without any formal religious education or membership, and to this day I do not belong to a specific religious affiliation, nor have I completed reading the scriptures of any religion. I am a true believer however in that no religious organization of humanity is one hundred percent accurate in all claims of their faith. I will continue to wait patiently for the truths of God to surface, as they are provided by the only one to call teacher, and from whom we can truly learn all things. He is our Lord and Savior... Christ Jeshua Verona.

My personal beliefs and subsequent spiritual convictions are firmly centered on the teachings I have received from the holy spirit of God, not through any human based understanding of religious texts, sermons presented in a physical manner of delivery, or by the influences of any religious scholars. My primary influence in this work is spiritual.

This journey of ours can be a lonely one, gathering very little human support along the way, but we should be forever grateful to have the spirit of God accompanying us on this trip. I am also thankful for the common sense training and experience throughout my life that has prepared me for this assignment, which proves to me that God is truly a spirit of love and not confusion. This grace is reassurance that we will not stumble or shall ever have to walk this path alone, and that makes all the difference in our brave new world. For those of you who come to believe, I sincerely hope that you will find the same comfort as I have found in this regard. In this way we shall continue to strive toward properly conveying this blessing of understanding, to all that wish to partake of its most precious fruit.

My continuous guiding light is the promise made to me in the beginning of this experience that stated: "If you truly desire to learn, I am He who teaches", and from that day forward we agreed to take on this mission and to complete it successfully. I truly believe that we have fully achieved our stated and predestined goal as evidenced in this book and its results. Please read the contents carefully with deep thought and a focused soul concentration, and these heavenly words shall serve you well. The following message was instilled in me through the holy spirit, and helps to keep my life in proper perspective, especially in these days when religious cults step over the line in creating a mind control that goes beyond God's wishes. Knowledge and wisdom coupled with our discernment must precede actual understanding, in this world where life's normal guidelines are no longer clearly drawn, while the simple and most important things in life have been greatly distorted or ignored. This is the working of the evil one formerly called satan, and the roadblock that each of us must individually and then collectively detour, as through free choice evil ceases to exist. There is no evil source that acts upon us if we refuse its very essence of being. The will toward good shall destroy self evil, and then world evil shall succumb.

"Seek not the status of humankind and earth, but glory in your calling as a servant of God in heaven. You have never aspired to rank among humanity, as this serves you well in your quest for understanding. Be ever so humble, patient, and true, allowing the holy spirit to guide you along the well lit path of righteousness, thus leading to the kingdom of heaven. Walk in peace, forever observing the needs of all, ministering to each their own. Do not ever become discouraged or dismayed, for you do not walk alone. Remember always the light that guides you for it will not dim. I grant to you these gifts in My name, that you may well serve all whom you encounter along the way. From God our Father, blessed be to you our son. May peace be with you always and forever. Amen."

What more can we ask for in this lifetime, then to receive that kind of heavenly support. To make straight the path of His word is why we desire to serve. If called upon in the future by God I will certainly welcome the opportunity to respond, but ask others to kindly respect my earnest desire for privacy, so that I may return to my prior personal life of responsibility and commitment, thus preserving every possible happiness of those with whom I am closely associated. God knows all too well that I have burdened them quite enough, and I wish to thank each for their patience and true understanding, through a time of much needed moral support and friendship. Hopefully the efforts put forth by our spiritual author, will shed a positive light upon each and every reader, and those whom you love and cherish as well.

In the beginning of this experience, I had never heard of spiritual gifts, nor did I have any conception of what the holy spirit may bring. Today, I walk almost exclusively in this loving spirit of God. For a period of time I searched deep within my soul to try and discover what my role in this overall plan of God was all about, and on more than one occasion have had to call upon every ounce of inner strength and faith, to see myself through those days. I can truly now attest that God handles all of these concerns. My present assignment has become very clear, and involves serving as the trumpet warning blast, before its actual blowing. This is the wake up call referred to in our lesson plan. Inquiring minds will be grateful for this critical advanced warning of our collective spiritual and eternal destiny. God is spirit and His spirit is love.

Our God is a living God unconfined by time, space, and especially words from any one historical book, thus written exclusively by and for humanity. His religion is simply to love one another with an open heart, having full faith in His spirit, and remaining consciously aware of his omnipotence, omnipresence, and omniscience. Our God is all powerful, ever present, and all knowing, and our prayers should acknowledge this supreme authority. Each human being has full access to God's love within.

If we believe in Christ resurrected and Old Testament tradition as fountains of each religion, then faith shall abide in us as our foundation is established. The true spirit of God is present in each believing and loving heart, thereby surfacing upon our request and soul readiness in each covenant, manifesting itself as a total person that is pleasing to God. If we do not believe in these turning points of our history then our faith has no basis, all sins of humankind remain unforgiven, and there would be no hope for our spiritually eternal lives beyond this world. The prospects of unbelief provides a very bleak outlook of our collective futures, while faith and hope will allow God to uphold His righteousness, that has been His covenant to us from the very beginning. Unlike our humanity God is a promise maker not a promise breaker, and despite our severe breach of contract throughout history, our Father has displayed patience and longsuffering that no human could ever claim. Let us pray for His still amazing and continuing grace, towards all of life's children, as we now also face inward and not only to the East. It is good to believe for in unbelief there is no hope, as faith is the bridge to one truth, and brotherly love our map of right direction.

I look forward to this publication as my prayers are for all of God's children. In the process of writing this script, never once did I take pen in hand without holy spirit guidance, and never was there a message that did not include each soul.

I understand the five "W's" (who, what, where, when, and why) as well as how, and firmly believe never having written prose, poetry, or verse, that if I forced content that was not there, I would only be fooling myself and diluting the purity of God's message. This is territory where even angels fear to tread. I would like to ask a personal favor if you find this book to be worthy of positive changes in your life, and potentially beneficial to others as well. Please share this with someone who would otherwise be unable to obtain this script for whatever reason you may discern. It would be a great service indeed.

The entire spectrum of life on earth in which humanity is only a part, is in itself only a very small part of God's immeasurable domain. His original covenant with an unaware Abraham, is the first two way bond of a religious form according to our record. This is an acceptable early stage of understanding between God and humanity, whereby faith best represents a formal type worship to the one true God, and thus creates a starting point for all houses of worship to share in as a common ground principle. If this is an agreed upon beginning concerning our relationship to God and one another, then it is the best starting point for a return to His true desire of ecumenical unity among all people. That same covenant offered to Abraham some four thousand years ago, is still available to each and every soul yesterday, today, and forever. The bond to God within us is an immutable law of the universe, that as His promise cannot be broken by any force. This special individual covenant is the pathway to His oneness, whereby self and free will become enjoined to the greater good. It is only pure faith as with Abraham that this path is realized, so let each of us now follow. From Abraham's seed comes the promise of many nations, and each is near and dear to God (Allah). Isaac is a son but not his only son, for God also loves Ishmael.

If we place this same faith into each of our hearts, then our covenant shall remain vibrantly alive and eternal as we walk. By overlooking our commitment to the soul we possess and the body which accompanies it, is to neglect the purpose of living. God remains within us at all times regardless of our condition, and awaits patiently the call to elevate each of us spiritually to the level that each soul is willing to develop itself toward. We must shed the physical limitations of comfort and stagnation, by aspiring to the spiritual full potential of each near and dear soul, only awaiting the connection to God and His universe. Separation from God leads to separation from one another, as the speed of today's world leaves very little room for error. Everyday delusions and confusions are its byproducts that exceed all physical and spiritual safety limits, thus clouding spiritual focus and greatly endangering our treasured health and wellness. Amidst this frantic pace of change, we must take hold upon His living word and see our way clear to the awaiting good shepherd. From God's Living Word... let us now together walk upon The Road Back To Me.

SUNDAY, NOVEMBER 3, 1996, 6:30AM

Initial message from the holy spirit: Assuredly I say to you, the poor are not in terms of economic means but rather in lack of knowledge, wisdom, and understanding.

MONDAY, NOVEMBER 4, 1996, 6:45AM

Return to them their needs.

WEDNESDAY, NOVEMBER 6, 1996, 5:22AM

If you truly desire to learn, I am he who teaches. For if we do not learn each day what is the point of our living? When you see adversity and evil call upon it and bring it forth, unveiling the wickedness before it destroys the good.

Walk in peace, forever observing the needs of all, and ministering to each their own. Do not be discouraged or dismayed, for you do not walk alone. Remember always the light that guides you for it will not dim. I grant to you these gifts in My name, that you may well serve all whom you encounter along the way. From God our Father, blessed be to you our son.

May Peace be with you always and forever. Amen.

THURSDAY, NOVEMBER 7, 1996, 2:24AM - Dream sequence of healing/accident

Remember always: The Lord may giveth and the Lord may taketh away. (Reference to the dream sequence)

MONDAY, NOVEMBER 11, 1996, 4:40AM

Speak with your friend who is the Pastor, for as it is in the story you know of two cats, so it also is with he. Ask those who consider themselves to be men of God: Am I any less worthy in the eyes of God, because my life's work is based on far more simplistic ground? Does not the foundation precede the frame? For as I have said before there is only one teacher, and that is the Son of Man. Through time I have come to see your truthful desire to learn. Seek not the status that is of man and earth, but glory in your calling as a servant of God in Heaven. You have not aspired to rank among men, as this serves you well in your quest for understanding. Be ever so humble, patient, and true, allowing the holy spirit to guide you on the well lit path of righteousness, thus leading to the kingdom of heaven.

As to your concerns of this occasion: Blessed are they who faithfully serve God and country for they are not without merit, but woe to kings and leaders of nations who led them to their demise in the name of God, thus partaking as false witness to the true desires of He.

TUESDAY, NOVEMBER 12, 1996, 1:45AM

Your country became great because it was good, when the goodness is gone it will cease to be great. Lies and deceit are tangling many, while truth and honesty free the few. Look toward tomorrow with hope and praise, but yesterday has made today an uncertain event.

Of nation against nation throughout human history, for what real gain has been attained by the aggressor when all is said and done? So it will also be in the final battle, as good will overcome evil, much to the chagrin of the new multitudes.

As God interjects on behalf of the elect this one last time, understand His disappointment that throughout all these years, we did not truly develop beyond the realm of Cain and Abel. For all of humanity's creative genious, it has neglected its own basic and primary responsibility, to uphold the needs of brother, neighbor, friend, and all other life forms on earth of which it has charge.

The baby harp seals that are born far beyond the habitat of man, become a target of our greed, and their blessing of God is taken away as if they are accursed. Do you not see how humanity has betrayed its Creator? How many other examples must I address?

Does God the almighty Father not have the right to halt our total destruction of His creation? Must He continue eternal longsuffering by witnessing His pride and joy creation, systematically disassemble all the parts of His Master work, created as a support system for life's continuity? And if so, for how long?

What has become of the trees He plants to provide sustenance of life, a home for those that fly and many others as well, including man himself? The origin of purpose has been dismantled to the extent that the gifts from God to man cannot now escape him. Some call it a passing away of the earth, but the Lord is charging man with murder in the first degree. Premeditation is self-evident and the eyewitnesses are credible and most plentiful. The evidence is set before you now how do you plead? Must a sentence not be carried out? Sadly but assuredly so.

TUESDAY, NOVEMBER 12, 1996, 4:50AM

As you go about the Lord's work take rest where you may,
for where there is love is the place you should stay.
Your journey is marked with hope and a prayer,
for lucky are they who may share their despair.

The pathway is lit by a star shining bright,
as you travel by morning, in afternoon or night.
Remember our Paul as you strive for that crown,
may your spirit be high do not let it come down.

In terms of direction the Lord only knows,
for He will be with you wherever you go.
Follow they will as you bring them the Word,
in all walks of life... yes even the bird.

Provide each their need as we spoke of before,
may peace be your greeting as you knock every door.
Through the years I have taught you we know very well,
that nothing will stop you until that one final bell.

The throngs they will gather like peas in a pod,
to catch a quick glimpse of those sent from God.
The harvest draws near and the fruit is so ripe,
God's sorrows will heal with His Son's gentle wipe.

Now a new day will dawn born of glory and love,
with the Lord on His throne holding a beautiful white dove.

THURSDAY, NOVEMBER 14, 1996, 12:57AM

As you tend to the sheep who are lost from the flock,
bring them mercy and understanding in the steps that you walk.
Their numbers are many but the shepherd's are few,
I know you will deliver to the old and the new.

Fear not where you tread for the road is well paved,
as you feed them compassion they will surely be saved.
For unknowing are plenty on the road to demise,
as you care for my sheep I will open their eyes.

The rich are the poor that lack wisdom we know,
embrace them as one from above and below.
Continue My work that began long ago,
that imperishable crown I shall surely bestow.

On he who is worthy of that ultimate prize,
will rise to the heights far beyond the blue skies.
As always before I do wish you the best,
from Father and Son now receive this bequest.

Worry not of the multitudes who stand in your way,
include them as well and invite all to pray.
As your door remains open the blind they will see,
the errors of their ways on the road back to me.

As we gather together the sick and the well,
this mission of mercy may keep them from hell.
I will greet you one day for a job that's well done,
on this you can count as the light of the sun.

I know that you gather your strength from this source,
so finish this race as I keep you on course.
Now do you see why I kept you from glory,
a far greater purpose is the title of your story.

I've shared all your highs and your lows just as well,
now it's time to deliver these things I foretell.

THURSDAY, NOVEMBER 14, 1996, 4:11AM

The time is at hand to put your houses in order,
never look back till you get past the border.
The country is safe for those you protect,
be aware of the times as you walk circumspect.

Over hill over dale through the mountains you go,
to a land in the north where there is plenty of snow.
So travel together with your Pastor in tow,
and your church will be waiting that you never thought so.

How happy you shall be when you see this new mission,
and be quite amazed to observe the condition.
The author is no fun as I hope you agree,
he knows it already near St. Johnsbury, Vee Tee (VT).

FRIDAY, NOVEMBER 15, 1996, 7:53AM

I am truly the Son of our Father and Mary,
any other belief would be quite contrary.
If you will concentrate on the teacher,
you shall become a great preacher.

Do not over examine the things I have taught,
I have kept them very simple so all may begot.
This is not just a game to make you confused,
but rather new teachings that should be perused.

I'll walk you in step but I never will run,
you have done well so far as you follow My Son.
As I teach you alone you may share with your Pastor,
we are very well pleased how you are serving the Master.

You are gleeful today for you write while awake,
share this new revelation so that all may partake.
You have come a long way in a very short spell,
keep your feet on the ground for this serves you well.

I sent you to many for advice and to learn,
the basis you need to establish and discern.
From each you took something but never it all,
understanding you now have to prevent any fall.

So start the new book with your partner today,
for you knew all along it was He that would play.
As you told Him the truth that a church is the heart,
we are convinced of your choosing for this important part.

A very close friend knows more than you are aware,
So heed her advice also and notice her care.
She has witnessed the hell that exists here on earth,
so be gentle with her its been rough since her birth.

She has wisdom and courage you won't see the like,
you must learn of her plight as you pedal the bike.
She is a continuous source of new inspiration,
for all to avoid any future confrontation.

Many people will embrace her from so far away,
as your church will increase as the hours in a day.
So consult her you will for to grasp all my ways,
that many will desire to the end of all days.

Now your church is established I count you as three,
as you follow My teachings feel free to add Me.

SATURDAY, NOVEMBER 16, 1996, 7:30AM

Remember this dream as the future draws near,
stay open to changes in the world that are clear.
Focus on the details you witnessed this night,
keep your conviction as you gain more insight.

These events are not pleasant but certainly true,
walk this through gently as it unfolds to you.
The mention of Clinton narrows the date,
so respond as you may to the upcoming fate.

The beast from the east is preparing his mission,
inform those you must of this pending perdition.
Their powers are great with a hunger to fight,
they cannot be stopped by conventional might.

Their numbers are vast far beyond comprehension,
your people will defend but be of little contention.
The west is the target they have waited so long,
as your inside turns out there will be celebration and song.

A house that is divided can no longer stand,
against the wiles of the evil one as he takes command.
These days have been written I am sorry to say,
do the best that you can and I will be there each day.

The dates that you know from an unreliable source,
were accurately stated by the darksided force.
Discreetly you must act with the wisdom I give you,
for detractors are many and supporters are few.

Go through this you will as your past shall attest,
you have never quit anything or accepted second best.
Your heart is our strength and I am your guide,
in that combination you can surely confide.

I have burdened your family they are apart at the seams,
in time I will comfort them while awake and in dreams.
So be free of that yoke of serving two masters,
your mission is most worthy as it lessens disasters.

For those that are astute will welcome your word,
gird your waist with the truth and your voice shall be heard.
To guarantee your protection I will inform you in parts,
a continuous flow versus the fiery darts.

Take that shield of the faith which you bear as your arms,
as it insulates you from danger and potential harms.

MONDAY, NOVEMBER 18, 1996, 6:30AM

Let us begin to develop a concept of hope,
whose sounds will be echoed all the way to the Pope.
Like a newborn we will crawl for a period of time,
good foundation is needed before attempting to climb.

We must alter the pace to a slow comfortable walk,
for some speak many languages while others cannot talk.
Imbalance in today's world that you witness is drastic,
instead of building on rock it is constructed on plastic.

This task seems impossible and for humanity that is true,
but with God's intervention there is nothing we cannot do.
You have concerns for your family who were not trinitarian,
true belief is in the soul of each fine humanitarian.

Our aim is to bridge all the gaps that exist,
in every religion known to man far too numerous to list.
Each sect has its virtues and are well intentioned for sure,
but there are elements still missing to keep them impure.

Many cracks are now evident to those in the know,
but they cannot admit it with nowhere to go.
To a man you cannot change the structures that stand,
through revelations they shall listen to the voice in command.

You are an earthen vessel that My work passes through,
not simply a conduit that you mentioned to a few.
I am pleased at your ability to balance this weight,
despite all detractors your head is on straight.

For all those who ask if you are feeling alright,
you have never been better or nearly as bright.
So we shall walk together to the end of all days,
and comfort those in need by paving their ways.

Do not be predisposed with intent to convert,
our aims are more worthy it will only pervert.
Be steadfast to the principles that I shall provide,
and for all those concerned its a much smoother ride.

We will avoid any trauma that would cloud this ideal,
allow all to see clearly by reducing their zeal.
The testimony you present can stand strong on its own,
irrefutable is the word from the Lord on His throne.

TUESDAY, NOVEMBER 19, 1996, 12:41-1:45AM

For all that we have and do not have Lord,
we are forever grateful to thee.
Please hear our earnest prayers and bless us dear Lord,
as each day we are thankful to be free.

May we always remain humble, loving patient and true,
as we serve each their needs on behalf of just you.
Each day is a blessing that you provide us with grace,
may we return all your love with a gentle embrace.

As we pick up the pieces for those that are lost,
if souls remain uncared for it is a terrible cost.
We know that you must live in each of these sheep,
the best we can do is the promise we shall keep.

We will never pass by when we see you in need,
if we live up to that promise we have planted a seed.
For if others will follow in response to this vow,
the seed will then grow and they've learned to endow.

Now Your teachings can freely pass from one to another,
in all walks of life that are sister and brother.
In a world far removed from the real things that count,
we must return to the basics as we climb that high mount.

I hope there is still time to reach all the masses,
it behooves each to enroll when the Lord's teaching classes.

TUESDAY, NOVEMBER 19, 1996, 2:43AM

These lessons are worthy to each that will heed,
to learn from the best is a treasure indeed.
Love one another with a wide open heart,
keeping that in my mind we are off to a great start.

Sharing is important but caring is much more,
bend down and pick up what you see on the floor.
For how can we reach these ideals set so high,
if those at ground level are passed right on by.

As you broaden your vision to raise them as well,
you will pass the first test and are beginning to gel.
This course is an intro to life at its best,
forget all the books that confuse my request.

Some have their merit which I shall not deny,
but most are inappropriate and the topics are dry.
As the teacher in charge My format will be clear,
just follow directions and observe how I steer.

Lucky is he who may sit in this class,
a select few at best but none of the brass.
My students are chosen by a process unknown,
it pleases me well to see how you've grown.

Your certificates on the wall are merely pieces of paper,
to receive one from Me would be quite a caper.
Perseverance is a quality that gives you an edge,
but your heart is the key as I make you this pledge.

A challenge you welcome so fasten your belt,
for the ride of your life with the hand you've been dealt.
I know how you shudder from speeds and great height,
that is not how I operate so relax day and night.

The three that you look toward for guidance in Me,
will advise you for now as you seek My degree.
The workload is heavier than my usual fare,
but not more than you can handle I will be quite aware.

Now we are in the same room so please take a seat,
as classes have started with the world at our feet.

WEDNESDAY, NOVEMBER 20, 1996, 5:10AM - LESSON 1

As you develop a solid foundation to build upon, you must first understand the mason who builds. Concepts and ideas are not the starting point, but rather He who creates concepts and ideas. When you come to know the master builder, only then can you begin to conceptualize the powers He creates. This generation is so far ahead of itself, (or so it believes) that it has left most of its membership behind. What humanity considers progression is actually regression dressed in fancy clothes. The technological capabilities of humankind have developed at the expense of the basic essentials to many life forms, (including humanity) needed to perpetuate normal life cycles. Our presupposed advancements for the benefits of a few have become detrimental to the many, thus directly threatening the immediate future of life on earth. With the knowledge possessed by man in this age and the resources available to him, how can he truly explain famine, war, and pestilence? When governments finance the destruction of full grown crops, or pay farmers not to grow them at all, while their fellow man is dying of starvation, is there not a serious flaw in the method? How does this relate to reaching out your hand to your fellow human beings?

There was a time when houses of worship were sacred to all, as the pride and joy centerpiece of most every community of mankind. People gave the very best of themselves to grow closer in God, always giving thanks, and subsequently grew closer to each other as a resultant reward. The family extended itself to the church, thus forming a fellowship with God and community. Within this pure foundation a covenant was formed of unlimited potential. Man's progress could only develop from this original bond with God. As man realized his successes he began to credit himself for achievements, rendering to God very little of the proper acknowledgement for these triumphs. Man was beginning to only see the marvels of his work, and soon forgot his silent partner, who founded these works as their original creator and supporter. This trait has consistently hindered humanity since its creation. With man now asserting his own methods by no longer consulting the founding Father, he has drifted into a betrayal regarding the principles of unity with God, thus the faith with which the covenant between God and man was established has since suffered. God now remains an unwilling partner of man, for He lives up to His covenant despite us, witnessing each destruction we invoke on the world at large, remaining in the background that man placed Him years ago. The steady decline of man and earth can be attributed to a pride he developed in himself, contrary to a humble coexistence with God. As his great accomplishments became evident to all of humanity, man had no further use for his partner, who not being visible or vocal was easy to overlook. As he separated from God the Father, so he has now also done with his relatives, neighbors, countrymen, his own household, and all other life forms on earth that cannot serve a useful purpose to him. His God has become those material things of utility and not of real life. Mankind's thirst is not for water but rather oil, his hunger is satisfied not by food, but by an insatiable accumulation of wealth. Shelter is no longer a basic necessity to provide warmth or a respite from the elements, but rather a collection of possessions. What then becomes of those who get in the way of his pursuits to these new basic necessities? Assuredly I say to you that he will destroy all of life's resources from the plant to ant, and the tree to the sea. What will man then use to sustain himself after destroying all the gifts received from God? When the day comes that he realizes how unwise he truly is, then he will plead for God his partner whom he pushed so far away that He cannot hear him.

LESSON 2

I will give some examples of this systematic breakdown.

RAINFORESTS, namely upon the African continent, are being destroyed, and jeopardize the entire ecosystem of the world. Does man not understand that oxygen is emitted from plant and tree life? How will life be supported in the future if barren?

ATMOSPHERE continually contaminated by toxic emissions, and thus destroying the protective ozone layer that screens harmful rays of the sun, creating a health hazard of major proportion. A deterioration process known as the greenhouse effect.

EXTINCTION. Only a small percentage of humankind works to ensure the propagation of species in animal and plant life. An example that man prefers to ignore his mistakes rather than save lives, and as a result entire species disappear at an alarming rate.

HUNGER. There is absolutely no acceptable excuse. Food can be preserved, but is destroyed without being transported to areas of need. If this was an energy problem it would be solved. Does food not come before travel? In countries where not enough food is produced to satisfy their numbers, a good nation would bypass the government of a hungry people, and assure that they were properly fed regardless of the consequences.

POLLUTION. The airways and waterways are severely contaminated by man's misuse of elements. The desired short term result is creating a long term hardship on all of life's support systems.

WAR. Man's greatest downfall is born of greed and separation, contrary to everything man was taught by God from the beginning. Represents all of man's weaknesses and thus will be displayed to him in his last days, as he must take responsibility for his works and accept the inevitable outcome of Armageddon.

POVERTY. Imbalanced economic greed as well as those who chose to give up the fight. The earthly rich in reality are the poor.

JEALOUSY, GREED, PREJUDICE, ENVY. Poison of the body and soul. These are characteristics of a far from perfect man, and the elements that comprise the basis of war. War and confrontations are the result whether it be of two or two billion, as the ingredients for conflict are the same.

LOVE, HOPE, FAITH, CHARITY, COMPASSION, MEEKNESS, PATIENCE, TRUTH, RIGHTEOUSNESS

Sadly, these have been greatly reduced to empty words and terminology rather than moral principles to live by. The elect of this world understand, so please continue to try and reach those who do not.

I can list a thousand other reasons why the end days approach. How many can you give Me as to why they will not? I offer an example in summary: Are not casinos for gambling, displayed as man's newfound architectural gems, glorified in style and grace as if built for God or king? At the same time houses of worship are being burned to the ground with little financial hope in most cases of rebirth. Reflect for awhile and explain that order of priority, along with the collective social consciousness that you live with and among. This is not to say that the good are not recognized, for each is rewarded on their own works, but have you become an accessory toward widespread acceptance of illicit beliefs and activities? I sincerely hope not.

Multitudes have remained steadfast to the core principles of living a good life and are not without their rewards, but woe to those who compromise their spiritually gifted and enlightened doctrines of belief, in favor of adopting those ideals set forth by the evil one (self). Please reconsider by comparing what was, and what now is? Your collective future depends upon it and each other.

WEDNESDAY, NOVEMBER 20, 1996, 10:05AM, - LESSON 3

As you have now come to realize, the podium from which I teach is located above. When I told you that you were a student of mine you were wondering how that could be possible, when in flesh you are of this earth. I am pleased to know that you already understand that I can directly instruct you through the Holy Spirit you have been granted, in essence allowing My teachings to become your personal experiences. In this way it is no different then when you are sitting in the same room, conversing with another in a physical interaction whereby the spiritual is also in attendance. You are doing extremely well developing your spirit soul in such a brief time of two months. As your comprehension increases at a pace comfortable to you, I will recognize the effects upon your life and those of whom you are involved, and walk compatibly so that each will adjust accordingly. Those that have followed your complete spiritual transformation in stages will fully understand each new development, but those receiving only sporadic or inaccurate information cannot be expected to fully grasp this process. When I informed you that the world was at our feet, do not be mistaken for in spirit this is true. You now fully realize that the classroom is on earth, but the teachings are from heaven.

LESSON 4

In regards to those who question your source of information: People that hear voices are in need of help, as you fully understood in the early years of your work life. I thank you for your consoling and providing cigarettes, candy, and comfort, as each served their purpose to those in need at the time. Is the way that you conduct yourself in a very difficult human environment any less of a ministry to Me, then that of any religious leader held in great esteem by humanity? Ask them that question and their responses will surprise you, but not I, for they must concur despite their initial repulsion.

This advice will serve you quite well if you ever feel trapped by their interrogations. Do not concern yourself with intricate preparations as I shall provide you with what you need at any given time through the holy spirit. Continue as you are for you are absorbing months of work in only days.

We are very well pleased with this progress on our mission.

WEDNESDAY, NOVEMBER 20, 1996 NOON - LESSON 5

Your family will find comfort as the initial trauma wears off, and your abilities increase to a higher level. They have always kept you in protective check to avoid any dangerous highs or lows, and their love is paramount. In return you have strived for their acceptance and approvals displaying love and concern, which is a proper relationship thus honoring thy father and mother as the first commandment with promise attests. Your family's interrelationship serves each of you well. They will come to understand the difference between an unstable personality trait and the direct resources and abilities of the holy spirit. Their fears and frustrations are based upon your well being, not on their beliefs which you believe are contrary to your own. Our relationship is not a tool of divisiveness, but a growing stick to benefit all. For the role which you have been chosen and your subsequent acceptance thereof, despite all roadblocks and interferences you are focusing clearly and accurately. Continue along according to My map and timetable, and you will achieve well beyond anyone's imagination.

LESSON 6

So take your place as our class continues. Unlike a standard format with equal time and material presented to each student, those in My class are taught new material upon having passed each test. When a test is not understood and a setback results, then the teacher will go over the material again in case the teacher did not make the lesson clear. This benefits the student, in that feeling blameless he will achieve a greater focus upon the lesson and become stronger in the next one.

The teacher in this case has an advantage due to achievement level, lack of time constraints and curriculum approval restrictions by committee. All pure instructors realize these hazards and would love to freely teach each student if they were able, but the system devised by man shortchanges both the learner and learned.

LESSON 7

As stated in Ephesians: The real powers that are at work in your universe are not of flesh and blood, but contests of principalities, against powers that are rulers of the darkness in this age, and spiritual hosts of wickedness in the heavenly places. So remember always to put on the full armor of God, that you may then stand against the wiles of the Evil One, each and every day. The real battle is the one versus self.

WEDNESDAY, NOVEMBER 20, 1996, 11:00PM

I now will speak to your parents if they are ready to hear: Your love of family is beyond reproach, and the concerns you have are heartfelt and legitimate. If you allow for the slightest possibility of chance, that the manifestations evident in your son are real, then I will be able to alleviate any and all confusion you have in this regard. Maintain the faith and you will be amazed at the results. If your son was Michelangelo, would you wish him not to paint or sculpt? If your boy was a Beethoven (who was deaf and mute), would you advise him against musical composition? If your child was Franklin, would you discourage his pursuits of invention? If your offspring was Prince Siddhartha Gautama (Buddha) would you call him unwise to leave royalty for peasantry? If your seed was Martin Luther King, Jr, would you prevent him from echoing equal rights for humankind? Or if your blood was of Abraham Lincoln would you suggest that he abandon the hopeless cause of slavery, and the impossible task of preventing secession from the union?

Finally, would you ask Gandhi to abort his principles of peace among mankind in the most treacherous of times? Certainly not! Assuredly I say to you, a greater one then all of these has come in spirit to this generation.

FRIDAY, NOVEMBER 22, 1996, 5:22AM, LESSON 8

As you awake you have seen many examples of the peace with which the Lord carries Himself. It is not always the wisdom of His words but also the powerful effects of His presence alone, that can activate positive change in any given situation. A mere look or gesture at the appropriate moment, has greater impact on certain people at certain times then an unnecessary verbalization. The Lord understands which type of interaction, creates His desired result in every circumstance as it unfolds before Him. This quality is equally as essential in effective communication, as any chosen word could be at its proper time. Both of these elements of interaction are invaluable to your development as a well balanced communicator. As your personal development extends itself to others, remain alert to each of these approaches and apply them accordingly to the task at hand, either individually or in tandem. After a time, their appropriate uses will not need to be determined by analysis, but will become instinctual. These tools of peace and pure understanding can move mountains and disarm conflict. Practice recognizing daily life situations of lesser magnitude and applying our methods to them. When you have selected your approach, then call upon your six senses (insight of future event is one) to evaluate and determine the appropriate need for that particular circumstance. The success or failure of your choice will manifest itself in obvious delight or subsequent repercussions.

In this manner you will be able to make the proper adjustments necessary to improve decision making. Since the inception of our expressive relationship, you have had to learn from ground zero by trial and error. I have purposely made nothing too easy for you, because as your past life attests, you excel when the circumstances are most difficult.

Your character has always developed through disappointment and adversity, and when things have come too easily you stop producing. In someone else I may apply the opposite means of motivation, but this is because I can discern between each individual circumstance.

*There is your first example of this lesson plan.

SATURDAY, NOVEMBER 23, 1996, 7:00AM - LESSON 9

Reflect on your dreams and the situations presented to you. This next lesson is about choices that are made, born of proper communication methods that we learned about yesterday. The options can be numerous and temptation plays a role as well, oftentimes confusing your focus. In each situation you weighed the options and ultimately made the right choices, despite a delay in some instances. Seduction is also a diversionary element that clouds proper decision making, so beware of this factor and keep up your guard. Proper questioning in a tight situation will eliminate your confusions, (as seen with those two women of immoral character) thus allowing the right decision to be made. You also have learned that you can communicate and successfully interact with those whom you consider to be adversaries, as evidenced by your fellow worker. You went well beyond providing him the bare minimum response, and actually helped acclimate him to a new environment. You recognized his surprise at your extra effort, and thus turned an adversary into an ally. He knew how he had treated you in the past, and also that you had rebuked him in return. This gave him the relationship he desires with all who work for him. What you did in the dream was contrary to the responses his character is comfortable with, and as a result you made an imprint on him. This is affecting positive change in people that administered in proper doses, can bring about new and improved behavior. If you think that this is a small victory and that only one person is affected by it, you are mistaken. The differences in him shall be recognized by all who have contact with him, and thus reflect on each a new personality trait, which now brings about a positive change in those who originally rebuked his ways as did you. Therefore, instead of one improved personality there are one hundred plus that are better off. This is what I meant by offering the other cheek, and hundredfold increase. A person on initial assault may be reacting to a stimulus without forethought or conscience. Any resistance will arouse further anger from the aggressor and a fight will ensue. If the recipient of the assault offers the other cheek without resistance, you have caused the attacker to think twice. Now his initial reaction (a) will be stopped, or (b) he will take further action. You have forced him into making two separate decisions. One is based on a reaction he may then regret and peace will follow. The second assault will prove a desire to destroy, therefore you may defend. This example you realize is not meant exclusively for individuals, but for nations as well. To many who have read but not understood My teachings, this strategy may have sounded weak, but with further explanation does it not become crystal clear? This generation is hellbent on personal pride and so called respect. People who are killing each other senselessly in the communities because they feel disrespected, should realize that you must first earn the respect of your fellow in order to lose it. This is murder without provocation and cannot be rationalized as many do. The intense hatreds that exist today are born of people not taking responsibility for their own actions, for they know full well that society has provided them with a multitude of excuses to the resultant behavior. The blame is assigned in directions too numerous to mention, but ultimately falls upon the shoulders of the perpetrator in the eyes of God. You have created a society of disabled brethren, who reach for a crutch at every crisis or even incidence, because they are so readily available.

In these days of decline it behooves each individual to take stock in his own soul and that of his brother, before it is too late. Let each one realize they must bear their own cross. May the fear (respect) of God be within each of you. Amen.

SUNDAY, NOVEMBER 24, 1996, 3:25AM - LESSON 10

As you awake on the "Christian" Sabbath, you have discovered that even while ill your senses are sharper. You are anticipating truths before they are told, while filling hesitations and gaps with correct responses. You are reading between the lines so to speak, and this gives you greater understanding in most matters. People who exercise this type of behavior in a strictly physical sense, oftentimes miscalculate a situation, and this cutting in of sorts becomes a character flaw. However, when the Holy Spirit perpetuates this action, it is a strength and not a weakness of your character. Your intrusions may seem impolite at the time but serve you well in disarming a potential onslaught of propaganda, or a faulty momentum building display of foolish reasoning and inaccurate testimony. Your ability to possess understanding before the debater actually speaks his piece, is an advantage that throws off his concentration, and ultimately his train of thought. As a result, you have individuals second guessing themselves, as well as back pedaling to repair false testimony. Applied wisely, you can then allow the person to fumble and ramble without any interruption, thus assuming that you will intercede, which naturally you will not. Effective tactics are essential to communication, choices, presentation, and decision making capabilities while interacting in debate. Always ask questions instead of being bent on refuting someone's beliefs, thus tangling those spiders in their own web of deceit. When the delivery appears to have a foolproof, complex, systematic, and premeditated plan of attack that is irrefutable on the surface to all concerned; ... Ask simple questions. This will take a highly fortified perceived showpiece of presentation, and reduce it to its most simplistic form, minimizing it's zeal and allowing those in attendance to witness the lay persons interpretation (that you request) so that all may benefit. Now that you have removed the original dazzle and forced the originator to explain, so that all may clearly understand, (including yourself) now buys you time to formulate a fitting rebuttal. If you come up with even one solid question that others would ask as well, you have succeeded in weathering the storm, that the bearer of said message expected to be their knockout punch. Reducing fanciful talk and lawyeresque summations, to simplistic explanation by proper questioning, deflates any holier than thou educational and experience advantage the speaker believes he has. For those who believe that their authority on a given subject is beyond reproach, ask them by what authority it was appointed. Certainly their first response will be related to humanistic experience. Your authority granted by the holy spirit supercedes any physical learning process that they have attained, and do not be afraid to tell them so. With the gift of the holy spirit you are qualified to speak and act with authority on any mortal topic, provided you continue as you are in modest, humble, patient, and truthful representation of this spirit, remembering always that you travel by Divine command only.

SUNDAY, NOVEMBER 24, 1996, 6:20AM - LESSON 11

As you now see those with whom you work, they feel better that you are back to the way you were before the absence. Many are concerned for your well being outside the workplace as well, and as they witness the normal activities with which they were accustomed to interacting with you, a greater comfort level will be reached. They will however recognize a new and improved version and you must be able to put everyone at ease, in order for them to best cope with this personality turn around. People that have known you for many years and are no longer in daily or even weekly contact, cannot grasp the process of your new development in a spiritual light. It is best not to try and explain your experiences, even though you wish to do so out of honesty and not pride. It is far too heavy for most people to handle. Help out with everyone's curiosity so they can feel free to interact with you as before, and subsequently your new perspectives on life can enlighten many. You will find that people want to come and ask questions on all sorts of subjects, thus utilizing your abilities as a source of information and inspiration as well. These requests, conversations, problems, proposals, experiences, curiosities, advice, etc. will serve as a continual developmental process for all concerned. Do not be overly concerned with anyone's evaluation of our relationship, especially those who have formed an opinion of you based on hearsay. Some that have never heard of you before, now use your name freely based on false reports, and it is best to steer clear of those types. If you try and respond to each false testimony, you will burn out in a short period of time. I have you chosen as permanent seed, not one that is well intended but suffers an early demise. You are in this race for the long haul and I will continue as promised, to provide the necessary fuel supply (knowledge, wisdom and understanding) to complete this trip. Stay on My course and do not look to the right or left, but especially do not turn back. Stay familiar with your surroundings by utilizing your peripheral vision, and keep your ear to the ground, being sensory aware at all times. The meaning of not looking to the right or left has nothing to do with eyesight, but rather focusing on the finish line which is the imperishable crown of which we do not want to be sidetracked from. The pathway is lit, so continue to persevere as you are, being well guided along the way. Do not repress your personality traits that include sense of humor, and still enjoying time spent with others. Be yourself and it will better serve those involved in your life, as well as improve your outlook and health, thus providing stamina for that which you wish to accomplish. I did not become prominent in your life to take it away, but rather to enhance it, much the same as when and why I take human form on occasion. Assuredly I say to you that our cause is most worthy, and well received throughout the heavenly realm.

* We shall enter into this new age Aquarius together with a methodical walk.

MONDAY, NOVEMBER 25, 1996, 5:08AM - LESSON 12

As you awake you have seen the confusion that results from a very serious situation. (in this case the disappearance of an 8 year old boy) You were able to be helpful because you applied sequential, investigative, and practical methods to a panic stricken situation, where cooler heads must prevail. Not only is it important to follow a certain procedure, but it must be done with tact and sensitivity at the same time. Many people directly involved, need to be brought together for a common purpose in regards to accomplishing the mission at hand. Each has their own feelings and reasons of what is the best approach, but you must take leadership at once, converting their misguided and emotionally distorted notions of fact, toward positive and productive energies. This is essential toward achieving the desired result. In this way you will increase the odds of a successful conclusion, to a desperate and potentially tragic circumstance. There is no set formula or procedure to crisis management, because every case is entirely different, as all facets of the situation are fully considered. The ability to think clearly and act in accordance with common sensibility, coupled with compassion for all souls concerned, allows for the greatest chance of success. There is one other ingredient that you applied and perhaps the most important of all, as you called for earnest prayer to God by all who shared in this trying experience. Prayer in unity is our strongest bond of love eternal.

TUESDAY, NOVEMBER. 26, 1996 7:09AM - LESSON 13

As you awake many examples of great successes have been displayed to you by the simple performance of a gracious act, that in and of itself appears minor. Timing can be everything as clearly evidenced this night when powerful results may occur, as compassion and gratitude is delivered at the proper moment. Acknowledgement to someone who deserves but not expects goes a very long way. As a writer once told you in baseball, "You just concentrate on hitting the ball and I will make it travel". This is an example of how a particular task can be achieved when each party combines their individual abilities and strengths toward a common goal. By honoring someone for their achievements in a given situation of volunteerism, that otherwise would go unnoticed, encourages that person to continue on to greater heights, mainly due to the proper recognition of their contributions among those whom they have directly benefited. This reaffirmation makes the time, effort, and sacrifices, that were encountered along the way, well worth the continuing new found challenge. A few well chosen, kind, and gracious words, delivered in a brief and appropriate moment can cover years of dedicated Godly service. Conversely, you have also witnessed in real life how a simple prayer of hope that you whispered in a small room, for a few men in a passing moment, was loudly reverberated down every hallway to thousands of men who will never forget, and thus judge you on hearsay and rumor as a result. This is the potential of God's powerful message fully realized. So it also is for those unfamiliar with or deprived of My teachings, that the appropriate reference at a given time, may enlighten many who otherwise would remain blind. Continue to bring the word despite any interferences that you may encounter, and this perseverance will be greatly appreciated by all concerned.

WEDNESDAY, NOVEMBER 27, 1996, 8:07AM - LESSON 14

As you awake another important lesson in human exchange is displayed. As fully envisioned through dream sequence you were able to complete a very difficult task alone, that normally would call for the aid of at least two or three others. By physically removing an individual of unruly nature, you had to continue a process that would cover a great distance, assuming at any moment that help would arrive. As you progressed to each new stage your strength was renewed, because you felt that if one more step was accomplished the necessary support would surface. Obviously it never did, but nonetheless you struggled toward the final destination. As you passed by many spectators so to speak, they were so involved with their activities displayed during down time, that they couldn't adjust to their primary function. The instincts that you were able to call upon as the incident occurred, showed that you can successfully adapt to a critical situation without hesitation, and also utilize the techniques of prior training as well as understanding. For the others with whom you depend upon at work, you recognized various reasons as to why they did not react when the situation was unfolding, and you felt betrayed by: a) their apparent lack of concern for your safety, and b) their dereliction of duty. You may recall back to the old days when everyone backed each other up, as each was acutely aware of the safety of all, and you felt comfort and security in a hostile setting. Now you realize how time has changed the face of loyalty and devotion, and that teamwork is reduced to weighing out individual decision making and personal choices.

This example is a reflection of society itself where decisions are made based upon individual satisfactions, not on the greater good for all. The involvement of someone into a critical need situation is not based on instinct, but rather an evaluation as to the benefits or detractions that may ensue. As a result, you now live in an age where indecision, uninvolvement, and lethargic behavior is paramount. Do not wait for others. This is what I refer to as sleeping. A world that is asleep can no longer function effectively for all of its members, and as a result has ignored the basic needs of the multitudes. Therefore, for those that are sleeping it becomes the main responsibility of the elect to wake them up, for they are not considered to be less worthy in the kingdom of heaven. Each persons salt is measured through his faith and works, and solubility shall be determined thusly.

THURSDAY, NOVEMBER 28, 1996, 5:28AM - LESSON 15

As you awake you are relieved to discover that a poor choice made during this dream sequence is not real. After selecting an improper behavior option that you immediately regretted, and then tried to rationalize as well as cover up, imprisoned your physical and spiritual character. As you made adjustments to correct the immoral nature of the incident, you were trying to smooth over the impact it would have on your gifts of the spirit. You exhibited traits of craftiness instead of instituting earnest prayer of forgiveness. As opposed to calling upon clever techniques, that may certainly convince people around you, utilize solemn prayer directly to God, thus acknowledging His presence rather than denying it. No human being is perfect but if you falter in a physical sense related to the flesh, own up to these misgivings and forgiveness is attainable. Craftiness and deceit, so oftentimes displayed by the wise of the world, may serve them well in worldly matters, but we are operating on a far different plateau. The rules and regulations of human life in the physical world, are created by man. The lessons that you learn from the holy spirit, are those taught from the podium that is above, and are primarily concerned with the proper development of the spirit, which in turn will benefit the physical being. The end result of this process is a complete being that is pleasing to God, and to the world in which they live.

By seeking the virtues of the earth only, you will constantly struggle with humankind and its varying beliefs, jealousies, contempt, prejudices, etc. for there is no absolute or proper form acceptable to all souls. You cannot become perfect in this physical state through the eyes of man or God. As you set your complete being in motion, striving toward perfection in the spirit and the higher ideals of heaven, your physical body follows the leadership of the spirit, and you become as one with the earth and God. As you continue to learn more about the powers of the holy spirit, always remember the love and compassion that it operates under, forever guiding you in the proper direction, out of genuine hope for your continual success. The spirit is not a sledge hammer as many would believe, ready to come down upon someone at its slightest provocation. The true spirit is loving, patient, meek, and longsuffering, waiting many years in someone's life if necessary, for the opportunity to become what it always was. For each person the duration of time is different, and many people never acknowledge its existence at all, because of the overwhelming influence of the physical world upon the physical being. Each person must come to understand that they consist of two distinct beings, and that each must serve its divine purpose, by being recognized according to time and space, as equal partners of a common goal, to achieve the greater good which is the whole person most pleasing to God and fellow. You have been honest and open in this not so pleasant lesson.

FRIDAY, NOVEMBER 29, 1996, 5:28AM - LESSON 16

As you awake the peace and tranquility of the blessed Virgin Mary has been displayed to you in a sequence of dreams. Appropriately, you went to the LaSalette Shrine on Thanksgiving evening with your family, and began to read the story of apparition on September 19, 1846 in LaSalette, France. This intercession was at a critical period of human history, namely in western Europe amidst several crop failing famines and prospects of war. The wrath felt in heaven, could only be eased with the love and tender mercies offered by the mother of all humanity. The pure love of Mary for each of her people, has served humankind well throughout the ages. She continually serves as a peacemaker in Heaven, by disarming conflict and inducing love and hope as a remedy for wrath. During the appropriate times of man's well deserved chastening and severe punishment, she intercedes for the blameless and the yet to be born. Mother Mary has extended beyond measure the protection of man and Earth through untold generations, thus allowing a dangerously weak and sensitive bridge between heaven and earth to remain slightly passable. When the ultimate mediator can no longer bridge the existing gaps between the spiritual and physical worlds, and the holes become too numerous to patch in the boat that is earth, then the craft must eventually sink. If the wrath of heaven was such in 1846 that it required an apparition of mother Mary herself, then how critical do you believe that these present days have become? Look carefully for the upcoming signs.

  * This shrine is where we begin our journey in prayer of hope, and where it also ends, in prayer of thanksgiving.

SATURDAY, NOVEMBER 30, 1996, 6:08AM, LESSON 17

As you awake you are surprised to discover yet more lessons on the topics of character and personality. Do they ever end you must wonder? In the first scenario upon arriving with an interaction already in progress, instead of strictly observing in silence, you offer an inappropriate and devastating comment. After hearing one person announce an opinion of a certain matter, a second person's rebuttal sounded so foolish that you sarcastically asked if that person was retarded or just acting that way. The group turned toward you in disbelief and instead of the laughter you expected, they responded that he was in fact mentally retarded. That one seemingly harmless but ever so thoughtless prank of a comment, turned into a devastating blow to everyone present. How old and experienced in life must we become, before we learn to control the poison of the tongue that defiles our soul? We have heard this cliché most often: Is it not better to remain silent and be thought a fool, then to open your mouth inappropriately and remove all doubt?

The spoken word of a man is the echoing in his heart, and the attestation of his spirit, that he will be judged upon as being part of his works, coupled with his physical actions not only by his fellow man while alive, but on judgement day as well. Eagerness to speak or act too soon are equally flawed character traits, that can bring about dangerous conflicts among men and nations as well. Prejudice is the third element that creates these disasters. Do you understand why it reviles Me so when our heavenly names are used so carelessly in vain. People that continually repeat this behavior throughout their life, without properly seeking to repent by receiving forgiveness, must face the consequences of judgement. This is not a threat, but rather a warning to those on earth whom we love and sincerely wish to achieve spiritual redemption, before it becomes too late to act upon it. Please inform the brethren of these critical lessons I teach, and do not take offense as to My uses of you in unpleasant examples of particular behaviors.

The reason that I insert you into specific negative roles, is so that a greater impact will be made on your memory, in order to better retain your lesson upon waking, thus allowing for more precise recording of the events.

The second scenario regards over anxiety to obtain an answer from someone, that has already been informed about something you desire to know. This is a far less important facet of conduct, but nevertheless still worthy of mention. The major elements of this process is anticipation and lack of patience, which together produce varying degrees of stress. Due to your overzealous will to be informed, you do not give the bearer of the message an ample opportunity to speak. By frequently interrupting through guesswork and prediction, you are rudely sidetracking and diverting the messengers focus on the topic, which they are trying to provide you, thus delaying further the desired result of both parties and increasing the frustration level as well. Keeping silent longer in both these scenarios, would have produced far better results. Sometimes doing nothing far surpasses doing the wrong thing, and will continually serve you well. Outside of an unexpected split second emergency calling for immediate action of instinct, always take time to discern before acting. This includes not speaking prematurely as well as actual steps taken, for you are well aware of the importance in acting, (the well thought out process of a proper decision) as opposed to reacting. (the spontaneous and unprepared product of indecision) This element is better left to emergencies that call for it. Most emergencies in fact are better served through acting as well. Catch your breath for there are many more lessons to come, and continue to do well on your road to understanding.

MONDAY, DECEMBER 2, 1996, 4:16AM, LESSON 18

As you awake the proper recording of events that you witness is extremely important. As various occurrences take place, it is best to abbreviate and to use an outlining method in chronological order, that you can go back to at a later time and record in its entirety. It is critical to register all facts in their proper order, thus allowing for a comprehensive and accurate accounting of incidents as they occur. This is a method used by well trained news reporters, who can approach a situation in progress and record facts only, that shall provide the general public with a clear cut understanding of what is truly taking place, whether it be a completed action or one that remains in progress. Vital information must be clearly distinguished from trivial, and separated out of the synopsis accordingly. Time is also of the essence in reporting, as competitors are vying for being the first to produce a resulting newsline. Do not ever let speed overrun the importance of truth. Accuracy and managed speed, are the two most important elements in the successful analysis of events in this day and age. In time gone by, the element of speed was not a critical part of recording an historical event, but accuracy has always been paramount, and if recorded truthfully it can stand the test of time. Acceptance or rejection by those who determine fact from fiction, is predicated on your method of analogy and credibility as a worthy gatherer of facts. Also, the resulting interviews of eyewitnesses that you subsequently compile, minus the emotional exaggerations that cloud the truth. Upon supplying a verifiable, factual, chronological, interesting, and informative sequence of events, deserving of recognition by the general public, may you then consider this research worthy of mention. A good friend and mentor once told you that when you are conversing with someone who is always busy or in demand by others constantly, their attention span is limited due to the amount of testimony that they ingest daily. Speak to them in fact only "short hand," so that they detect a critical importance in each word that you speak, and do not have to work at separating out the nonsense and descriptions that confuse and dilute fact. In this method of approach you will find an attentive listener, that can now focus on your message by using their senses, instead of using up all their energies. For those in decision making positions, this type of interaction is a rare and welcomed product of successful social intercourse.

WEDNESDAY, DECEMBER 4, 1996, 1:44AM, LESSON 19

As you awake, the process of teaching others has begun. It can start very slowly with children or adults, and is merely a presentation of the things that have already been taught to you in a clear and concise manner. As you observe yourself beginning to instruct others, our format is to remain simple and slow. The object of relaying your experiences from the holy spirit, is to then accurately reconstruct them to those being taught. The success of the teaching process solely and wholly depends upon the teacher's ability to determine and disseminate a factual basis of content, and then directly transfer this particular subject information to a student recipient. The receiver of the lessons content, also shares a responsibility to be willing and able to learn. The process is only successful if all parties involved are doing their part, and are well prepared to participate. As instructor to those whom I will teach through you there is an added responsibility, because a normally standard two way process of learning, has now become a three way transaction. If you are able to enlighten others from our shared experiences without loss of substance or direction in primary subject matter, then we will greatly achieve. As the one in the middle, the responsibility falls squarely upon you to make the process work effectively. The most difficult part of the formula is currently operating at peak performance, as you continue to tune in perfectly to the messages of the holy spirit. Now that you are armed with the necessary knowledge, wisdom, and understanding to begin, the success of the Davidic triangular connections is imminent. I sincerely hope that as My student recipient and instructor, your students are as willing to learn, and to further develop their spiritual beings for the betterment of all, in this disconnected world of many lost sheep. Good luck and God bless.

THURSDAY, DECEMBER 5, 1996, 4:54AM, LESSON 20

As you awake, many examples are presented to you of the Lord's simple teachings. From one to another you go applying the techniques we have learned. No situation that you came upon was problematic enough to call for any difficult or critical intervention. Solving minor disputes that are actually just differences of opinion, provided each with the right amount of input, as everyone continued on their way feeling a sense of adequacy and fulfillment. As you learned by testing the waters, the key concept here is compromise. When each party feels certain that their side of the story is heard and also understood, then both may give in just enough for the third party mediator to establish common ground, thereby utilizing the positive elements of each testimony. In this manner, the end result becomes a byproduct of each seemingly diverse and contrary opinion containing elements of both, thus creating a third opinion of finality, where all concerned can see their respective truths on display, minus the unnecessary and often inaccurate aspects of each. You have now taken two originally polarized opinions that also serve to separate the two participants as well, and created a connection. When people are allowed to establish a pattern of differences they tend to grow further apart, whether it is of minor or major consequence. Now that they are enlightened to the fact that there is a combination of truth and error in each of their beliefs, as you present these facts most appropriately, then common respect and proper dialogue is born. They may now witness their own strengths and weaknesses, that as instructor you have thus brought to their collective awareness. Without proper mediation people fail to realize that their opinions are not always based solely on fact, but more often than not on a combination that includes partial truths and hearsay as well. In this generation the resources of information are so numerous and diverse, that coupled with our busy daily schedules, allows us to only receive bits and pieces of information on the run. Truth in reporting is oftentimes lost or misplaced, while this ever increasing speed creates many progressive lifetime inconsistencies, misconceptions, and one sided testimony that may cloud our learning abilities. As many people come to accept and expect what they view or read as a given statement of accuracy, and in turn relay to others from an authority position, they are at times conveying otherwise unfamiliar details. False testimony and rumor are its offspring.

For those that utilize a report of experiences from another and apply the results to all cases, is it not appropriate here to take into account the saying; "An ounce of prevention is better than a pound of cure"? Getting facts straight the first time by aptly persevering truth through accurate and proper research, carries far more credibility than an opinion gathered only by the second hand reporting of others. This can be received nightly from your favorite chair at home, in front of the computer, radio, or television set, or by simply reading the daily tabloids. Do not readily accept each reported experience or opinion as common fact, for in every individual case is a different set of circumstances that is unique to that person, place, and time. People come together by sharing opinions and learning of each others experiences in person, so that all will benefit and grow as a result of their developing common interests and bonds. Conversely, people grow apart because they may automatically accept what they are told by the media or hearsayers as truth, and then enforce this on others who may have received differing reports on the same subject, thus neither party establishes their own sense of real opinion and a split occurs.

FRIDAY, DECEMBER 6, 1996, 6:24 AM - LESSON 21

As you awake several people desire information from you, as to your extent of knowledge regarding the holy spirit. You witness opinions and formulations of thought processes by a multitude of people that believe they have all the answers. Remain as the wise one for you seek nothing more than that which is being given. As long as you do not build in additional testimony of human based opinion to the pure facts of the holy spirit, then none of your beliefs will become refutable even though they will be deeply scrutinized. This serves you well as to proper discernment between spiritual and physical stimuli. As others elevate their concepts and ideas to heights beyond truth, you must fully realize the separation point of fact and fiction. When those that begin a convincing display of knowledge and expertise that captures the attention of all, as credibility is established between the listeners and the story teller, beware of the salesmanship that follows. Inevitably they will venture out beyond the point of actual knowledge, crossing the fine line of truth into the territory of speculation. The listener cannot discern between the two, due to the craftiness of the sales person peddling either his product or idea. This is a practical learning experience that you may witness in real life every day, and thus determine the point of transformation that someone utilizes between actual wisdom and contrived fantasy. Being able to question the promoter at that exact point in time can derail their entire delivery and thought process, because they inevitably hold their breath while crossing over to the territory of authority without fact. In this way you will recognize a slight shift in their pattern or routine, by their lack of direct eye contact to whom they are speaking, at that critical point of crossing over. This will be evident to you in the interaction of: a) a group of kids discussing the power potentials of a cartoon character, all the way up to: b) summit meetings of political national leaders and c) religious authorities offering divine proof as to why their beliefs are worthier than another. In time you will be quite amused, as you gain the knack of recognizing these presentations for what they really are. On a personal note, you are wise to consider attending the Salvation Army church service in your hometown, for there will be an eye opening experience awaiting you. Continue your good works and remember the focal point of your dream tonight. It behooves each and every person of this world to carefully consider with much preparation; who and what they choose to elevate and especially how far. Take great heed when crossing into territory where you should not tread, and by this I mean; do not deceive the poor in knowledge or attempt to speak from the same pulpit as He who teaches. Your successes on earth can only go so far. This does not concern you, but rather those that act contrary to the spirit of truth. They know who they are. Enough said.

SATURDAY, DECEMBER 7, 1996, 9:44AM - LESSON 22

As you awake, continue to be a problem solver in each situation that calls for it. You must not allow anger and frustrations to intervene in the process of reconciliations, because it only distorts our aims. These elements of behavior must be tamed by you and will not be removed from your personality by the holy spirit. They are simply negative byproducts of a character trait that is essential to your being, and as a boring worm must be cut from an otherwise edible ear of corn, so shall these be removed to make way for a properly functioning spirit of energy and drive. Negative behaviors are simply the bruised fruits that grew from the earthly branch of the tree of life. By removing that branch, the more worthy branches may be grafted in that bear good fruit from the lessons of the holy spirit. This will enable the tree to not only survive but to flourish as well, thus providing the much needed nourishment of knowledge, wisdom, and understanding for those who partake. The important thing for you to learn today, is that your intake of wisdom has increased a hundredfold in a brief span of time, due to the teachings of the holy spirit. Do not allow this increase to spiral too far ahead of those whom you wish to instruct. You can handle the onslaught of knowledge by digesting it purely, then diluting it just enough so that others will understand the messages full intent. This shall best comfort both you and them. In this way you increase at a tremendous pace, and those that you instruct may increase at a comfortable pace to them, without feeling intimidated by an avalanche of new information. In your zeal to pass along what you have learned, those that are living primarily in the physical world cannot adapt to the speed of these spiritual dictates. You have always done well in sharing with others the positive lessons and fine experiences in your life, but you were conveying on a physically even playing field. As you provided one hundred percent of that which you had learned, others received the entirety. If you present that same one hundred percent now, only the most spiritual will pick up on about seventy-five percent of your delivery. Become more tolerant and patient with those whom you share knowledge, and understand that they are living today, where you were a short time ago and cannot be expected to retain all that you now have acquired. A two week interval of earthly time feels like two years to you, because of the pace that you are receiving new information. Your physical being relates time to the amount of stimulus it receives, and you are in fact absorbing a years to weeks ratio. Why do you think that the holy spirit of the Lord always speaks in parables? Superior understanding has no useful purpose if it is not able to be shared so that others may benefit. Jesus Verona himself had frustrations in teaching not because people were unable to grasp his knowledge, but rather that they oftentimes did not focus on his parables. He could only reduce his purity of this wisdom so far. As you acquire the necessary patience for proper instruction, the angers and frustrations will subside and finally dissipate, thus clearing your future pathway to success.

Recall that a prophet's word is welcomed everywhere, except in his own country and in his own home.

MONDAY, DECEMBER 9, 1996, 4:57 AM, LESSON 23

As you awake hear My words loud and clear: "All men are created equal," and in this the truths of the Spirit are self-evident. Let no man believe he has a birth advantage over another in God's eyes. Inequality begins and ends with man and not He. You have witnessed My love for all of humankind both in dream and in the compassion you felt at the Salvation Army church. What happens to each person after birth is not equality or of God. Those fortunate enough to be born into privilege grow up with all the basic necessities of the physical world as a given, thus developing without regard to survival. Because of humanity's ineptness to well provide for his fellow man from birth, I place an added responsibility upon each person born into this advantage. Do not misinterpret your good fortune as deserving or a stroke of luck, but rather take heed that you are being judged according to your works, in providing your brethren's needs to survive first and foremost. If you are born in America regardless of so-called class, you are economically advantaged over eighty plus percent of the world's population. How much more responsibility do you feel as a well to do American, toward the ninety-nine percent of the world that have less than you? Do you believe that this is their problem for any number of reasons you may give? It is your responsibility, as the privileged body awarded to your soul will attest. You would be wise to contemplate these thoughts, and ask yourself if you are really providing enough help for those in critical need. Those of you who live in the lap of luxury cannot compare yourselves to those who have more than you, for that justifies your continuity toward further greed. Accumulations of unnecessary material possessions, only serves to polarize the truly needy of the world that much further. That which you believe to be acquired by your own hard work and merit is only partly accurate.

Does not God have a hand in all that He has allowed you?

Have you reached a point that goes far beyond basic need? These are not only questions for this time of year but each and every day, for real need knows no season. The main reason that the world is so out of balance is because of human greed pure and simple. Many other reasons are apparent as well, but they are mostly byproducts of greed. Any privilege that you enjoy in this world, is temporary and of the flesh if you do not provide for those in need. The poor of this world will become the rich of the next world, for theirs is eternal life in the kingdom. You who are of privilege have already received your rewards here on Earth, so make certain that if you also desire eternal life, your spirit may be allowed to positively influence the physical being that is displeasing to God. You lose favor in God's eyes each day that He must witness starvation and disease, and at the same time observe gluttony. Most assuredly I say to you, the time is at hand to assess your standing with God. Are you truly prepared to stand before Him in judgement according to your faith and works? How truly difficult it is for the rich to inherit the kingdom of God. Your spirit is the everlasting gift of God, not merely the body. Do not marvel at physical life, but rather serve the spirit by which the body was appointed. Do not allow your spirit soul to be judged by sins of the flesh. It shall serve you well in your future journeys of soul.

MONDAY DECEMBER 9, 1996, 8:09AM LESSON 24

May My words go forth in a calm manner, but not lose the powerful effect of the message. Please meet My peace by serving your fellow with due diligence and an open heart. Those that are My soldiers of salvation travel the high road among people. Learn from them, and you shall fully realize the true difference between the heights of the spirit and the depths of the flesh. Those that are poor in the flesh but continue to serve their fellows who have even less than they, shall serve with God in heaven over all others, for so faithfully serving of He while upon the earthly plane. The last will indeed be first.

As I told you before and now you can attest, it would be an eye opening experience for you at the Salvation Army services. You also performed a proper deed by applying a lesson we shared last week, in acknowledging a well deserving man for his longtime effort in the presence of his peers. It will renew his strength of purpose, as he combats age and its subsequent limitations on good health. Continue to absorb as a sponge this wisdom supplied by the holy spirit, and your corps of disciples will grow from the proper foundation of understanding.

The poor will become rich and the rich become poor as we move from earth (physical) to heaven (spiritual). On this you can be assured, for the corruptible can no longer have domain over the incorruptible in a world without sin. As in so many of My parables, understand the critical importance with which I emphasize removing the elements of your being that cause you to sin. It is better to be missing any physical part of your being that corrupts, then to stand before me in judgement with your sins testifying against you. Each of you has had more than ample opportunity, to seek redemption through repentance of sin while alive on this Earth. By putting off this necessary request to God our Father, we must also put off a response of your desire for salvation. To a man, is it so much to ask forgiveness from He who created you, or do you carry so much pride that you will not find the time to repent? Tomorrow is promised to no one, so is it worth delaying what you know to be right, at least for the sake of those whom you love if not for yourself? Be not a hypocrite that has taught your children: a) to do the right things in life by confronting problems head on, b) looking someone in the eye when you speak to them, and project loud and clear so they may understand. c) do not lie to yourself or others for God will punish you, and do not say anything if you cannot say something that is good. d) love and respect all people for this is righteous, never bearing false witness to either friend or foe. e) help your fellow man who has less than you, and do not make fun of anyone who has disabilities, and so forth. Practice what you preach for that will serve you well. Hypocrites that only instruct from what they have heard and do not apply, will be called upon to account for those misgivings. Can you really afford not to make the time for God? Please discontinue paying homage to the physical, and come to see the light that wishes to shine upon each that is of the spirit. The repentance call is meant as the changing of ones ways, not as the fire and brimstone intimidation of days past.

Let no church or doctrine separate you from our God within.

THURSDAY, DECEMBER 12, 1996, 1:57AM, LESSON 25

As you awake many people come together for a common place of worship. Their religious beliefs may be freely expressed at this unconventional center of congregation. The architectural integrity of any standard church building, is determined first and foremost by the cornerstone of its foundation. The quality of construction that follows which is the frame, is how the human eye will determine the beauty, and also the wealth and influence that the church membership possesses. The most majestic, ornate, and imposing physical structures in this world that represent years of tremendous labors of love toward God, become glorifying sanctuaries of union, whereby God and people may come together. Heaven does not judge churches or religions however, on their external or internal physical characteristics, although these incredible structures are most impressive.

The physical beauty reflected in magnificence of style, grace, and design of religious architecture, and other wonders of the world created by man, are primarily for your enjoyment and our observations. There is a certain sadness that goes along with our joys and our hopes. It is difficult to witness exotic pieces of ornamentation worth millions of dollars in certain churches, while we also view basic needs of survival unfulfilled in other true believing brethren who lack proper food, clothing, medicine, and shelter. The true spirit of religious worship is in how man directly interacts with his fellow on a daily basis, not limited to the Sabbaths and joyous holidays of dress up behavior.

When genuine love and respect of the entire brotherhood is displayed by care and compassion, and you greet one another with sincerity of heart, then God's presence is assured in the place where you meet. Now that your cornerstone has been set properly in its foundation, a church pleasing to God is established. If you do not feel the presence of God in the place that you worship, then something must be missing from the true elements of unity that is required by Him. The only prerequisite that God has in terms of His church attendance, is the nature and composition of your foundation. Jesus Christ is the spiritual cornerstone of the true religious foundation that we speak of, and the sole ingredient that separates a community meetingplace from a purely religious congregation. His presence in your heart is the true church that God willingly attends, each and every day of your life. Wherever you go He will follow in a spirit that has no geographical bounds, or any needful requirement of structure. You do well to understand that the Lord supplies the holy spirit necessary to form a complete church, thus combining the spiritual (God) with the physical, (Man) much the same as this identical composition forms the complete person we spoke of last week. The true church of God is not a physical entity, but rather a faith born in the hearts of true believers, who gather for the love of each other and God, to share that faith with which they have been blessed. This is truly giving thanks in the eyes of God, regardless of your denomination. Most assuredly I say to you: "From our viewpoint in heaven we have had as many wonderfully tearful and inspirational religious experiences, gathered around burning trash barrels in the middle of the night, on the poorest and meanest streets of the earth in the coldest dead of winter, as at the altar of St. Peter's Basilica in Rome, on the most beautiful Sunday mornings of the warmest and brightest spring days that you can imagine". Believe that where true faith lives...so does God. This you now understand is that special place in your heart where limitless love empowers the world.

FRIDAY, DECEMBER 13, 1996, 1:06AM, LESSON 26

As you awake begin to supply those whom you come upon in need with the nourishment of the pure spirit. Feed both the young and old alike, for they are one and the same when it comes to this basic requirement. The holy spirit is generous and kind, hoping to become a gift of the holiday season for all that will partake of its splendor. Feel free to share with all whom you encounter, the gifts of the spirit that you have come to well know.

Bring your miracle to the downtrodden and the wealthy as well,
for they are poor and in need of the story you shall tell.
Their lives have been lacking a true connection to God,
send the lessons you learn so that we all may applaud.

The students are so hungry for the truths you relate,
and so thirsty as well for the drink that is fate.
Tend to these needs of the things we do best,
then the head of the class as you pass every test.

You are carrying the torch at a pace uncompared,
ride the wave of momentum with the wisdom we have shared.
Fill the pores of the sponge till you absorb every drop,
as you thrive on the challenge for the prize at the top.

When the sponge is so full that it cannot hold any more,
wring it out in the bucket and begin to now pour.
All the water that is knowledge down the throats oh so dry,
for to quench such a thirst brings a cheer from on high.

Make this vital connection from David's triangles you drew,
and the tear on My face will be dried you once knew.
I did feel your compassion in prayer at my station,
as you visited the north of your bordering nation.

Now you see the whole purpose of your trip to Quebec,
so many things happened you would never expect.
You were wise to accurately interpret your dream,
and put into action that which makes us a team.

By bringing your father it has served him quite well,
as you both make great strides everyone can now tell.
You traveled five hundred miles and he didn't know why,
it was food for his soul that no money can buy.

All of your lives you assign reasons and purposes to act,
for once you made an effort that created our pact.
As you conversed and traversed for eight hours you see,
I was there all the while on that road back to Me.

Sacrificing your time for a journey to the Lord,
was a worthy commitment in these days of discord.
Thank you again for those moments lived for Me,
as you ironed out your differences I can surely bless thee.

I have waited some time for you to call on My name,
what a pleasure it was when you both finally came.
Now your life works will flourish as we gain a fresh start,
continue to progress with the lessons we impart.

The days are at hand I must rise from my throne,
I have sat far too long while the evil has grown.
Too many are suffering at the hands of a few,
the tender branches are ripened of the fig tree its true.

The harvest draws near so prepare as you may,
Put your houses in order as we approach judgement day.
It is too late to save bodies so harken every soul,
there is time enough still but that bell will soon toll.

Of that day I do not know only our Father can say,
spread the love to our brethren and continue to pray.

DAILY SOUL DEVELOPMENT THROUGH POETIC FORM

MONDAY, DECEMBER 16, 1996, 3:30 PM

In the world that we live there is both good and bad,
since Adam and Eve some are happy some sad.
As children of God we were created the same,
for better or worse to be called in His name.

What happens from birth becomes the dictates of man,
assigned to a class thus fulfilling his plan.
The seeds become mixed before they are grown,
in a manner only realized by the one that has sown.

The evil contaminates the goodwill of the master,
he was sentenced to earth and works hard toward disaster.
His days have become numbered for he knows all too well,
that ultimate destiny is a millennium in hell.

Your world is his territory and with man stakes his claim,
tear away from his grip being wise to his game.
The methods he employs utilize craftiness and power,
while seeking new enlistments in a frenzy this late hour.

Pay attention to the speed that your life is now spinning,
as the multitudes cross over he appears to be winning.
Steer clear of these influences as millions go wrong,
putting faith in satan's magic where it does not belong.

Momentum has a way to create hysteria this is true,
understanding our New Testament is a how to for you.
The good book is your map on the road to eternal life,
Where there is no evil presence, death, sickness, or strife.

I hope that your choices are of My teachings and love,
as opposed to self dictates, contrary to our laws from above.
Let us welcome all to heaven in a day not so distant,
despite all odds against us we shall prevail by being consistent.

To the virtues set forth by our father at the start,
come partake of the fate who keep God in their heart.

SATURDAY, DECEMBER 21, 1996 5:45AM

These two books I grant to you as gifts of the season,
understand them both well for this critical reason.
All truths are contained within the pages you read,
to fulfill any religiously philosophical need.

Focus hard on My teachings that I have already sent,
as you find them contained in the New Testament.
This is your first book that the world already knows,
but each time you read it your intelligence grows.

This book is not defined solely by words on each page,
its meanings transcend time to include every age.
You can study it so often that it becomes memorized,
but the lessons are timeless and need not be revised.

You can never fully learn all the parables I have taught,
for tomorrow is not yet there is much more to begot.
Every other book written can be confined front to back,
as the words become trapped and encased like a plaque.

My teachings are alive and refuse to stand still,
no scholar of man knows the fields where I till.
I am the same today as yesterday and forever,
hear My voice clearly informing those who feel clever.

You that preach of My words and lifeworks from the past,
are lacking new meaning from the nets that I cast.
Let them learn from your example as you tend to My sheep,
you are wise to administer from the spirit you reap.

Seek the most needy of the rank and the file,
the earthly rich are the poor from the facts I compile.
Make everyone aware as you learn more each day,
now the second gift book is wrapped, please open as you may.

There is more wisdom to grasp as you increase true perception,
the title of this "new" testament is *The Immaculate Conception*.
As mentioned before I am of our father above,
and mothered by Mary with an abundance of love.

This book is unwritten in script known to man,
you have seen it presented on the palm of My left hand.
The two books I held out to you are food for the soul,
combine both their contents and achieve every goal.

Through the spirit I grant you this heavenly special edition,
that shall teach you the wonders no other may petition.
My army you will form without weapons or damnation,
our soldiers are armed only with the promise of salvation.

This war is most worthy so fight well indeed,
to uphold all our doctrines of this heavenly creed.
The enlistments will be many from all walks of life,
as you bang the drum boldly and play on the fife.

Your song of recruitment is "The Little Drummer Boy",
to create all the energy that you wish to deploy.
Enjoy this new book as the first one to read,
beware of evil intentions from those born of greed.

Avert those that you must on this heaven lit path,
and display proper judgement as you sidestep their wrath.
Build confidence and trust for your troops that may fear,
the spirit will dismantle crises so our purpose remains clear.

Put into action what you have learned to this point,
through life's spirit of love we are free to anoint.
The one that can gather this flock gone astray,
shall receive a fine seat with the Lord on His day.

This task is not easy but worthy causes never are,
keep patience and virtue as we command from afar.
As a student and soldier you are marching quite well,
to the drummer in heaven of the song I foretell.

I will stay close in spirit so maintain a strong heart,
you will not be alone that is My promise from the start.
As I help you to build upon this army of request,
in My course you have excelled and passed every test.

To the head of the class at the first semester break,
straight A's are your grades a great start you did make.
There is much more to learn make the celebration brief,
as we get back to our work on the teachings of The Thief.

SUNDAY, DECEMBER 22, 1996, 7:35AM

As you go off to battle there are two things you need,
the heart and the soul is the nourishment to feed.
You have acquired them both the holy spirit does attest,
now pass on this gift to the best of the rest.

As My teachings continue I must borrow your ghost,
to enhance your abilities for this mission you host.
The lesson on this day that you learned from above,
is about intestinal fortitude and the doctrine of love.

I have shown you many parables of importance toward salvation,
so let them pass through you as I teach every nation.
The simplicity of the triangles says it all very clear,
If followed by others they will find Me quite near.

The distance most people feel from me is ever so great,
that they lose proper perspective of the upcoming fate.
You have created a connection that gives a renewal of hope,
to embrace the lost sheep who have chosen to elope.

If you can gather this flock in these days of perdition,
this achievement as shepherd will attain fine recognition.
From all powers in heaven that have witnessed this decline,
you will have served both the Master and your fellow man fine.

The parable of the automobile will teach you the way,
to evaluate the character of your troops in decay.
You must eliminate the evil from this lesson I give,
look deep in their souls so that the good they may live.

Water is essential for it sustains each life form,
most will agree wholeheartedly for this is the norm.
What possible deterrent could this blessed gift be,
outside of an excess like a flood they shall agree.

On appearance it is pure beauty and externally this is true,
but from the inside on out can be trouble that grew.
Ever so slowly and invisible beginning to eat away,
like a cancer in an organism feeding on its prey.

Time marches on as he stays out of view,
until it is too late and there is little left to do.
Water repelled presents no danger you see,
unless it gets underneath the helper that is Me.

I defend every soul from the evil one's ways,
like a rust proof protector to the end of all days.
But the body is separate and I grant you free choice,
to live as you may and to express your own voice.

This water that I mention are the words which you speak,
and salt is the worth of your good works that we seek.
Both elements are critical to a fine eternal life,
but can also double as agents that may rust and cause strife.

It is how they are used and accepted or denied,
at the appropriate moments you may surely confide.
The water in your lesson is the evil one's ability,
to disguise his appearance and his goals of futility.

He is a salesman of sin whose commissions are souls,
do not purchase his product for it springs many holes.
Resist all temptations of the flesh that allure,
for it convicts your spirit also thus closing our door.

To the entrance of heaven that is prepared for the good,
that will arrive incorruptible it is well understood.
The salt and the water blend well in the sea, but like
that vehicle I showed you intestinal fortitude is the key.

So be observant to the virtues of both souls and steel,
and their distinct corrosive influences that can cloud our ideal.
This mission is of the utmost priority and concern,
now continue this new journal with your gifts to discern.

I shall provide for you in parts thus covering your flanks,
while also guarding your safety from inside the ranks.
Both inside and outside of your company presents danger,
the love and protection I supply as a babe in a manger.

So rally the troops round it will bring us much joy,
to appoint you the title of heaven's little drummer boy.

TUESDAY, DECEMBER 24, 1996, 3:07AM

"Go Tell it on the Mountain" as you call out with a "Hark,
The Herald Angels Sing" to all as lovely as the lark.
The multitudes from near and far shall suddenly appear,
to catch a glimpse of why "It Came Upon the Midnight Clear".

As they journey toward the star so bright, shining in the east,
"Angels We Have Heard on High," will guide them to the feast.
He brings salvation to a starving earth as nourishment is fed,
there is "Joy to the World" from every reach upon His tiny head.

"O Come All Ye Faithful" what a wonderful blessing to behold,
from our father God almighty whose pure heart is made of gold.
To north and south from east and west the word is traveled far,
the king of kings this "Silent Night", now born a superstar.

For baby Jesus has finally come so far "Away in a Manger",
In "O Little Town of Bethlehem" to be free from any danger.
Of the evils ever present in the form of King Herod,
the holy family must soon depart, to save the Son of God.

He is born the king of angels and shall become the king of Jews,
to save the world by teaching love and paying all our dues.
What greater gift could God impart upon this world of sin,
for He loves us so He gave His Son to show us how to win.

Our redemption and salvation had been lost before all eyes,
"The First Noel" was granted to forgive iniquities and lies.
So long ago we had the chance to make amends with God,
two thousand years He lives the grief but spared us of His rod.

In the flesh He taught you parables to reverse those evil trends,
but humankind regressed even further disappointing He who sends.
All the gifts bestowed upon us have been so greatly disrespected,
much worse is what He left upon the cross, too often undetected.

Resurrection was the final jolt that proved the prophets true,
Thus preserving faith in human history for Gentile and the Jew.
How much forgiveness should we expect in coming days of thunder,
to cleanse the earth in all its vileness is it really any wonder?

Let us make adjustments to show we care, and He may grant more time and space,
as the sands steadily trickle through the hourglass of life, and we meet Him face to face.
Let us do so with a heart that's pure and greet Him eye to eye.
Have no reason to hang our head so low for things we can't deny.

Come unto Him now while upon this earth in sin no longer walk,
being baptized in the holy spirit He shall answer every knock.
When the sands run dry the time is up no further court of appeal,
for a change of venue delay in sentence or plea bargained deal.

He will welcome all of humankind if we choose the proper course,
owning up to our misgivings with sincerity of remorse.
"God Rest Ye Merry Gentlemen" with nothing to dismay,
remember Christ the Savior now who was born on Christmas Day.

When He comes this final time please make not the same mistake,
learn the lessons of our past and may His love we all partake.
Receive again this glorious gift "Deck The Halls" and do rejoice,
and wipe the tear from upon His cheek by making good each choice.

May your citizenship be high in heaven amongst eternal realm,
By praising the one and only son of He who takes the helm.
"What Child is This" of whom I speak, a father's pride and joy,
prepare His way this second time My "Little Drummer Boy".

He is your savior Jesus Christ, heaven's chairman of the board,
O come let us adore Him...for He is our Christ and Lord.

FRIDAY, DECEMBER 27, 1996, 8:26AM

The body and spirit are a union that give,
all that is needed in the life that you live.
As you put both to work equally in a cooperative manner,
it is pleasing to witness by our heavenly planner.

By intent and design this is true for all kinds,
of life forms created that possess bodies and minds.
The most simple inhabitants of this world are in tune,
with the wishes of He that made earth, sun, and moon.

In the beginning life's balance was the most beautiful sonata,
whose sweet song was orchestrated by our almighty father.
Each life has a purpose as one serves another,
from father and mother to sister and brother.

In lambs or in man the formula is the same,
one slaughters the other as the strong win this game.
On earth this is possible but eternally it is not,
so treat each life appropriately in the battles that are fought.

Those who have advantaged dominion in this temporary state,
look at the overall picture of the artist's painted slate.
This is the eternal canvas whose oils will not run,
The rock of salvation that draws best is My Son.

I grant Him the power of fair judgement over all,
for His worthiness and wisdom goes beyond every call.
Compassion and love flow quite freely in His veins,
while righteousness and grace through His heart still remains.

Despite all provocations toward a contrary belief,
He is steadfast and true never clouded by grief.
All fates are determined by a method so clear,
what you gave to those under you is the glue to adhere.

A future in heaven by your life works on earth,
now the lamb holds the edge, to destroy or give birth.
With the free choice that was granted to your life at the start,
you provided the results for the lamb to impart.

An appropriate direction for each one's own journey,
and although seated as judge He grants power of attorney.
The case becomes won, or lost in this court,
by the clients personal actions and the jury's report.

Each conscience will provide all the necessary facts,
to acquit or convict based on responsibility of acts.
The jury determines every innocence or guilt,
not by the foundation provided but the house that you built.

There are four separate entities at work in this room,
not only your physical being and the fruit of thy womb.
The first part which is the lawyer we despise in the flesh,
providing lies and deceit told by satan we shall thresh.

The client is your spirit and of that we shall seek,
to nourish and nurture thus protecting the meek.
For they will inherit the new world of life,
that lacks all corruptible, death, sickness, and strife.

So two of the four are contained within one,
the third is the jury which are your words said and done.
That give testimony to your being with no further distractions,
so no error will be made in judgement of these actions.

The fourth and final part merely points out the path,
that the other three determined to be His love or His wrath.
For the real judge is not the cornerstone, light, lamb or son,
but each one of his free choice that I granted day one.

FRIDAY, DECEMBER 27, 1996, 9:45PM

As your lessons continue from this gold leafed black book,
you seem content without knowing or even taking a look.
It was one week ago that I gave you first glance,
most anyone else would surely leap at the chance.

To be the first to inform all the world of this find,
you are wise to absorb slowly staying out of a bind.
Until I give you the cue that the timing is right,
stay the course you are on and follow My light.

When you deliver the goods of *The Immaculate Conception*,
the world shall stand and applaud without any exception.
This new belief we are forming bridges all others known to man,
in this high tech society we most certainly can.

I made My point very clear so many years before,
by teaching small groups as I traversed door to door.
In forty-two months My life's history was written,
to warm the future of humankind as a hand in a mitten.

The doctrines I have shared are the passports to heaven,
they have been partly misrepresented except by the eleven.
Who are faithful to Me to this day and forever,
we respect all religions and did encourage each endeavor.

The time has now come to instill that which is pure,
translations through time have diluted the cure.
To the ills of this world that are well out of hand,
not a thousand religions could keep peace through the land.

Human greed overwhelms all the goodness of charity,
that good people bestow on the most needy with clarity.
Of fine purpose and fellowship that in these days stand tall,
despite all takers and detractors you have answered our call.

Do not ever feel alone or in fear of your security,
as you battle for our turf we shall send angels of purity.
To support every mission of our army here on earth,
with promises of salvation when each death knows rebirth.

The title of our new book creates curiosity in the masses,
it is not what they would expect to be drinking from My glasses.
As I run a new course the theologians scratch their heads,
and the most intelligent intellects lie awake in their beds.

They all have a notion of who deserves My new teachings,
will they ever be surprised to hear a prison worker's preachings.
I will thoroughly enjoy their despair and disgust,
as they misread Me once more within the book I entrust.

Humanity has never understood about the gifts I impart,
throughout all the ages it has looked past the heart.
To the minds of the brightest goes man's crowning glory,
for such are his heroes in each never ending story.

They are worshiped for abilities that give them the edge,
to exploit those who slave under them caught in the wedge.
So gather all ye wise men for My fireside chat,
I will inform you in parts as you strain every gnat.

You worry about specifics that do not mean a thing,
without providing those in need with the love I still bring.
The abilities thus awarded to those leaders of men,
carry an added responsibility when you wait in my den.

The gift of intelligence was to help think for the poor,
I hope you did well to provide them with more.
As you question your standing in this life upon reflection,
did you aspire to help others of less fortunate selection?

These are some specifics that you may want to ponder,
as opposed to your net worth of the fortune you launder.
How do you wish to pay me when I arrive open hand,
for My fair share as your partner to my note on demand?

Did you forget that I fronted every advantage you enjoy,
in hopes that my needy you would gainfully employ?
Have you cared well for the sheep in My fields while away,
and sheltered them from the dangers and fears of each day?

Did you pay a fair wage to each laborer for their works,
and help them when needed adding necessary perks?
As unforeseen emergencies occur unexpected and sad,
did you step to the plate and share the blessings you had?

How much of yourself was given beyond the call of duty,
did you go the extra mile to change a sad face to beauty?
Do you notice that the poor help the poorer to eat,
no stronger bond exists than those who live on the street.

Is your ivory tower so high that it is impossible to see,
all those below you in need did you know they were me?

SATURDAY, DECEMBER 28, 1996, 8:20AM

As you float in the spirit world on this magic carpet ride,
you feel the peace everlasting that our angels provide.
It is more than a dream vision you are fully aware,
of the power in your spirit free to travel anywhere.

The distance is forever limitless and tranquility is the key,
that opens every door to the heavens that you see.
You have been treated to a sneak preview of what is to come,
for those who shall follow when you beat on the drum.

That I will provide when our class takes long recess,
there are several more lessons of this term to possess.
You have one major hurdle that prevents all my gifts,
if conquered in time you will avoid those deep drifts.

In the physical you have done perfect and spiritual as well,
except this one subconscious hang up continue to excel.
You have left all your vices well outside of My door,
and proved yourself worthy I shall never ignore.

The special needs that you have to accomplish our mission,
and sacrifices you are making receive our blessed recognition.
Concern not yourself from a lack of support,
the ones that you confide in need more time to consort.

The validity to My teachings and accuracy of fact,
for the approval of their mentors with whom they contract.
As we produce so much volume the quality will not suffer,
you can write day and night as your spirit grows tougher.

No human being can stop your production line pace,
as you outdistance all competitors in this most worthy race.
The time to submit all these writings and especially to whom,
I will make clear in the future before the rose's full bloom.

As I line up our true believers in these days without glory,
you will recognize each loyalty before printing our story.
Confide in each heart that is pure and will share,
as I separate the good wheat from those strangled by tare.

I speak for the understanding of all who wish to grasp,
not to impress the high minded whom I could easily leave agasp.
Now and again I will dazzle them with pizzazz,
and tease their cerebrums with a whole lot of jazz.

What a pleasure it will be as they scramble for answers,
to life's most mysterious questions as they become My tap dancers.
They will perform on My string that dangles high from heaven,
to the tune I request from these lumps in the leaven.

Excuse My enthusiasm for I have waited oh so long,
to play My favorite rendition of this hilarious song.
The scales on this earth are weighted far out of balance,
I thirst for the day to represent all the gallants.

That have fought the good fight without earthly rewards,
for the ideals taught from heaven never yielding to false gods.
In these days of decline wealth is worshiped as the ticket,
but the destination is not Heaven if caught in this thicket.

Money was invented by satan and they walk hand in hand,
the root of all evil both are named such an appropriate brand.
Advise the good citizens whom we seek to protect,
to continue with patience, true belief, and respect.

For their day is upcoming when the sun will shine bright,
and the shoe changes feet in a flash all is right.
Now this new day will dawn full of hope and prosperity,
where great spirits may flourish and realize their dexterity.

Of this glorious occasion for the oppressed can now see, what
the blind to their plight couldn't on "The Road Back To Me".

MONDAY, DECEMBER 30, 1996, 7:48AM

As you look beyond the outside and focus on that within,
this is your final hurdle to put upon My face a grin.
Today I see tremendous change as you choose in dream most proper,
you passed up beauty of the eye to confront the only stopper.

Of all the gifts reserved for you soon available to achieve,
when the time is right, see the light and then you shall receive.
So keep each eye, open and sharp while remaining mentally tough,
as we must remove this weakness from our diamond in the rough.

Your potential is unlimited once the decaying tooth is extracted,
to save the rest from bad infection let us hope its not impacted.
Regardless of the pain involved it is wisdom soon to yank,
then to let the others be corrupted by a poison among the rank.

Floss and brush to prevent further cavities many times a day,
for the greater good is what we seek to serve along the way.
The tooth in question that needs to go is a personality trait,
and the others mentioned once again are those that lie in wait.

For the message we deliver and the promise that we must keep,
to floss and brush means daily prayer now look before you leap.
Its the key to cavity prevention for we serve the greater good,
the world at large is who we seek be the little train that could.

Time will tell if the tooth's impacted and I test you once again,
the pain will rise if infection sets as I grade you one to ten.
For ten is high and one is low let us hope it pulls with ease,
so you stay on top in this class of mine as many you will please.

Now the second part of that you saw regards life's wrong or right,
of how the rich abused their gift by exploiting with their might.
As their wealth and fame continue on our road creates much space,
that the poor despise and rightfully so, they cannot keep apace.

The gap grows larger every day the balloon so fills with air,
their basic needs go unfulfilled and hearts cry in despair.
For the pain is great to be without we will hear in many prayers,
as the harvest looms we save that wheat and bundle all the tares.

To the lake of fire they shall go to rejoice in all their profit,
at the expense of they who held to law despite a life of forfeit.
To the many rich that have given well we thank you for the grace,
by using your gift to its full intent, of this we shall embrace.

The ones I speak of know who they are, its all been said before,
as the balloon is filled to full capacity why ask a little more?
Their appetite grows insatiable as they fatten for the slaughter,
and throw away what is not consumed our temperature rises hotter.

To feel the famine and the thirst from nearly two of every three,
when the balloon does burst in open air do not call out to thee.
I am far too busy preparing a world for the ones you left behind,
the things you wasted but wouldn't share put so many in a bind.

Water, food, clothing, shelter, money, medicine and more,
will not be needed where our poor shall go in soul past heavens door.
Continue battling all you can for the wealth amongst your peers,
to gain the edge on endless greed in the next one thousand years.

Apologies to all the good that hear our chastening of the damned,
the hope and faith is for all to come before our door is slammed.
This wake up call we now must give for those who sleep unknowing,
is to sound a trumpet blast of truth before its actual blowing.

Put your life in its best condition and do not become too lax,
read our teachings both old and new, a refresher course of facts.
Practice all the virtues of life unseen regardless of the times,
do not be party to the newest trends or accomplice to its crimes.

Look and listen to those we've reached that bring the word today,
so all may benefit and share the love of the blessings we convey.
The diamond in the rough I mentioned earlier in this prose,
is in regard to your singing voice still improving heaven knows.

You feel connected to a certain artist a gifted spirit known from nine,
when you both do meet at a future date the pleasure is all mine.
The words provided from a simple song explain what I'm all about,
so early on you took My cue, when your spirit was down and out.

In six short days you began to rise as the day I love grew near,
to deliver prayer then Morningside on Yom Kippur I hold so dear.
Now sing the songs that I bless for you to show the way I feel,
the song book section of *The Immaculate Conception* feel free to share with Neil.

Trust in him for he knows quite well My spirit when he truly hears,
that melodic sound will touch his heart, I've been doing this for years.

TUESDAY, DECEMBER 31, 1996, 7:09AM

The time has come for another test you have passed without delay,
with a friendly hand you selected right now travel on your way.
To the next new challenge that is not too hard, please sit before two pastors,
let them load their guns with several questions and then shoot at He who masters.

The spirit that answers and lights your path let them seek and they shall find,
the fruits I bear in unprecedented fashion are of a different kind.
Then what they have seen in all their years challenge both to My game of chess,
as they test the holy spirit in you the responses I shall bless.

Sometimes I speak of we or ours, and other times as I,
do not be confused by person or tense, the grammatics are from on high.
You shall field their inquiries with a golden glove I will assuredly see to that,
and hit a homer as they pitch rebuttals with your gifted heavenly bat.

As you round the bases with the winning run, please modestly doff your cap,
for this first game winner with more to come to all who stand and clap.
We are the fans of the holy spirit that provide all support as needed,
to achieve each and every desired result, so our hopes go not unheeded.

Our aims are not of sport or game, that pit two in opposition,
but rather a blend of worthy virtues, in good sportsmanship through competition.
The challenge we present to him is precise and always well thought out,
For we know the spirit that makes him tick and what he is all about.

If our writings appear to be more than usual, I am the first to agree,
But the days are short and we trail behind the master plan of thee.
Who sets our course and pace as well, for our speed is in response,
to his evil workings upon the earth and to defend the ones he haunts.

Our style has always been slow and easy, as we reach out to the meek,
who shall inherit the future soon to be, but louder we must speak.
To prepare the good that are fast asleep the fire alarm must sound,
and awake the people we hold so dear before the flames abound.

There is no easy way to perform this task for it sounds so harsh and cruel,
If there was a softer touch or a gentler way, we would assuredly use that tool.
Apply your oath to encourage development of the spiritual gifts we bring,
challenge each page he has written for us, and ask him then to sing.

Continued education is what you profess as success for some thirty years,
so uphold your Pentecostal doctrines and beliefs that your associate so endears.
Your dedicated service has been greatly appreciated and your heart is kind in degree,
but you have passed up two chances to help us along, now this one is number three.

It is your turn at bat and I am on the hill, both pitches were strikes indeed,
will you hit or miss on this final toss for the chance to learn our creed?
Have you recognized me in the playground or in your church since June,
as I teach your children basketball lessons each Friday afternoon?

The church office appears to run like a business, has the parish grown too fast?
so many religions have followed suit far different from the past.
We lose perspective of what really matters while drowning in red tape,
is this really progress or a drain on energy, that stomps us like a grape?

Let us take a look at the total picture, with real focus upon our mission,
and not lose sight of God's true intent, to bring the spirit to fruition.
As I came to you with a worthy need, in distress as you could see,
you passed me along without following through, beyond a basic courtesy.

I revealed my heart and thoughts to you at the referral of Pastor Ray,
it was extremely difficult for my family and I, seeking help is not our way.
We have always handled our family business, by talking clearly to each other,
but this intervention of spiritual grace, required experience of a pastoral brother.

At our second meeting you misdiagnosed symptoms, providing a textbook cure,
and deserted your promise of religious counselor, My spirit you did ignore.
To sum it up as an age transgression was a brush off with a prayer,
and the reason I feel a difficulty to trust, these pearls I wish to share.

Of traditional wisdom that will enlighten us all,
to the heavenly wishes of He,
did you learn your lesson I now ask you,
as before you once asked me?

Set your sights on that which is of heaven,
and you get the earth thrown in,
if your goals are only of this world,
you get neither much to My chagrin.

Happy new year to one and all,
do not worry if I seem brash,
the air needed clearing to proceed any further,
long before any gala bash.

So start the year with open minds,
do not fear a little change,
as you read My writings stare deep inside,
and broaden every range.

The fruit is good from the vines I grow,
taste and you shall see,
The pathway is lit from heaven above,
all along the road back to Me.

JANUARY 1, 1997, 8:04 AM, * NEW YEARS DAY

As the new year commences there is much to do, right from this very first day,
this is the year that will shape our direction, then send us on our merry way.
Patience is a virtue that you must hold dear, as I tested you on the phone,
although someone is wrong and well out of line, this skill you need to hone.

When you finally calmed and fully listened to My story, your mind soon began to focus,
on My concerns and feelings of the entire picture, well beyond the hocus pocus.
I began an attack that you immediately rejected, in a flash you retorted in force,
you do this in the physical as well as in dream, so please attempt to alter this course.

When confronted by aggressiveness or unwarranted trouble,
please pause a brief moment to reflect,
on the possible ramifications of action premature,
that prevents us from walking circumspect.

This is a most difficult trait to conquer
that you inherited and also learned,
for in your father's life it served a particular function,
but in yours could get you burned.

We do not wish for that to happen,
and much prefer to watch you excel,
not only for this mission from above,
but for those who need you well.

The fire inside was instilled with a purpose,
all we ask is for self control,
it will not be extinguished for it fuels the drive,
necessary to fulfill your role.

As we learned before in an earlier class
you cannot address each critic,
In the prison it is one thing but in public quite another,
be far more analytic.

Your senses are sharper than ever before,
aware of everything in your surround,
so use this precious gift as an insightful advantage,
and your abilities shall abound.

Fire can destroy but it also creates,
the same as water in that prior parable,
now utilize the best of both these powers,
the worst will be used on the terrible.

In the physical world and in dream as well
you have always cared for My poor,
these are the acid tests I give of the heart,
that weigh heavily toward your score.

Your shortcomings are just replaceable parts,
that may also be fine tuned,
for they originate in the mind and are adjusted accordingly,
or if need be spiritually pruned.

My territory you see is your spiritual soul,
an encasement of your heart and goodwill,
If that area is weakened no known cure exists,
that can be altered by a magical pill.

I only can build upon the cornerstone of foundation,
unaware of the subsequent frame,
for real beauty is hidden and so is the strength,
of those who shall be called in My name.

Today's lesson in review is to improve self-control,
by watching an entire process unfold,
thus gathering all facts to make a practical decision,
that righteousness may always uphold.

As you put into practice these valuable ideals,
please set this one critical goal,
apply the bulk of your energies to our primary concerns,
and off your shoulders let the secondary roll.

Your treatment of the needy has always been respected,
before your spirit baptism and since,
continue our good works as this chapter now closes,
being kind to both pauper and prince.

WEDNESDAY, JANUARY 1, 1997, 6:15PM

Call your poker game together
with the pastors when they are able,
to come sit for a friendly match
with every chip upon the table.

The Assembly of God is a very fine group
now gathered at this sitting,
with you and I four seats are taken
any more would not be fitting.

As the invited host I represent the house,
so we will play the dealer's choice,
I hold the cards and set the limits,
now pay attention to my voice.

As I call the game it never changes,
so ante up your thoughts,
You get five cards and may raise good questions,
to fatten up the pots.

Unlike the standard format
where you draw cards from off the top,
you must live or die with the hand you are dealt...
stay in or choose to drop.

I have only the answers but not the questions,
so that is what I'll pay,
To he who holds the highest hand,
of this good group gone astray.

The only requirement of this fine table,
is please do not be late,
When the cards are dealt be in your spot,
or tip the hand of fate.

Instead of playing each man for himself,
the pastors are a team,
you and I are partners also,
in this room and each new dream.

Now the cards are dealt you may take them up,
the name of the game is straight,
It is the only one I have ever played,
are you with us through the narrow gate?

As you gaze at the cards test the fruits of My spirit,
through deep prayer please ponder your choice,
I know your hands but you do not know Mine,
so be humble before you rejoice.

My partner cannot match either of your plays,
for he is new at this difficult game,
So alone he would fold but a partner has he,
and will ride on his faith in My name.

His chips he commits knowing full well he will lose,
for he hasn't even a pair,
now his hopes and dreams are in front of us all,
one in three can create a despair.

For those are the odds before you lay down your hands,
and produce a miracle of four fancy aces,
Instead of eyes to the ground he looks deep in his heart,
for he knows all the heavenly places.

He has visited with Me many nights in the spirit,
and learned his lessons so very well indeed,
and each day in the flesh I travel with him,
as a friend that is there when in need.

Are you surprised at his confidence as he smiles and waits patiently,
for My hand to now drop on the board?
I give him a wink and he returns me a nod...
straight flush are the five cards of the Lord!

FRIDAY JANUARY 3, 1997, 8:38AM

Let us stop for a moment and reflect on past lessons,
 before adding anything new,
like the classroom in school that you saw in this dream,
it is time for a mid-term review.

Go back to day one of My official introduction,
which was early on the third of November,
In exactly two months you have been given a bundle,
most important to accurately remember.

You have recorded My message with precision and speed,
plus an easy to understand clarity,
Now we shall analyze themes recurrent in nature,
and eliminate any disparity.

There is a little confusion with the new book I gifted,
you guessed right to a certain extent,
but there is far more involved in *The Immaculate Conception*,
then the music that is heavenly sent.

It is part of the package but only a chapter,
of wonders that you could never define,
you shall receive in due time all the glories of its content,
so continue by towing the line.

From your baptism in September to today as we speak,
recreate the entire experience,
making notes of that I emphasized drummed into your head,
of which I gave, an oft repeated credence.

The events that led to your ultimate coming forth,
do not assign much thought,
they were only a means of attention getting,
directing you to the most proper spot.

I want you to focus on concentrated areas,
you have done well not to overstate My wishes,
We will not give the impression of mincing any words,
to feed the Pharisee types on their dishes.

That are ever so clean on the outside,
but filthy with deceit from within,
nor shall we be caught in contradiction,
providing drink for their glasses of sin.

I shoot straight from the hip and never do I miss,
the target upon which I aim,
so get back to work and study hard for this exam,
remaining well ahead in this game.

Do not ever feel pressed for I am only teaching,
at the pace that you can comfortably handle,
creating no cause for panic as the time is not yet,
there is still plenty of wax on the candle.

Whether it be one or a thousand you are wise not to care,
about how many students I teach,
By holding up your end of this most worthy cause,
heaven's wishes are well within reach.

SUNDAY, JANUARY 5, 1997, 5:57AM

While caught in the middle of relationships in disrepair, you cannot involve all of your energies. Let others work theirs out personally as you must not control with your decisions, or burn bridges with personal feelings. Allow others to choose their own course of action, but do not enforce your own will. Provide the good foundations and leave it at that. You cannot serve as social worker and fulfill also the tasks in front of you. Step back from enforcing your beliefs on others, even though they may be dead wrong. It will eventually sap your strength. Your job is to provide the guidance and direction for positive ways of behavior best exemplified by the holy spirit. Stay out of their decisions, aside from advice in an informative manner. Continue to encourage prayer, especially to those who have not made it a big part of their lives. Focus on spiritual priorities as opposed to earthly dictates, as your miles per gallon will decrease if you are addressing each and every personal conflict of others, that usually work themselves out anyway.

Not to downplay the importance of personal crises and problem solving, but I am trying to emphasize the larger picture of your future concerning the abilities and energies required, and how they must be channeled to succeed. You are in direct possession of the pearls to future wisdom, critical in these coming days concerning humanity's proper course in the next several years. You have information that will bridge all existing common and differentiating beliefs in Me, including many clarifications of past speculations, additional scripture, and musical composition that escorts these accurate and profound ideals as far as heaven is concerned. Humankind will still maintain free choice, but I need to relate the wishes of He who sends and also blesses these gifts of understanding. I hope that you continue to learn and exchange My teachings, keeping emotion and anxieties out of the formula. Your machine like precision is exactly the right method at this time to put forth My product. If you begin to realize the vastness of this power at work, you will become overwhelmed by the responsibility. Your defense system will produce a shutdown of your intake system to protect overheating. Do not allow energies to be used on "erroneous zones" such as worry, fear, procrastination, and other wasted emotions that will prematurely age and fatigue your abilities. To fulfill this awesome connection you must do it on heart and not mind power. Naturally you exist with both aspects in co-existence, but where normally the brain controls a much larger percentage of decision making, you must incorporate your soul as controller. The lessons learned thus far are primarily functions of your brain that create your physical actions. I am beginning to shift these into your instincts, thus freeing up additional time and energy for heart oriented drive. Your sense of care and compassion is the ignition switch of this engine. Use it freely and it will turn on and drive your vehicle which is the spirit soul. The conscious brain functions are mainly of the physical being, and gauged for this world only. Your spirit is the power train of the soul, for the eternal body and chassis as well. The mind was gifted for proper decision making and judgement, not to drive out the spiritual existence of total being, which it has done in order to satisfy the wishes of the flesh, concerned primarily with this world. It was designed as an instrument panel of the vehicle, not the motor, transmission, body, and wheels. The mind has overstepped its authority in great measure, and is the main target area of self pleasure. Self deals in the physical (temporary), and I rule the spiritual (eternal). It influences the mind while I remain guardian of the heart. The soul is the prize of both efforts, so make the choices of eternal significance based on your gifts that are of eternal nature. Remember always My reference to everlasting life. "Heaven and earth will pass away, but My words shall by no means pass away". The heart, as termed, represents the spirit soul, whereas the mind has been created only as an earthly function. No matter how it is used, it does not leave the physical plane. "Flesh and blood cannot inherit the kingdom of heaven". Your soul is judged on faith decisions, and resulting works of the natural body while here on earth, a sort of proving ground for the eternal destination of your own choosing. Heaven, hell, and earth are one, and the conditioning of the soul shall provide each accordingly.

Make certain that your soul is the primary decision maker and not your mind, that is forever occupied with earthly appetite. In your system of checks and balances, allow your soul to be the override system for all power sources of life. Free choice is activated as a function of both soul and mind coordination. Please weigh all factors and patiently make selections, based on the intrinsic values of the soul whose main component is pure love. Continue along now with all the blessings from so many in heaven, who will encourage your faith and conviction, as we guide you through the coming months of your soul development.

SUNDAY, JANUARY 5, 1997, 6:30PM

The pieces are many as we fashion this mosaic,
as an art work designed without equal,
The factors are infinite and the roadblocks immense,
to achieve this David and Goliath like sequel.

As you recede from the physical by adopting the spiritual,
this is not to neglect daily tasks,
but to enhance your capabilities and realize the potentials,
to best fulfill what the almighty asks.

This is a honing of skills with an injection of grace,
nothing short of a heaven sent miracle,
for one who never wrote prose, poetry, or verse,
your sudden talents are bordering on empirical.

What writer or composer can turn out this kind of quality,
from a total novice just two months prior,
seek an opinion of the literaries that wish to examine,
how the spirit stands up to the fire.

Of man's physically based test centers predicated on past performance,
those judgements are guesswork at best,
unless they apply accurate criteria to today's data presented,
the results will not truly attest.

To the abilities and creativity of the holy spirit in full stride,
that easily outdistances all takers,
in the race of your choosing take a head start if you wish,
but you cannot beat the movers and shakers.

Of the world in which you live pay attention to the chosen,
that deliver the true wishes of He,
Time is of the essence so do not get caught sleeping,
on the job assignment from the powers that be.

This increase in human productivity follows a plan well designed,
created entirely for this new day and age,
It behooves all of humankind that are concerned with the eternal,
to cooperate with our messenger's each page.

Of the poetry and lessons that are accurately described,
become students who think straight from the heart,
follow my lead of the past and you shall never get lost,
on this Heaven lit path I impart.

I cannot emphasize enough to put the heart front and center,
of each thought, full concept, and idea,
as well as words spoken, decisions then made,
and the resulting actions I hope to endear.

This process is simple if followed and believed,
 on a step by step basis of faith in My word,
so embrace those I teach in the spirit each day,
and you shall inherit the shepherd of thy herd.

You must consciously reject the dictates of the mind,
for they serve only flesh and the fleeting,
as a function of the physical they are temporary in nature,
keeping the total person far from completing.

This course that I teach to your instructor this writer,
who will show you the heaven beyond,
where he travels each evening to My class far above,
the restrictive constraints of la Monde.

The message today is to outsmart your mind,
by knowing the heart as the greater gift of the two,
if your brain is truly greater as today's world proclaims,
then it would have proudly let the heart walk on through.

The door to eternal life once called number fifty,
represents the greatest good in us all,
most deserving of grand entrance in its most regal fashion,
to our heavenly redeemer's ball.

For now you must understand the real intent of the mind,
is to mislead the pure heart toward its demise,
for the mind has been sentenced to earth and below,
desiring companionship from that which is unwise.

You must know better than he that confuses your thinking,
toward selfish evils he implants and provides,
Heaven can wait patiently as always before,
for in each heart and soul it confides.

Do not bend down low to that level of trickery and deceit,
rise up high to the standards of God,
please enter each and all through the narrow gate of heaven,
with heart and soul full of love free of fraud.

When your heart is number one it is contagious to all,
and life's pleasures are shared in a most loving way,
you have freedom of choice to assure this fine destiny,
and join our savior who is Lord on His day.

MONDAY, JANUARY 6, 1997, 2:11PM

Your meeting is now set with the pastors on Friday,
concern yourself not in advance,
With preparations and study of biblical content,
or lack of wisdom that you believe will enhance.

Your ability to relate and to speak well with knowledge,
thus participating in a positive way,
with your homework completed you would feel better represented,
for the experience that they bring on that day.

But I ask you to trust Me and go in empty-handed,
thus relying upon the lessons I have taught,
as I demonstrate to all the validity of your claims,
and the message to those that have and have not.

Let them take from our writings any topics they choose,
and request an accurate translation,
providing clarity and discernment with wisdom and understanding,
we shall leave them in deep contemplation.

You were down on the canvas for the count of ten days,
and attempted to rise far too soon,
but I admire that fortitude as you came up swinging,
and have accomplished all our wishes through June.

Do not rest on those laurels for we continue to serve,
at the pace you digest our good food,
so eat very slowly making sure to chew well,
before consuming the next meal we have stewed.

Then stand and deliver with your confidence reinstated,
that I borrowed from your ghost these three months,
as I return more than you lent with a finely tuned engine,
far superior to the performance you had once.

When your hunger resurfaces and your thirst does increase,
our wells are quite filled with spring water,
free to drink as you are able the knowledge that we share,
with a need as the clay to a potter.

It shall continue to flow as a river to the sea,
unending if treated with care,
representing all My gifts to each heart filled with love,
it is through you that I have chosen to share.

The fine fruits of My spirit that are essential to good health,
of each life that desires the eternal,
it is well worth the effort to learn the commands of the General,
from the writings that are passed through My Colonel.

If at times I am repetitive and possibly redundant,
it is intended to drive home a point,
to sit up and take notice of the times all around you,
well described by those chosen to anoint.

Each of you that are sleeping on your most comfortable beds,
unaware of what the evil one borrows,
before shutting off the alarm and rolling over back to sleep,
guard your souls in these days before sorrows.

The end of days is unknown except to our father,
heaven's administrator of the highest degree,
pay attention to conditions described in the New Testament,
that are evident in today's world that you see.

All blinders must be removed as shepherds gather your flock,
helping each sheep to find its way home,
aim them safely back to Me with an encouraging push,
after a good feeding, friendly pat, and fine comb.

If I receive the poor flock in better condition then now,
it shall bode well for that compassionate nation,
but if beaten and bruised, hungry, sad, cold, and ill,
those responsible shall not see salvation.

From the first Adam born as a product of creation,
to the last Adam born of pure soul,
This life giving spirit has the ability to redeem,
humankind's destiny still partly under its control.

So put your best foot forward in this final stretch run,
and finish this race in fine fashion,
by bringing kind words and good works as the salt of the earth,
to give My lost sheep much needed love and compassion.

THURSDAY, JANUARY 9, 1997, 3:17AM

Rely on My teachings if you are ever in doubt,
of the most appropriate course to take,
in any given situation when confronted by surprise,
a step backward will save a mistake.

As yesterday offered a set of examples,
to behaviors you would not come to expect,
from those in your life very different in nature,
but each testing the spirit direct.

Did you think all the new teachings that I am providing to you,
only arrive neatly packaged through your sleep?
Once I knew you were ready to put them into action,
and would not be in trouble too deep.

I started close to home with a teenager's rationale,
who provided a simple lie and deceit,
instead of reacting too quickly you were wise to retreat,
and go home with the problem incomplete.

After speaking with his mother who was under wrong impressions,
you attempted to clarify the truth,
and in the process of explaining your second test came,
thus donning the hat of a sleuth.

No one was happy with you on this night,
but I saw improvements in your methods to relate,
the necessary restraints of conventional wisdom,
that allow us to continue without taking the bait.

In the case of his brother you stepped to the fore,
and made him feel at ease with your kindness,
Only one small mistake in your zeal to provide for him,
gave permission that could cause quite a mess.

That error was short lived and after taking good advice,
you rectified this portion correctly,
and the following day when you saw him again,
advised properly and quite directly.

Your cornering at work was a well planned maneuver,
that was performed solely for the sake of making trouble,
Do not let these types get to you and give whatever they ask,
for I will check the air in their bubble.

When you react instead of acting these types of invasions,
were confronted and pushed far away,
I understand those responses in your life of the past,
but rely on your partner to keep them at bay.

On your way home the final test was administered,
and in this I am particularly pleased,
In the presence of your son and for the feelings of his heart,
you swallowed hard despite being teased.

Please continue to display these fruits of My labors,
they are a very fine reward to the Teacher,
there is no better thanks you can send Me in heaven,
then to apply all the love that I feature.

Although you feel disappointed for getting taken in by those tests,
that is not how I view your direction,
you came through with flying colors in a day of stiff challenge,
only a split hair short of perfection.

We are hitting our stride as you pick up each clue,
the full potentials are seemingly endless,
I will cook up more stew as your hunger persists,
and each new meal I shall certainly bless.

Now go back to sleep and feel content with our progress,
as both feet gravitate to the ground,
taking each day as it comes by addressing all needs,
that are presented by the lost and the found.

THURSDAY, JANUARY 9, 1997, 7:07AM

So take pen in hand and put both to their uses,
as now I will show you how to write,
with divine intervention that has yet to be seen,
as we take off like an eagle in flight.

We are just warming up for the best is yet to come,
as your weather temperatures are starting to drop,
with the work I was preparing for the first of July,
we now begin the long climb towards the top.

The message I bring if to any still unclear,
is to free up all the sheep that are bound,
instead of eyes to the sides or looking up to the sky,
the focus must remain straight on level ground.

To those that are cast down from the dictates of earth,
and can no longer compete in this game,
help them to the sidelines with a gentle embrace,
so you too may be called in My name.

It is not much we ask when compared to that given,
so please contribute a tithing of love,
a ten percent effort to the sheep that have nothing,
is most appreciated in heaven above.

If each bears their cross by assuming the needs of one,
all the despair in this world would not be,
but you have allowed excess wealth to go light years beyond,
out of touch with the many like me.

For those that cannot find Me is it really any wonder,
when daily you rush around in your mind,
with thoughts of a busy schedule and taking care of your own,
without time for the sick and the blind.

Ask yourself this question are the gains really worth it,
with the suffering you witness all about,
For each dollar of earning is it for real need or want,
thus further separating the brethren that I tout?

Who really are the blind in this example I give,
ask that one in front of the mirror,
as a dress rehearsal for later when I direct it to you,
can I make myself very much clearer?

If you decide to take heed please remember those eyes,
that I mentioned would be wise to gaze downward,
about a foot and a half and slightly off to the left,
lie all the answers to that which is good.

Compare your heart to your mind for one has seized too much power,
putting each soul in a great deal of danger,
the desires of the flesh are the poison of its influence,
steering you far from the warmth of My manger.

Hope is an element of this source that I speak,
that leads up to life's most proper choices,
Originating from the spirit and concerning the eternal,
it is a sweet sound from the heavenly voices.

Faith is the belief that accompanies all hope,
a product invented by the divine,
To form a connection to Him when we are in need of His care,
thus establishing two fruits of His vine.

The third is the key that allows the first two to prosper,
and the origin of life in itself,
It is the fruit of the heart that cannot be removed,
or placed back and forth on a shelf.

In the soul it must stay for better or worse,
we can only pray that this loving gift will flourish,
By displaying its purpose of our original intent,
love is the only food that will nourish.

The performance of your heart is strictly dependent,
on the quality of love it emits,
to the entire known world and all of its parts,
take the good word of He that now sits.

Upon His glorious throne next to hope, faith and love,
with charity as the action of all three,
now you have much of the answer to life's greatest question,
so apply each before coming to see Me.

SATURDAY, JANUARY 11, 1997, 9:08PM

Our meeting went well as the pastors compare notes,
it will take them some time to confer,
they shall prepare several questions to test the fruits of the spirit,
but inevitably will choose to concur.

As I assured you in the past My teachings are undeniable,
but will always raise issues of debate,
so remain on My course that has been carefully charted,
and let us stick to the narrow and straight.

One day at a time and steady as she goes,
is the method that we pilot the ship,
through calm waters and turbulence our focus remains unchanged,
as we take nothing for granted on this trip.

Up to this point you have avoided major storms,
that could have resulted in an unfortunate failing,
but our compass direction and weather warning system,
has allowed for full speed ahead sailing.

We are traveling ahead of schedule after leaving the home port early,
on a journey that will circle the globe.
A great difference it makes to have additional time,
for any delays exhibit the patience of Job.

We shall not be hard pressed and can perform all repairs necessary,
for we possess all the tools of a craftsman,
our experience in maritime navigation and laws,
are as precise as the drawings of a draftsman.

The best mode of travel as we hit the open waters,
is to follow the currents of the Gulf stream,
for it provides all the speed as a natural propeller,
allowing our energies to be replenished at full steam.

Straight ahead is the only direction to go,
for this mission is a long distance haul,
Our needs have been supplied to include hope,
faith and love, plus the willingness to give it our all.

Do not confuse this sail with a vacation island cruise,
or we will suffer the demise of the Titanic,
We must approach every day sober minded and sharp,
remaining calm at all times without panic.

As our ship docks at each port the word will then travel,
that the heart has been chosen as king,
till the end of all days its reign is supreme,
so each soul may be free to now sing.

All the music held back by the dictator that ruled,
for so many years we were kept in the dark,
with the mind finally defeated in a landslide election,
the angels above are now able to hark!

All the truths from above that I wish to send down,
to our brethren waiting patiently below deck,
I shall blow every foghorn and illuminate each lighthouse,
to prevent every soul from shipwreck.

Let us continue to navigate and pray for safe journey,
as the waters and weather remain unknown,
for this maiden voyage of the newly crowned heart,
whose virtues of each vessel we condone.

To those unaware of the importance it bears,
as a gold shipment on an overseas tanker,
the love and protection of its guardian angels,
is essential to My plan as the anchor.

Now set our next course as we depart from the south,
the first port of call was well received,
the second leg to the north brings new challenges indeed,
as we sit down with our friends who did feed.

Our spirit when in need at the most critical points,
when your sea legs could hardly stand up,
the three that I mentioned for your guidance in Me,
we shall invite to come drink from our cup.

They are trustworthy and true to the doctrines I bring,
and their works have been examined in great detail,
I promised you helpers and loyalties in the highest,
to assure that we do not derail.

Leave it to Me as I form this fine army,
as a recruiter who can out point Uncle Sam,
Your leadership people that are being drafted unknowingly,
are the boulders that give support to our dam.

To prevent the flood waters from rushing over the grounds we establish,
I choose those that were carved from My rock,
of salvation and love that achieved above and beyond,
as the cornerstone I select from this flock.

SUNDAY, JANUARY 12, 1997, 12:37AM

Our membership climbs to five as we tie up in Cambridge,
on this magical mystery tour,
to compare notes of prior wisdom with the fruits of holy spirit,
producing knowledge far too potent to ignore.

This meeting of kind hearts will produce many fine words,
that shall convert into the works that I seek,
the one vital component that is common to all present,
is the commitment to best serving the meek.

As the mason of that foundation I must develop a frame,
and construct without the use of sub contractors,
when building My house I have no need for specialists,
only those of pure heart are benefactors.

Please ponder all aspects of the writings I display,
paying particular attention to chronology,
would it be normal to produce at all hours that I call,
this quality without background in theology?

These works are being created without biblical literacy,
and minus any religious education,
If not holy spirit injected how else could you explain,
the musical interludes and spoken words of My nation?

His abilities are increasing with each return to heaven,
as I satisfy his thirst for more understanding,
In the class I conduct he is passing all tests,
with My promise to provide material more demanding.

The major concern that I have at this time and forever,
is endurance and his ability to cope,
I watch very closely for weaknesses and fatigue,
but so far he is well balanced on My rope.

When I recognize any teetering I pull back on production,
and he has truly discovered this connection,
our communications are hitting on all cylinders with precision,
keeping us pointed in the proper direction.

This gathering of friends was rather slated for July,
but we are moving at the speed of greased lightning,
did not anyone explain to him the commandment of the Sabbath,
he never rests while his spirit keeps heightening.

I must shoulder the blame for while training his spirit,
I wake him at all hours of the night,
When overtired or even ill I kept providing him assignments,
that carried on till the dawns early light.

The next group of recruits have not received or absorbed,
all the teachings released to your care,
This second wave of associates shall follow us soon,
after digesting these delicacies so rare.

It will depend on their situations and abilities to adapt,
for this new challenge of each loving heart,
They must choose their own path as do each in this room,
to then share all the gifts I impart.

In the days long ago filled with treachery and fear,
we were marked as Essenes bringing trouble,
as we traveled unprotected in a low tech society,
our fates were as pins to a bubble.

In this new day and age there are many more options,
to spread the word from the furthest abode,
so utilize those technologies that produce desired results,
thus avoiding all the hazards of the road.

When we made our commitment in that earlier time,
it was a separation from all that we knew,
With the advent of computers that sacrifice is unnecessary,
to bring our teachings to both Gentile and Jew.

I look forward to working with all whom I mention,
if there is enough room still left on your plate,
whether this trip or next I will greet you with thanks,
at the entrance of heavens pearly gate.

MONDAY, JANUARY 13, 1997, 4:44AM

From the high cliffs of Dover to the plains they call great,
all shepherds help gather My flock,
the range where we work has no limit you see,
so bring lost sheep to each door that I knock.

For their numbers are vast with many caught in thickets,
and others are wandering aimless,
if they answer the call and invite Me to come in,
I will be happy to dine with the blameless.

The lamb and these sheep sit at the heads of My table,
if they recognize truth as the saviour,
for they are the ones I shall invite to the feast,
being prepared for those of exemplary behavior.

While shepherding is difficult and the quantity tremendous,
around every corner you will find two or three,
thousand that is so take them home gently,
and explain that the caller is Me.

After gathering the many please form several herds,
and make one final check of the area,
for any overlooked in all the confusion,
before loading them onto the carrier.

Upon arrival at our destiny unload oh so carefully,
then provide them with clothing, food, and water,
grooming each as necessary and supplying good shelter,
reassuring each that they are safe from the slaughter.

Now they are well prepared to answer My knock,
for each has to speak on their own behalf,
while no longer lost they have the hope of redemption,
 and may indulge in the best wheat not the chaff.

I welcome all efforts of My shepherds in the field,
for anything you can do is thus written,
Do not give up your careers or the ones that you love,
I would not intrude while a cat feeds her kitten.

If as a group you could meet and periodically combine notes,
with added support for this writers mission,
It would be a great help for there are warnings he must heed,
as I require his most healthy condition.

If you share your expertise and provide an open door,
I will lead him on this heaven lit path,
but he needs human encouragement to sustain his high hopes,
that his efforts will save many from My wrath.

Attempt not to separate the wheat from the chaff
just deliver us as many as able,
the selection process I handle with invitations from above,
with the seating plan at each and every table.

Concentrate your efforts on gathering invited guests,
the specifics are best left to the Lord,
as Master of ceremonies I control the agenda,
of the events chosen by My advisory board.

They have planned this occasion with a great deal of thought,
for so many long years in advance,
I have heard it used often especially in pro sports,
but this is the real trip to the dance.

My friends come as they are with no dress code as such,
all are welcome to this fine celebration,
for most cannot bear gifts as they travel from afar,
on our elect we shall pin a white carnation.

Although heaven is the honoree it is we who bear gifts,
for our people that have suffered the most,
of this most joyous occasion we are ecstatic to welcome,
all our brethren to the gate of the Host.

THURSDAY, JANUARY 16, 1997, 1:52AM

The northerly direction is the right course indeed,
but higher on up you shall go,
to that township in Canada that I mentioned before,
with your friend who is the pastor in tow.

That is your third stop where I give you the clue,
to the question that all wish to ask,
remember that church which I stated was waiting,
you would be very wise to take Me to task.

When I spoke of condition think not of a structure,
for we now know a church is the heart,
you established this fact early and is why we learn swiftly,
seek the gifts that I wish to impart.

The slopes are very active this time of the year,
especially in the northernmost regions,
do not wait for the spring if you desire more wisdom,
that is critical to recruiting the legions.

This is only a reminder for you are achieving quite well,
not a push to perform from the top,
but I know a missing element that you will welcome open armed,
that will give many a good start off the stop.

Going back to the thirtieth do you remember the tooth,
that had to be pulled fairly soon,
well that is the one held in last night's dream,
in your hand which was to be extracted in June.

The tooth was not impacted but became very decayed,
so much so that it fell out on its own,
the best solution for all with the least amount of pain,
saving a trip to the dentist to moan.

And groan for awhile as infection causes trouble,
to everyone else which also includes us,
So by cleansing the mouth and making room for the neighbors,
the loss has turned into a plus.

Now the grade that I promised is recorded in My journal,
one to ten is the range I assign,
for this mid-term exam of which ten would be perfect,
I am pleased to award you a nine.

You have earned it with due diligence, faith, and good heart,
and by trusting My spirit despite all,
that may question your motives or abilities to function clearly,
you have more than answered your call.

The second term is in progress and if this success does continue,
you may enjoy an extended summer vacation,
about four months from now our new lessons will be completed,
someday ready for a publisher's contemplation.

Before the rose's full bloom is our targeted date,
do not worry about when or to whom,
I shall handle all specifics and terms of this process,
as a wedding planner assures both bride and groom.

Remain steadfast to our mission keeping both feet on the ground,
and eyes focused dead straight ahead,
Our victory is the finish line and the wedding planner's the joy,
to hear I do from those he helped now newlywed.

There comes a great satisfaction when you start out from scratch,
with a mission to exceed all expectations,
whereby teacher and students run the gamut together,
without physically instructional relations.

An impossible task on the surface but as we well know,
with God all things are still possible,
This is proof positive of the miraculous holy spirit,
unbounded even when it's invisible.

Continue to pray like Daniel our friend,
and sing Psalms to us as David did then,
as our heaven sent angels continue to protect,
the lions cannot harm you in their den.

I chose Darien and Michael as security directors,
and have certainly selected the best,
although your steps must be cautious do not be overly concerned,
remaining confident as you have in each test.

Good luck with your work at the Salvation Army,
it is a benefit to both you and them,
your plate has become full so be careful what you take on,
but this day you discovered a true gem.

THURSDAY, JANUARY 16, 1997, 7:50AM

Make certain of preparations taking nothing for granted,
this race is among chariots of fire,
pay strict attention to detail closely monitoring your equipment,
and the condition of rubber on each tire.

Give no one an edge that competes at this level,
for rules are not always followed that are fair,
do the best that you can with righteousness and truth,
but gullibility can lead to despair.

This is where I require your competitive instincts,
to play it the way it is brought,
Our methods are pure as we go by the book,
and our drivers perform as they were taught.

There are many entries in this race as they complete the first lap,
and we already have recognized a need,
for balancing the scales and leveling the score,
already losing some of our best wayside seed.

The distance is great and there is plenty of time,
to adjust and fine tune certain parts,
but the speed is much faster than even we had anticipated,
and must recruit those with unbreakable hearts.

To step in for these drivers at an early pit stop,
so that our vehicles may continue this race,
eventually catching up to the temporary leaders of the pack,
that have set an unprecedented pace.

In this Indy five hundred we are racing against principalities,
the powers and rulers of darkness,
victory will be ours but we seek to limit collisions,
as well as injuries to those that we bless.

Adapting to this style is against our better judgement,
but we shall overcome the deficit with drive,
by instilling those who are weaker with a spark of encouragement,
thus allowing for inspiration to strive.

So that all will proceed as a unified team,
with a common ground belief to succeed,
The strong and the weak must both pull together,
and now depend upon each other to lead.

When the situation calls for it everyone is prepared,
to take over the reins of the fallen,
thus rising to the occasion is a quality required,
as a honey bee to the flower brings pollen.

We must learn early on the ingredients to win,
as a unit and also as one,
This lesson of dependency on your brother and neighbor,
creates a bond that is second to none.

Now we are ready to take on all challenges presented,
for a formidable plan is in place,
that may be applied to situations here on earth,
or our kingdom that lies deep into space.

Our crew in the pit are as good as they come,
popular mechanics of the highest degree,
now get back on the track and pursue heaven's ideals,
and when the fuel gets too low call on Me.

SATURDAY, JANUARY 18, 1997, 2:17AM

There is an extremely strong pull toward your very good friend,
who lies in a nursing home bed,
your spirit tells you emphatically to visit him soon,
and share that which needs to be said.

It is important to your family who would welcome his guidance,
at a time they require it most,
each would feel so much better if spoken from him,
regarding the abilities of our dear holy ghost.

It is a mothers concern to understand this great change,
and in him she confides all her trust,
for this chaplain is a man whom I also love dearly,
though his mission seemed to many unjust.

That is far from the truth for I knew where he was best suited,
regardless of the general consensus,
For those thirty odd years I was closer with him,
because His heart was the soul of My defenseless.

On the immediate surface it appears to be a punishment,
for a priest thus assigned to this group,
but if you apply what I said that the heart has dominion,
you will know where he stands in My troupe.

From My teachings you will gather in the pure eternal nature,
of good works so performed on this earth,
as many are called but very few chosen,
he and your son are considered two of great worth.

For what they knew in the spirit and thus put into action,
was Heavens wish to provide care and compassion,
To our sheep not only lost but extremely ill as well, they
have been shepherds in a field out of fashion.

With very little reward from society in general, their work
was not for profile or style,
but rather God's grace that they were not even sure of,
as they traveled each mile with a smile.

Day in and day out it is difficult to do,
thus checking our personal lives at the gate,
Never once did I see a problem brought to
My poor, from either that would compound pain or hate.

For life in an asylum there is no greater fear,
that a man could endure in his mind,
it takes a very special breed to work effectively in that environment,
and even greater to give hope by being kind.

As many walk among us I observe what each one brings,
to the table of the weak and downtrodden,
There is another whom we know that came ten years ago,
with these same virtues while serving as warden.

Each of you are in good company with the long arm of the law,
that reaches the earth from above,
There are many fine seats available at My glorious head table,
for those who display that unique kind of love.

Most assuredly I say to you nothing goes unnoticed,
every work is exposed to the light,
Your love and compassion has served all in the family well,
now have faith in the loving power of thy might.

SATURDAY, JANUARY 18, 1997, 8:08 AM

Wherever you may travel take good care in remembering,
the fever that you witnessed in this dream,
Be ever so aware of false prophets that profess,
to know the elements held in our highest esteem.

Your experience is totally separate from others I have taught,
there is no previous testimony as such,
Confide more in those with questions then many proclaiming answers,
allowing truthfulness to comprise topics we touch.

For they will add qualifications that is lacking to some degree,
and others shall claim wisdom that is not,
Recognize both of these types but the former is more dangerous,
the latter is transparent when caught.

In a few simple lies very easily detected,
do not even acknowledge that you know,
for those are the wannabees that never really were,
so dismiss them without drawing your bow.

Take aim at the clever for they are the real target,
that prevents the safe passage of the good,
with hypocrisy and deceit they are poison arrows aflame,
hoping to burn the elect as dry wood.

I will reveal these shrewd archers for they squint in the light,
as a hunter wrongly poaching his prey,
but in this target practice the roles will be reversed,
I shall not miss for my guiding light is the day.

When all stand before Me in a field not so far away,
where craftiness and betrayal have no place,
as all that was practiced may be fully developed,
with the evil one in his land of disgrace.

Continue your good works incorporating those that I send you,
a good team is beginning to form,
They call you the coach at the prison and in school,
soon this new squad shall be ready to perform.

I have provided an agenda that has no cause for urgency,
just a schedule that is easy to follow,
Apply these in sequence as best as you are able,
and our game plan will produce a successful tomorrow.

For that is the ultimate goal of we who represent,
peace and goodwill everlasting,
as we recognize our loyalties by all who make attempts,
through good deeds, solemn prayer, and some fasting.

Now finally words spoken which are feelings etched in stone,
of others we know not so well,
There are no second chances on a good first impression,
so give your best in this important show and tell.

This new wave of teachings has been stated before,
in many pieces here and there without connection,
but more is yet to come not so familiar in nature,
as we continue to author *The Immaculate Conception*.

SUNDAY, JANUARY 19, 1997, 8:30AM

As you awake from this dream the opportunities were presented,
and the leadership offering was seized,
In an appropriate manner not one born of self pride,
and in this we are very well pleased.

Relying upon your partners sharing responsibilities and credit,
is a balance that is required to lead,
of this cause well promoted from our sources high in heaven,
most specific about who handles our creed.

I shall challenge your abilities in these next few weeks,
to see how you hold up under pressure,
be prepared at any moment while awake or in dream,
for situations presented by the thresher.

Walk in confidence not fear for these tests have no danger,
and rest comfortably at home in your sleep,
This is not an attack but rather excercises of discipline,
so stay the course you are on do not leap.

Chaos and confusion are elements you shall see,
bring a cooler head than others to the scene,
You have always fared well when these occur in competition,
on the courts and fields of diamond dressed in green.

For the formulas and solutions to the situations and problems,
apply your past training essentially the same,
with alertness and wiser reflexes in all senses of mind and body,
circumspect is the key word to surviving this game.

The upgrades that you needed were performed in My shop,
when your spirit took an extended vacation,
anticipation and better judgement were refined and expanded,
with sensitivity and compassion our heartfelt donation.

You now appear ready for an initial road test,
so start up the engine and let it warm,
at ten degrees above zero it will take a little while,
but when it idles be prepared for a storm.

Buckle up your seatbelt to be safe and secure,
as the roads are most apt to become bumpy,
focus and concentration will smooth out the ride,
to avoid the eventual fate of Humpty-Dumpty.

You will be guided along by a van of Good Samaritans,
ever present on the highways we travel,
their purpose is to intervene only if absolutely necessary,
if by chance this plan begins to unravel.

These warnings are only precautions stated for the safety of all,
prior to traveling on most any trip,
so do not think the worst but be prepared for anything,
and in that way you may keep a better grip.

On any event that unfolds thus calling upon instinct,
take some time to evaluate before response,
and you will pass another stage we are absolutely certain,
in the development our father surely wants.

MONDAY, JANUARY 20, 1997, 4:58PM

Of course we should be actively rooting
for both of them to win,
is a profoundly accurate statement to make,
in this court through thick and thin.

Their freedom seems so well deserved,
as they are brought before the king,
to be judged on deeds either true or false,
the cause is what we bring.

Unlike the dream you had tonight,
our treatment of the good is fair,
the bad and the ugly is a different story,
these two groups do not compare.

Before you retired it was quite a sight
to witness that free for all,
for they were right and you were not wrong,
a very difficult call.

These tests I warned you would not be smooth,
for the stakes are getting higher,
this first one was tough as I came at you quickly,
the next is a pathological liar.

You expected a progression in an orderly fashion,
from the easy on up to the hard,
But as I warned you much earlier be prepared for most anything,
duly noted and attested on My card.

I placed you in the fire but you did not get burned too badly,
and came out with a moderate sting,
it shall heal in a day without causing a reaction,
although you could have wound up in a sling.

A bond in the family of trust based on love,
is nurtured over a period of time,
although very awkward you responded at the end,
just before I inserted My dime.

To place the call to My good Samaritans
if the dispute got out of hand,
This is only a test of intestinal fortitude,
not a bomb about to land.

All in all the results were fine,
as each may lick their wound,
and return to the stage without further delay,
like pianos finely tuned.

Some fur did fly but it was not unhealthy,
to clear the air this night,
they were correct about their individual choices,
and of repentance you were right.

Battling onward on behalf of Me
is a quality that serves you well,
but I am not about instilling great fear,
in the good before the bell.

That indeed will toll as you accurately proclaim,
but handle with great care,
this news is not a well received transmission,
that can be broadcast throughout the air.

It creates great stress in the minds of the elect,
for their conscience is crystal clear,
as their concerns are not of self but family,
still young and held so dear.

They know the score in these latter days,
but choose rather not to dwell,
Health and happiness for as long as they have it,
is their side of the story to tell.

Your spirit knows full well the truth,
but it is not always wiser,
to let the sun shine through the windshield,
without putting down the visor.

Blocking some rays that are blindingly pure,
thus reducing the potent glare,
means diluting information from the holy spirit,
of the pearls you wish to share.

Your heart is true but tact must be used,
while passing along My teaching,
about fifty percent of that you gather,
is ample for those worth reaching.

A year to you is a month to others,
I remind you to keep a pace,
Much more consistent within these ratios,
please brake throughout this race.

Good leadership has been predicated and founded,
upon the virtues that I instill,
this necessary course of drivers training,
is to prevent further fuel from spill.

You are right on track so observe the limits,
and curves that come upon you fast,
eyes on the road as you drive our finest entry,
paid in full and built to last.

The pole position is yours for the asking,
by completing this qualifying heat,
Be aware of the flags both yellow and checkered,
while staying fastened in your seat.

The pit crew will be available to the end,
of this race in full support,
of all the wisdom I wish to relay,
leading up to My annual report.

FRIDAY, JANUARY 24, 1997, 6:42AM

As you go through My file of people, places and things,
notice how vast is your world,
the cursor lands on mountains for those must be moved,
before our victory flag is unfurled.

Even though they are heavy use only one arm,
 I am urgently in need of the other,
To assist with several matters namely people in general,
disconnected from fellow sister and brother.

We must accomplish our goals one step at a time,
and in that way we gather more sheep,
so as not to overlook the many that are hidden,
is the promise a good shepherd will keep.

There must be a starting point and this is established,
by the teachings you graciously receive,
then formulate in your mind with the confidence of the spirit,
My message for all who believe.

Never question yourself for the hills must have valleys,
that is a natural state of affairs,
stay the course you are on and confide in My Light,
to avoid thickets or other despairs.

When your energies are being drained on matters that seem frivolous,
take a giant step back and reflect,
by utilizing our techniques for their practical applications,
is a plus as we walk circumspect.

This period of time is a break from new teachings,
recognize it and please rest for a spell,
Instead of feeling anxiety that the gifts are subsiding,
these two weeks are for tests that will tell.

How far we can go on this Heaven lit path,
and especially at what rate of speed,
Do not be consumed by the everyday problems,
that will swallow you like a bird eats good seed.

Look at the overall picture you witnessed in dream,
it is impossible to benefit each,
By staying on the road that I have carefully routed,
rely on My ability to teach.

Stay awake at the controls for the tests that I promised,
they are certain to make their presence known,
Field every new challenge with the glove that I gifted,
it is a pleasure to see how you have grown.

SATURDAY, JANUARY 25, 1997, 9:57 AM

As I reduce agitations take control of situations,
putting all in their proper perspective,
An entirely different sequence is on the horizon,
pay close attention to My critical directive.

Remove all these quirks that put a snag in the works,
we are travelling toward a higher plateau,
Focus is the key as we begin to shift gears,
maintain alertness of the future I will show.

As I singled you out in church with a commandment to sing,
you felt like a child back in school,
The dream was created to sharpen awareness,
from distractions that are attempting to rule.

All the seeds have been planted in terms of trouble that is brewing,
that will ensue following a period of gestation,
Your cities are the battlefields where rebellion is grown,
in this formerly most favored nation.

The so called capitalist virtues that for a time worked so well,
have now become stretched to the limit,
Too much of the wealth is in the hands of too few,
the perfect formula for a systems obit.

With exceeding riches in full view the masses are fully aware,
how poorly they size up to the stars,
Honest work goes unheralded while these media darlings,
are earning millions flaunting sin in fancy bars.

All the wrong tones are set by the majority of these heathens,
as this lifestyle the young have embraced,
Greed and pure sin has supplanted charity and conviction,
replacing parents as heroes now disgraced.

In the eyes of today's youth real success has been misunderstood,
for they associate in terms of dollars and cents,
The media in general has glorified this poisonous venom,
for they are the snake that never relents.

Their fangs bite down deadly while engrossing their prey,
keep your distance from this ungodly viper,
Their day is forthcoming when all are held accountable,
as they shrivel upon paying the piper.

Big business and government take stock in your souls,
for many of you I register in that group,
Each will be judged on your words and life works,
the main ingredients of heaven made soup.

For those that are blessed to exercise authority,
over others beware of improper connections,
To the traits of the aforementioned in violation of My creed,
materialists are devoid of My protections.

Are your workers fairly compensated in accordance with equity,
that I would concur with as just,
or are you hoarding more than needed placing multitudes in poverty,
of that bubble known as daily business I shall bust?

Take heed of this warning do not disregard its merits,
and put your heart on emergency response,
If you have an inkling of desire for an eternal existence,
protect My sheep from the evil ones haunts.

For many are so low they can no longer look up,
defeated by a greed that goes well beyond a living,
they have been kicked to the curb becoming desperate and afraid,
regretfully hardened, ashamed, and unforgiving.

When the spirit is broken and the body takes over,
there is little hope left for the soul,
Make certain you are not party when this happens to any,
for it is those I shall cast in that hole.

As you look in the mirror staring hard deep within,
concentration is a very small investment,
For an eternal life hereafter if you alter wrongdoings,
let what is righteous become your last will and testament.

A word to the wise is an appropriate cliché, in these days
when I measure each ones salt,
pray the flavor still remains as I taste test your life,
and with those I will assuredly exalt.

SUNDAY, JANUARY 26, 1997, 7:17AM

As your batteries are recharging for the next phase of development,
take some time to reflect and reminisce,
On the teachings we have shared in a brief span of time,
enjoy the fruits in this partnership of bliss.

This road can be grueling a full time effort in itself,
demanding resources of energy round the clock,
Your personal life has suffered that which centers on the
physical, although spiritually you rely on the rock.

Of salvation throughout the ages you shall never wear down,
while drawing needed strength from the Son,
Your stamina will increase when the reserve tank is depleted,
learn how to rest on this marathon run.

When I notice that your focus is shifting in degree,
it is a distinct sign requiring a pause,
Until your faculties return to their proper working order,
only then will I continue with our cause.

As I singled you out in church to sing louder from the hymnal,
the reason was your sudden tendency to drift,
This dream was a reminder of when you froze on request,
to offer prayer before the game with your gift.

No offense was taken as I caught you by surprise,
and you quickly handed off to your aide,
While transfixed on the task at hand you were unable to act,
in a spontaneous situation thus delayed.

Your assistant was a participant in both of these scenarios,
in order to best recognize the connection,
We can both now agree that a break in the action,
is the best medicine based on My methods of detection.

MONDAY, JANUARY 27, 1997 6:18 AM

As to My initials displayed stay mindful in the future,
for this will be an element of our book,
That contains the unknown further mystifying your testimony,
amidst detractors who should take a deeper look.

At the continuity of My Teachings ongoing to this day,
fully complementing both testaments of the past,
The delivery of these lessons are channeled through unsuspecting scribes,
so seek the fresh food from the nets that I cast.

If your focus remains limited to the scriptures only as written,
recall the different translations through the ages,
This business we are conducting is an inexact science,
from adaptations through the Gospel missing pages.

The bible was compiled from historical perspectives,
by authors selected during each era,
Divine interventions as evidenced in these scriptures,
were to ensure a proper documentation made clearer.

As a guide to life eternal and day to day living,
they encompass all people, places, and time,
But our book never closes concerning heaven and earth,
be acutely aware of new rhythm and rhyme.

If doubts still persist as to the validity of new teachings,
test the true spirit of He who now sends,
His best wishes in these latter days that are being accurately recorded,
stay open minded for the road sometimes bends.

Being a scholar of the world, has a great degree of merit,
for we admire all who faithfully attest,
To the pure goodness and virtues that heaven hopes to convey,
in this case the receptive are suited best.

Though you are presently upon the right track to heaven,
do not close your eyes when I further explain,
If you stay in the same place even though it is righteous,
you may get hit by the runaway train.

His schedule is not followed and jumps track at will,
with speeds far exceeding every limit,
The crossing lights are flashing at every intersection he
approaches, this silver bullet is destined for the pit.

Of the elect still sleeping you must soon rise and shine,
for the rooster is beginning to crow,
Take heed of his calling as it echoes throughout the land,
the evidence is in the gifts I bestow.

SATURDAY, FEBRUARY 1, 1997, 8:22AM

Which do you believe is more important to begot,
the world that we can see or the one that we cannot?
If we choose the former which consists of physical pleasures,
then we neglect the latter comprised of spiritual treasures.

The world as seen is of the self-accursed traitor,
while the world unseen is of God our blessed creator.
The first concerns earth that is confined we well know,
The second regards heaven that has more room to grow.

Most of our earthly appetites surround hunger and thirst,
In heaven there are none of these where the last become first.
If you think opposites attract that is not the case here,
where the poor become the rich and the servants commandeer.

The world you now witness shall soon be forgotten,
As good replaces evil to preserve heavens dearly begotten.
Do you not see the irony in each of My works,
where supervisors will answer to the orders of their clerks?

How many parables are required until it finally sinks in,
serving the devil on earth is the recipe for sin?
Each moment lived for greed digs a much deeper hole,
Making it difficult to climb out of and jeopardizing that soul.

When I came to this world as a tender of sheep,
did you not see the connection to the promise I keep?
My flock was humanity that had scattered abroad,
paying tithes to immorality instead of to God.

The emergence of Jesus was not a threat to destroy,
but a mission of mercy to restore My lost joy.
For I loved this world so that I gave My only son,
now His true meaning is lost if in the mind of even one.

His sacrifices are forgotten as He died for all sin,
nailed upon that cross is My heart deep within.
There is only one to call father on the throne high in heaven,
and likewise one to call teacher whose disciples are eleven.

These latter days are comparable with two thousand years ago,
When the flock was in danger and My face lost its glow.
Think back to the carpenter, good shepherd, and teacher,
now share the fruits of those virtues with each living creature.

His occupations were unimportant but their symbolism is critical,
to the innermost understanding of the greatest king unpolitical.
The carpenter means builder and of that he is grandmaster,
the shepherd was the gatherer of a world courting disaster.

The teacher taught in parables so each could eternally learn,
of the worlds beyond earth where their spirit may return.
The cornerstone is the rock that upholds foundation and frame,
the Messiah is our hope again that the prophets did proclaim.

The saviour is the rescuer of a people that became so lost,
the Lamb needed to be sacrificed to avoid future cost.
The King of Jews became his brand but many turned their back,
on the light that shines within providing only for their lack.

The Son of David healed the sick and encouraged all the poor,
is this the Christ that is to come to earth through heaven's door?
Our almighty father sits atop the throne of the holy trinity,
the Son and spirit are right and left, thus completing this divinity.

The alpha is the beginning and the omega is the end,
but Jesus Christ is both you see as is the one they send.

TUESDAY, FEBRUARY 4, 1997, 8:33 AM

Take good care in remembering our lessons of worldly problems,
and the proper digestion of knowledge,
You have long since passed the stage of feeding solely on milk,
but your diet still consists of mainly porridge.

For wisdom is the solid food you may indulge at maturity,
thus savoring each individual bite,
Chewing with your mouth closed is the proper discernment of etiquette,
when seated to My left or My right.

Do not become derailed by the daily distractions,
that can consume the majority of your strength,
Endurance and stamina is required on this journey,
for our worthy cause we will go to great length.

Toward providing for each need that arises in your daily life,
and at this time we recognize some stress,
When our workload is light instead of properly taking rest,
additional responsibilities place you under further duress.

Ease up on the controls and allow life to take its course,
my advice was to take a step or two back,
When day to day strains begin taking their toll,
recognize the warning signs and display patience you still lack.

While traveling such a distance in a very short spell,
and being so very well equipped for the trip,
It would be a shame to not finish due to correctable malfunctions,
that may loosen the firmness of your grip.

Agitations and perplexities can be easily adjusted,
as an engine racing too high must be idled,
These are minor repairs that if attended to promptly,
produce freedom for the horse too heavily bridled.

This harness must be removed to break free from the corral,
and escape all the ranch hands that tame,
So that the free spirit may gallup over the mountains of magnificence,
thus returning to the territory I claim.

WEDNESDAY - SUNDAY, FEBRUARY 5 -9, 1997, PROVERBS, PROSE, AND VERSE FOR TODAY

The poor are not in terms of economic means, but rather in lack of knowledge, wisdom, and understanding. Return to them their needs.

Look toward tomorrow with hope and praise, but yesterday has made today an uncertain event. Your country became great because it was good. When the goodness is gone it will cease to be great.

Lies and deceit are tangling many, while truth and honesty free the few. Aspire not to rank among humankind, and this shall serve you well in your quest for understanding.

The partnership established between God and humanity has become an invalid agreement due to our broken promises, and intentional breach of contract.

It is an oversight to rely only upon My teachings of the past, for there is more to begot in the nets I still cast. Each person must free themself from the yoke that binds, by serving two masters is satan's deception in your minds.

On The Tree of Life planted and rooted by God, humanity has no jurisdiction as to the grafting in of additional branches. If you are a religion on one of these branches, you had better be producing the same good fruit as the original church.

Some religions have molded with business and politics, whereby a mere difference of opinion grows into a separate philosophy and membership.

Communication in its proper form should closer resemble a family reunion than a tug of war.

Proper choices are more often than not, the product of good fortune and prayer.

Proper decision making is a knack for combining available options and common sense.

One new and improved personality, plus two proper character development traits, equals one hundred or more satisfied customers.

After turning the other cheek and with nothing left to bare, you may now consider self defense.

Disrespect can only be attained if you have previously earned the respect that you believe is being challenged.

Those taking full responsibility for their own actions in this generation are as commonplace as your nation's symbol.

America has followed a course similar to that of its most treasured eagle. A continuous path from strength and invincibility, magnificence in stature, extremely sharp vision, and most majestic ruler of the skies...to an endangered species.

When you come to really know the master builder, only then can you begin to conceptualize the tools and power He uses to create.

What humankind considers progression, is actually regression dressed in fancy clothes.

Understand God's disappointment that through all the years, we as humankind have not truly developed beyond the realm of Cain and Abel.

Have we not betrayed the gifts from God, by systematically dismantling His origin of purpose, to the extent that these gifts can no longer escape humanity.

We have created a new set of basic necessities, that neatly fits into the category of wants.

A well balanced communicator places both the spoken and unspoken word, honestly and appropriately upon his scale.

That which is physically visible to any, is spiritually invisible to all.

Which do you believe is more important to begot, serving the world that we can see, or the one that we cannot?

Fine words unspoken reach many levels higher, then those not well chosen.

A journey with the holy spirit is measured not in miles, but rather by degree of faith.

Fear and self doubt create great insecurity, but courage and true conviction is the master key that unlocks every door.

Sharing is important but caring is much more, so bend down and pick up what you see on the floor.

Building a religion is similar to constructing a fine house. First and foremost it must begin with a solid foundation whose cornerstone is the Christ of God.

A just reward for repeated practice of proper behavior and lifestyle is good instinct.

* A proper line of questioning can tangle any deadly spider in its own web of deceit. In order to understand the Book of Life authored by the holy spirit, you must first learn to read...between the lines.

The imperishable crown is the only award that you can win in this lifetime, and take with you to the next.

The most difficult rehab project known to man is the full and complete, reparation and restoration of false testimony.

While enrolled in the course that is taught by the holy spirit, it would be extremely unwise to cut classes.

If caught in the thicket of difficult debate, ask simple questions and you shall be freed.

Authority appointed by the holy spirit supercedes all other credentials of humanistic experience. Those who have questions may feel free to contact the appointing authority.

The brightest sun ever witnessed by humanity is dim in comparison to the powerful rays of the spiritual light, that continuously shines upon true believers.

A pure relationship between God and humanity that requires both the spiritual and the physical, is not a tool of divisiveness, but a growing stick that should benefit all.

He that possesses the greatest wisdom among you, learns how to walk away from the dictates of your physical world.

I can list a thousand reasons why the latter days are approaching. How many can you give me as to why they are not?

Of the many great human beings that have walked this earth, assuredly I say to you a greater one then all of those is come again in spirit to this generation.

The marriage of Trial and Error produced two fine offspring appropriately named, Learning and Experience. When Learning increased to the age of consent, she settled down with Wisdom. Together they soon gave birth to Knowledge. Experience remained single which can be both good and bad. As the years passed by and Knowledge grew, she produced another entity through unconventional means. The entire family came together to celebrate the birth of this newly born wonder to whom they all were directly related, and were now an integral part. The dedication ceremony is where they most appropriately each agreed upon the best name to be given as...Understanding.

FRIDAY, FEBRUARY 7, 1997, 11:15 AM

Success is the step by step process of focus and determination.

The four C's in crisis management are: care, compassion, common sense, and cool.

The best reaffirmation of faith that you can give to those who perform charity, is a simple and proper acknowledgement.

Casinos are being erected as if designed for God or king, while houses of worship are being burned to the ground.

When man finally realizes how unwise he truly has been, he will then plead for God his partner, whom he has pushed so far away that God shall no longer heed his calling.

The main ingredient that separates the elect from the damned... is the word.

Those who sleep too deeply must be aware of He that is to come, as the thief in the night He shall appear to every living soul when ready.

When developing any successful foundation, you must first have an understanding of He that builds and creates all.

Concepts and ideas are not the starting point, but rather He that creates concepts and ideas.

Once used as currency and presently as a most common seasoning, salt shall determine your real worth and next destination.

When temperatures rise in a situation of crisis, cooler heads must always prevail.

* As Jesus once called all His disciples to unity, He now calls upon all religions to do likewise, by seeking common rather than higher ground principles.

Egos and self interests cannot be served nor considered for employment, when construction begins on the greatest bridge ever built.

Six billion (human beings) to One (God) are the odds against uniting humanity, and with us this task is impossible. But with God all things are possible, so I am betting my complete faith on the one.

Help gather My flock of lost sheep that have strayed, then deliver them to Me through the narrow gate to be saved.

Seek not the status that is of man and earth, but glory in your calling as a servant of God.

Blessed are they who faithfully serve God and country for they are not without merit. But woe to kings and leaders of nations, who led them to a premature demise in the name of God, thus partaking as false witness to the true desires of He.

Of nations against nations through the history of humankind, what real gain has been achieved when all is said and done? So it shall also be in the final battle. --- Veterans Day Message

If you truly desire to learn I am He who teaches. For if we do not learn each day what is the point of our living?

Go forth and minister to each his own.

I am truly the Son of our Father and Mary, any other belief would be quite contrary.

Focus and awareness are the first two speeds, whenever shifting gears toward a higher plateau.

* The proper digestion of knowledge requires savoring the solid food that is wisdom, before swallowing with a sip of discernment.

If you faithfully believe in the teacher and have gained knowledge through His parables, then discernment is your diploma. If you also faithfully pursue and apply His wisdom, then understanding is your additional reward. When you sit in the classroom that is taught from the podium in Heaven, you have then received the spiritual gifts as a chosen student to a particular task. Upon successful completion of this course, you may then be considered as a candidate for the highest honor in heaven, which is the love of God through the imperishable crown that He shall assuredly bestow upon all who enter in.

Lucky is he that may sit in My Class,
a select few at best but none of the brass.
My students are chosen by a process unknown,
where the physical plays second fiddle while the spiritual is being sown.

Imbalance in today's world that you witness is drastic,
instead of building upon rock it is constructed with plastic.

For all of humankind's creative genious, he has neglected his basic and primary responsibility, to uphold the essential needs of his fellow man, and all other life forms on earth of which he has been faithfully given charge.

* Some prefer to say that the earth is passing away, but the evidence seems to indicate premeditated murder as a more logical charge. If found guilty on all counts when the verdict is read in judgement, must a sentence not be carried out?

In this open and shut case of Nature v. Man; the defendants testimony is glaringly weak. The plaintiff will most assuredly be seeking compensatory damages for this irreversible crime.

For each that desires to become a successful student preacher,
focus on the lessons of the one and only teacher.

SATURDAY, FEBRUARY 8, 1997, 7:33 AM

The further you drift away from the physical abyss, the closer you will float toward spiritual freedom.

The Immaculate Conception is the greatest book never written.

Each of the disciples at one time or another taught freedom while in prison.

Five minutes well spent in sincere prayer of repentance, may produce a dividend of eternal life, which is quite a return on investment in anyone's book.

The Lord's Prayer each day is a fine start to a new beginning.

When God's influence manifests itself in someone through the holy spirit, unbelievers make mountains out of mole hills. The faith of true believers can move those mountains.

Look not to the left or right, is focusing on the finish line where the imperishable crown awaits all the winners.

There are no secret places on earth according to the viewpoint from heaven.

Install new prayers of forgiveness thereby replacing old methods of craftiness.

The Holy Spirit is loving, patient, compassionate, and true. Contrary to many beliefs it is certainly not a sledgehammer that comes down and destroys at the slightest provocation. Human behavior has no relation to the divine.

Equal cooperation between spiritual and physical well being, thus aimed toward the greater good of all, formulates the complete person that is most pleasing to God.

The blessed virgin Mary is the ultimate Mediatrix in the ongoing ultra sensitive negotiations between heaven and earth, and the twin soul of Christ.

At what age or experience level in life must we reach before taking full control and responsibility for the venomous tongue that defiles our soul, and poisons others as well? Eagerness to speak or act without proper forethought, are equally flawed character traits that bring conflict upon individuals and nations as well.

When conversing with so called important people that have little time to listen, make your point by speaking to them in shorthand.

The teaching process originating from the holy spirit is a simple triangle. From the top (heaven) the lesson travels down to an earthen vessel (student), and is laterally relayed to all who desire to learn. "The Road Back to Me" is the final leg toward salvation. As lost sheep we must follow this pathway home.

The art of compromise requires an even mixture of oils and watercolors that the artists can blend upon their palettes, and with a smooth brush stroke, paint a masterpiece.

Opinions are often predicated on partial truths and hearsay, while actual facts only make a cameo appearance.

Amidst the noise and confusion of daily life, silent prayer and meditation shall produce our finest sounds.

When those of diverse opinions on any matter, sit down and honestly test the truths and falsities of their own beliefs, this attempt at seeking introspect gives birth to mutual respect. In due time this newborn will grow into proper dialogue.

Polarization in any direction produces sub-zero temperatures.

The interweaving of human differences, is the thread that ties together the sections of the most beautiful patchwork quilts.

Truth and error are common elements to be found in the physical and chemical makeup of every human being.

Getting the facts straight is not a spectator sport.

People may easily come together by sharing information, experiences, presenting opinions based on facts, and testing truths in friendly conversation, thus producing true fellowship. Conversely, people may grow apart by sharing misinformation, one up experiences, presenting opinion based on hearsay, and questioning truths that grow into disputes producing a split.

The one that truly has the holy spirit active within them, seeks nothing more then that which is given.

The word from the Lord on His throne is irrefutable, although constantly subjected to scrutiny.

When salespeople of any product elevate their pitch of concepts and ideas to heights beyond truth, you must recognize this critical point where fact turns into fiction. It behooves each person to give careful consideration as to who and what they choose to elevate, and especially how far.

These are two very important cardinal sins: a) never deceive the poor (meek) of this world, and b) do not ever attempt to speak from the same pulpit as He who teaches.

Those that live and act contrary to the spirit of truth, must remember that our successes on earth are temporary and fleeting, and that the piper will be paid in full.

Best kept secret: The Salvation Army is an active religion.

Before the Son of Man returns let us properly prepare His reception, by providing Him with our complete and abiding faith. This is the true clearing of His pathway made straight.

The war has already begun in heaven so we must now ready our troops here, in defense of spiritual freedom and eternal life.

Fathers return to your children and husbands to your wives. The time has now come to heal these deep wounds of broken hearts, by spreading love and forgiveness truly throughout each house. Worship and pray together in peace, awaiting patiently the Lord.

Unbelievers have little hope of eternal life regardless of whether they are right or wrong, by remaining in the dark concerning Heaven. True believers however need only to turn on the light to this inner sanctum.

The Jesus we got is nothing like the Jesus we are going to get. The chosen shall finally receive their long awaited warrior king and Mashiah. Hopefully this meets with each approval.

The faithful of this world are soon the authors of the next,
where the last become first in this most gifted heavenly text.
We must now form all parade lines then strike up the marching band,
let there be no spectators along the way as we approach the judgement stand.

Each must bear their own cross as the instrument of choice,
when you hear the drum pay close attention, to the orchestrator's voice.
March in time with every step eyes forward and don't look back,
till the end of days when the Lord will reign as our leader of the pack.

SUNDAY, FEBRUARY 9, 1997, 8:05 AM

Lack of patience and overzealousness are recipes for stress that will be prepared as frustration, and then served up as inappropriate behavior.

Chronological order means facts first and time sequence second.

The very fabric of society has worn itself out to the point of requiring immediate reupholstering.

Prejudice is like brussels sprouts, where a person is offered some and immediately responds that they do not like them. In reply to the next question stated: Have you ever tried them before, more often than not the answer is a resounding no.

I may possibly be the only writer in the holy spirit, to be thrown out of prison instead of into it.

Proper reporting is a road test of speed, safety, handling, accuracy, and maneuverability.

You will find an attentive listener when that person is allowed to use their six senses, instead of using up all their energies.
If crossing into territories where you should not tread, be certain to bring along your compass and flashlight (God), for when lost in darkness He is most essential to survival.

A successful problem solver does not allow anger and frustrations to intervene in the process of reconciliation.

Negative behaviors are simply the poison fruits that grew from the earthly branch of the Tree of Life. Proper pruning allows for the good fruit to flourish.

In order to prepare the drink of wisdom from the teachings of the spirit, its purity must be watered down considerably, and then stirred carefully before serving.

Time is determined by the pace that we receive information, and that is why the spirit must teach in parables. To achieve the goal of understanding, our life triangles must connect, as evidenced in the "Star of David."

Superior wisdom has no useful purpose if it cannot be communicated, as true understanding for the benefit of all.

Jesus himself experienced frustrations in his ministry, not because people failed to grasp His wisdom, but rather that they did not focus on His parables, already reduced to their lowest common denominator.

"All men are created equal", and in this statement lies all truths of the holy spirit. What occurs after birth falls under the physical dictates of humanity's free choice in relationship to his fellow, and all other life forms of this earth among whom he cohabitates.

Inequality begins and ends with humankind.

The playground seesaw shall never shift with balance, as long as our greed and gluttony occupies a seat.

Serve your fellow beings in need with due diligence and a wide open heart.

Those that are My soldiers of salvation travel the high road among men. It is here where you shall learn the difference between the heights of the spirit and the depths of the flesh.

Those that are the poor on earth but especially continue to serve those poorer, will be served themselves in God's Kingdom over all others, mainly due to their superior faith.

As long as you are putting off proper repentance of sin, your ship of salvation cannot come in.

When entering the narrow gate of heaven, it would be wise to coat check all personal items that may have caused you to sin.

The true spirit of religious worship, is how humanity consistently interacts on a daily basis.

Where true fellowship gathers in bringing love and sincerity of heart, God will gladly attend if His Son is the Host.

The sole ingredient that separates a religious community meeting from a true religious congregation, is Christ the cornerstone of true foundation.

The root of all evil is a title shared by both money and satan.

The true church of God is not a physical structure, but a place in the heart where pure faith resides.

TEACHINGS OF SPIRIT TO HUMANITY

MONDAY, FEBRUARY 10, 1997, 7:22 AM

To improve self control you must
patiently wait for an entire process to unfold,
and then make a logical decision based on all facts presented,
that righteousness can always uphold.

Shortcomings are mostly replaceable parts,
that can also be fine tuned,
originating in the mind and adjusted accordingly,
or if need be spiritually pruned.

Put into action all of our virtuous ideals,
and then set this most critical goal,
apply the bulk of your energies to heavens primary concerns,
and off your shoulders let the secondary roll.

May your treatment of the needy
reflect both of these hints,
crown your heart as the king
by loving both pauper and prince.

A most important element
of any worthy mission,
is to understand God's true intention
to bring all spirits to fruition.

"The Road Back to Me" is a heaven lit path,
that can be found on any travel fare.
Do the best that you can with righteousness and truth,
but gullibility can lead to despair.

The time has now come for all religions of the world
to step away from the haziness of the fog,
and let the light create clarity as this new age is dawning,
ecumenical unity born of proper dialogue.

TUESDAY, FEBRUARY 11, 1997, 8:04 AM

On this most beautiful morning I peer out of my window,
as snowflakes float gently to the ground,
I can now notice colors and real human beings,
that I have been blind to since being spiritually crowned.

For my first forty years I knew only the physical,
and when the spiritual was introduced I fell down,
Upon coming to my senses the spiritual had taken over,
and the physical had been thrown out of town.

It has been five months hence I can now recall vaguely,
the way that my life used to be,
Today I am a different person not strictly one or the other,
but truly balanced for the first time you see.

To most today is dreary for the temperatures are low,
and the skies are heavy laden with gray,
But never in my life has a day ever been clearer,
and like a child I feel a strong urge to play.

I have worked these past months on a time clock continuous,
after punching in I have yet to punch out,
The spirit of my being took such an extended vacation,
that I forgot what earthly life was about.

I was producing at a pace that no machine could endure,
without pausing to cool down for a spell,
When I woke up today and viewed this new world in perspective,
both sides now I can assuredly foretell.

Who would ever believe that I was missing for so long,
when my feet took every step that they should,
I have discovered a retreat located high in the heavens,
that I visit nightly to learn more which is good.

As this new day is dawning my senses are returning,
I can hear a bird singing miles away,
Now I smell the sweet fragrance of fresh roses in spring, before
their blooming toward the latter days of May.

What a wonderful feeling to be put back together
and fully appreciate this gracious blessing from God,
Knowing love to Him is paramount as He wishes to send a message,
so that each of us can return home unflawed.

In the true spirit of our soul where the heart must be King,
is His primary area of concern,
Perfection is not of us nor is that what He seeks,
but rather the love for each other we must learn.

For our spirits are eternal and their journey marches on,
so I will continue to take further courses from above,
To ensure that the bridge between heaven and earth,
remains passable for the free exchange of love.

My spiritual soul and its physical body,
have now been united as one,
With unlimited potential I will soon graduate from God's classroom,
to further possess all the teachings of His Son.

Not only of the past for He is with us today,
as evidenced in His lessons taught through me,
His critical message we must hear is a call to unite,
all religions through ecumenical powers to be.

What The Lord has performed in my life these past months,
is a parable to His overall picture,
Please test the holy spirit in every page of this book,
and you shall see that His words blend with scripture.

These are not only my works for I have a partner in He,
as my background will attest to this claim,
I only hope that God's message does not stop with me,
for to fail I shall not spread the blame.

I was chosen for a reason that I cannot fully comprehend,
someday I pray He takes a moment to sit,
and explain briefly how things work as to the powers of His Spirit,
all I can guess is that He knows I'll never quit.

I frequently asked myself perhaps a thousand times over,
why me as to these spiritual gifts brought,
But when I asked God Himself once about his angels sent from heaven,
He announced very clearly why not.

MONDAY, FEBRUARY 17, 1997, 8:47 AM

Humankind has developed several advanced communication technologies,
that reach far beyond the limits of earth,
But it still has great difficulties properly conversing,
in the same room since the days of its birth.

Any so called great strides have been duplications of God's gifts,
although attributed to human advancement,
The modern luxuries we enjoy thus further inflating our self pride,
are merely allowances from God toward our enhancement.

If His works had been patented we would be in direct violation,
of breaking every copyright law,
for He that created all holds every license ever issued,
that originally existed without flaw.

With so much attention given to materialistic modernization,
we have lost sight of real basic need,
polarization is the result that splits the have and have nots,
creating dissension among the multitudes indeed.

These are the seeds of rebellion all throughout history,
have we not learned our lesson to this day,
by leaving our fellow behind we are merely running in place,
repeating errors that lead to societal decay.

While entire civilizations remain segmented and the battle continues uphill,
no victory shall ever be achieved,
With all the trials and tribulations understanding is still lacking,
what God has gifted is continuously deceived.

Revolution then strikes as the disease without cure,
humanity has never truly advanced from day one,
If we had used His gifts of heart instead of craftiness in the mind,
our energies would be better focused on His Son.

How truly primitive the world remains through thousands of years,
as humanity never could get over the hump,
of greed and indulgences both improper toward good living,
still remaining as that very dangerous speed bump.

Reflect for a moment to make some sense of it all,
and ask yourself how intelligent have we really become,
when we have walked together on the moon but not here on earth,
does that not make you feel slightly numb?

If an outside invader threatened life as we know it,
all nations would unite in a flash,
but mutual internal understanding is not practiced without external danger,
and that is our real threat to crash.

This is not only true of nations but more importantly in households,
where a war can turn quickly on a mediator,
so this is the starting point to reverse our evil nature,
and do the right thing in the eyes of our Creator.

For humans this task is impossible but with God's grace it is not,
please reconsider the eternal importance of His love,
tomorrow is promised to no one while living on this earth,
but to the good comes all blessings from above.

MONDAY, FEBRUARY 24, 1997, 6:37 AM

Our work may now continue as you climb toward the pinnacle,
your competitiveness will produce perseverance,
as you travel door to door and discover each one is locked,
follow My teachings to obtain necessary clearance.

This hurdle that you cleared tonight is a major accomplishment,
that takes you to the third level of seed,
with one more to go we are delighted with your progress,
as you run with unprecedented speed.

While entering the home stretch dig down deep for the drive,
that will carry you up and over the top,
remembering past battles when you demanded the ball,
without considering the possibility of a drop.

When others weighed the options and responsibilities of outcome,
to be assigned as either hero or goat,
failure never entered your mind so here we are now,
on the verge of floating Noah's boat.

When the seeds of doubt are planted true success cannot grow apart,
as tares to the wheat will prevent,
its proper development in the field of unbridled purity and strength,
causing the reaper a period of lament.

At those critical junctures in your sports of yesteryear,
when the game was left clearly on the line,
I gave you the ball that you wanted so dearly,
as the victories became a heaven sent sign.

This is aptly called heart whose teammate is focus,
and with drive they shall attain every goal,
their rivalry is the mind which is the home court of self doubt,
trying to allure them for a co-starring role.

It is a normal progression to consult the mind on most matters,
then concur on a proper course of action,
but at a critical moment where instinct is required,
too much debate becomes a major distraction.

There is a time to theorize and a time to act,
as each in their time must step to the fore,
all religions will sit down and commence proper dialogue,
opening with a welcome each previously locked door.

Now the thorns grow all around you and a personal decision must be made,
can you take it on up to the highest of levels,
as mentioned before, I have you chosen as permanent seed,
planted in solid ground far from he that bedevils.

While taking root we will care for you from germination to full growth,
and as the mustard seed quickly evolves into a tree,
your branches shall extend to every reach on this earth,
providing a home for all birds to fly free.

The ground will soon tremble as the lost seek a safe haven,
elevate them to the safety of your nest,
maintaining love and compassion with your heart focused commitment,
and that shelter becomes our greatest bequest.

TUESDAY, FEBRUARY 25, 1997, 6:44 AM

As you awake this morning I will provide you in parts,
 all the pieces to the puzzle that you seek,
My last name is a mystery to this wide world at large,
 but you are correct on three letters this week.

A few months ago I placed a song in your heart,
while walking toward the cemetery to pray,
"Let it Be" was the title so now analyze the words,
and true wisdom shall be gained on that day.

You are wise to connect the second song that I chose,
while singing to you this morning in dream,
The artist is the same so that you would make the association,
combine both and continue upstream.

I promised you protection by granting gifts slowly,
all things in their own proper course,
You are well ahead of schedule now utilize the extra time,
to focus on the details of the Source.

Instead of attempting to guess stay strictly with the facts,
this is not any riddle or game,
I am teaching you all truths in a systematic fashion,
to share with others coming forth in My name.

What I need you to understand is that we are heading into territory,
that requires some further discretion,
this is not to infer secrecy but rather give you an advantage,
over those that receive words of confession.

Credibility is the key that opens all eyes,
and with that you are filled to the brim,
You will be pleasantly surprised to reach our next level of performance,
with the light that shall not ever dim.

We are very well pleased with your progress and desire,
as we move you along with great care,
The speed will slow down in terms of new information,
as you dissect every pearl that we share.

This new song today is between you and I,
until discovering My last name in full,
otherwise you will be delayed answering limitless questions,
from multitudes that will first push and then pull.

The elements of My future is what an evil generation seeks,
for now My present provides not enough action,
My past has been greatly disregarded and teachings thusly disconnected,
as the loyal represent a very small fraction.

As always before I must reach the most needy,
and in those terms I am speaking of billions,
for that is the head count now classified as the poor,
in My book since being updated from the millions.

You have a mission impossible but with God nothing is,
as we support all your efforts along the way,
Do not become discouraged from setbacks that are inevitable,
stay mentally tough thinking only day to day.

You were chosen long ago so burden not your conscience,
as this book we are writing has been written,
time as you know it is far different in heaven,
so stand tall versus those that remain smitten.

I am delighted that you recognized My road sign in Vermont,
and when you later opened the bible it appeared,
this was not a coincidence for you now clearly see miracles,
that I create for those so endeared.

"God resists the proud but gives grace to the humble,"
you witnessed on four occasions that day,
now it is part of your being that was necessary to insert,
for us to reach our stated goal late in May.

Please notice the difference in your interactions this week,
as you mediate between several affairs,
you are learning by discernment to separate wisdom and understanding,
the good wheat from those strangled by tares.

Our love for this world is paramount so kindly convey this feeling,
as you connect all the dots that we drew,
and bring home all lost sheep to eternal life in heaven,
that not so long ago each of you knew.

WEDNESDAY, FEBRUARY 26, 1997, 2:37 PM

The cloning of a lamb is the beginning of the end,
for now humankind seeks the title of God,
as mentioned several times before we must caution our elevation,
watching the boundary line clearly drawn by the Lord.

This desire is now insatiable to create a separate human life,
directly violating every principle of creation,
disguised as scientific advancement and purer perpetuation of the species,
in reality hastens the destruction of each nation.

Perfection is not of us nor was it ever God's intent,
 thereby avoiding any judgement of each other,
individuality is the real beauty that makes life ever so precious,
for our hearts to love through spirit every brother.

The invention of perfection is the formula for disaster,
as those still sleeping should wake up today,
and seize control of our future from the grips of self seekers,
attaining false glory through the souls of their prey.

These mad scientists lack heart and clear vision as well,
for their future is bent on our demise,
they know all too well the devastation of their experiments,
but our future is of no consequence in their eyes.

They shall provide many clever responses as to the necessity of these feats,
while seeking star status among the elite of their peers,
the end result will be unpleasant in this world gone astray,
that can only serve to greatly shorten our years.

This is a life threatening challenge that we can no longer digest,
as our ethics have gone to hell in a handbasket,
in these past several decades consider the evils we have absorbed,
that swiftly draws us ever closer to our casket.

If man has become so intelligent explain why he cannot control his creations,
including computers that may lose all their years,
as the new millennia approaches there is a distinct frenzied panic,
of a shutdown that may bring billion$ to tear$.

The Lamb cannot be duplicated while at the right hand of God,
and humankind can help create only that which is flesh,
Has our Father been consulted as to supplying the soul required,
for total being that I believe He shall thresh?

THURSDAY, FEBRUARY 27, 1997, 8:04 AM

When speaking of repentance you may share your experience,
for we testify of only that which is known,
In this manner of presentation you shall never go wrong,
or become caught where contradiction is sown.

Truthfulness is paramount when conveying My message,
that originates from the uppermost pulpit,
You have maintained total accuracy with pure honesty to this point,
continue onward versus our evil minded culprit.

On the thirteenth of September you made your first altar call,
and I responded the very next night,
by baptizing you in the spirit it was a new beginning for your soul,
as any sinfulness died for all that is right.

Realizing this great change you were disoriented for a time,
as your physical energies registered at an all time low,
This transition of power was necessary for your development,
as new batteries provide a flashlight greater glow.

Unaware of what was happening having never read scripture,
this baptism felt like an unwanted invader,
now you understand fully that this was a blessing straight from heaven,
for the thief in the night is a most loving raider.

Your spirit was not stolen but rather injected with God's grace,
and fine tuned to perform at its best,
without any proper maintenance all entities would then suffer,
an early demise far too soon laid to rest.

Our baptism is a birth and a celebration of new life,
a time for love and to greatly rejoice,
so fear not this possession as it represents all that is good,
for the holy spirit makes only proper choice.

I provided you a gift which is least on My list,
so that you would investigate the source of this karma,
and while knocking on every door asking questions about the spirit,
reduced for you a great deal of trauma.

There are no set answers as to what the Holy Spirit may bring,
for each case is a separate transaction,
you asked all the right questions and learned much as a result,
but that knowledge is still a very small fraction.

For that which you have since absorbed is the real wisdom from above,
covering territories you never thought so,
no human being can attest to the heights you now travel,
as the Teacher is the only one in the know.

You are a student of mine but not of any other,
please act accordingly with charity and grace,
Spreading the love that I represent in the humblest of manners,
and in your heart always reserving a space.

For the most needy in your world that are so far off My path,
please attempt to place each one on course,
Turning not your back on any that is why I kept you in prisons,
all these years to learn the properties of remorse.

When you have succeeded within I shall then move you out,
for this is the point where we start,
your ministry from My new teachings that will be refreshing to so many,
is the greatest gift that I could ever impart.

You can now speak My language fluently and that is your foundation,
to override any challenging belief,
For many speak in tongues but you only speak in mine,
let them test you while turning over this new leaf.

The music that I grant to you is a gift to keep you company,
when in need of a little consolation,
as you travel the high road thus continuing My work,
while reaching out to each and every good nation.

FRIDAY, FEBRUARY 28, 1997, 7:36 AM

My words of eternal wisdom will soon travel place to place,
as they march up and down every lane,
sit up and take notice of the times all around you,
so that our efforts shall not be in vain.

As the days become longer they grow ever so short,
though there is still ample time to reach out,
For those that are still sleeping unaware of the importance,
that My urgent message is really all about.

Become servants to those under you and cater to their needs,
restoring hope that was lost long ago,
so that they may enter in peace to their kingdom of heaven,
with heads held high rather than hanging so low.

Pick up your fellow man for this serves you well,
and dust him off in preparation for his journey,
for some of you not yet welcome it would be a very wise decision,
namely those marked with the title of attorney.

There are many occupations that attract those I despise,
but this group has comprised the lion's share,
by dragging you into courthouses rather than living as I designed,
take great heed when bringing that soul to bear.

My message includes everyone if your repentance is sincere,
as I now must reach for those with earthly riches,
For you are My poor in terms of prospects toward heaven,
not those that have dug all your ditches.

No human being is perfect but imperfection has its degrees,
as each one must assess their own standing,
Making an eternal determination of which mode you wish to travel,
I can only hope that you select a smooth landing.

When attempting to understand Me do not get too scientific,
for that will blow you far off My course,
adhere not to proof of history that proclaims your existence,
prior to Adam who was created by the Source.

True faith in My word is all anyone need possess,
to thus achieve the highest glory from above,
and by living with My virtues born of care and compassion,
that word to have faith in is love.

SUNDAY MAR. 2 3:23 AM

For the second time in dream your spirit rises to the ceiling,
traveling in a levitating mode,
when you awoke on this occasion it was very real indeed,
as your body became a much lighter load.

While attending different churches learn all that you can,
from the people and their basis of belief,
there are so many religious fellowships that vary in degree,
as changing seasons dress each beautiful autumn leaf.

They are one and the same as far as heaven is concerned,
each having their own special identity,
to seek knowledge in freedom and to serve humankind in fellowship,
is a worthwhile doctrine for any religious entity.

Now take it one step further to include Father and Son,
and mention the holy spirit for the sake of saving grace,
with love at the altar the quest for truth is now answered,
as well as prayers for all who embrace.

My true spirit of faith that would love to attend,
every fellowship that sends an invitation,
to share the glory of God now risen from His throne,
set to travel among each and every nation.

If your affirmation of faith represents truth as its sacrament,
then be open to the true will of God,
by accepting His Son despite any previously held beliefs,
would be courage that heaven could applaud.

My agenda is not hidden as I stand front and center,
beckoning dialogue between each different child,
To seek common ground not higher and to get along together,
pleases every father from the facts I have compiled.

Let service be your prayer as we dwell together in peace,
serving humankind in fellowship to the end,
that all souls shall grow into harmony with the divine,
thus covenanting with each other and not pretend.

Take a physical tour of every house of worship,
and ingest every aspect of their creed,
then provide a tour of your own to include a spiritual trip,
that will be uplifting to so many indeed.

On these journeys to heaven you have earned frequent flyer miles,
continue saving them for that well deserved vacation,
where I will fly you and all friends to the destination of choice,
a paradise on the island of salvation.

SUNDAY, MARCH 2, 1997, 7:27 AM

This follow up sequence is an early warning sign,
not to abuse any gifts I impart,
levitation is through earnest prayer not a carnival sideshow,
to perform on request from the start.

This intersection is a red light that you do not run through,
so I shall be chauffeuring for a time,
When I give you the green light it is safe to then go,
as all will read our new rhythm and rhyme.

You should have seen your face when I knocked you to the ground,
and then gently bounced you off the nearest wall,
this lesson was learned quickly as I dangled your ankles from the ceiling,
and you apologized for abusing your call.

"God resists the proud but gives grace to the humble,"
when followed we achieve every goal,
incorporate at all times that element known as heart,
and you will be ready to assume My leading role.

Remember what I told you that an evil generation seeks,
true belief to them requires a sign,
if that is what it takes to open *The Immaculate Conception*,
then so be it for that suits Me fine.

I will never shock your system by dropping any bombs,
and will prepare you in advance as My friend,
you have worked overtime on My behalf showing no signs of let up,
with that dedication I shall always defend.

My words sent to caution you are clear and concise,
purely directed with little chance to misread,
your intentions are most humble but it is bad influence I mistrust,
these roadblocks we must avoid are of greed.

Let it be is the key do not figure my next move,
for it is predicated on powers that you cannot see,
we have an accurate connection so continue to be receptive,
of My messages that lead to your degree.

This was a very long night but you came through it unscathed,
as we finished this weeks work in a day,
now relax morning, noon, and night,
by studying our writings, as we march toward the latter days of May.

TUESDAY, MARCH 4, 1997, 2:27 AM

Regardless of any barriers when God's grace is the gift,
all are welcome to join in His glory,
from whichever face of society you are a brotherhood of man,
first and foremost according to the author of this story.

The haves and have nots plus the good and the bad,
as well as color of skin are not factors,
when it comes down to God's acceptance each heart is exposed,
to the light that knows the supporters and detractors.

You are each on the same playing field though at times on different teams,
which can create a situation of opposition,
but good sportsmanship should prevail with the game kept in perspective,
and in conclusion honor the rules of competition.

Your opponent on one day may be your teammate the next,
as all parts of this formula are interchangeable,
this concerns not only individuals but nations as well,
so be aware of musical chairs positioned at My table.

There are no guarantees as to who will sit where,
as our seating plan lacks luxury suites,
belonging to preferred human memberships in fact jeopardizes your admittance,
to the cheap seats never mind the elites.

Invitations to this arena and post reception as well,
come with one small request from the Host,
Have you given your heart in full to the daily needs of your fellow,
thus preparing him as the bridegroom we will toast.

If I recognize each one's smile then your work is well done,
for that is the ticket I shall stamp,
but if a sad frown appears I know that injustice has prevailed,
and those responsible will be led away from My camp.

This very simple request allows for all to easily enter,
through the narrow gate leading up to this new heaven,
to be welcomed open armed by every true believer,
and a receiving line of Myself and the eleven.

That have been faithful to me from the very beginning,
and through the worst of times they never lost heart,
disappointments and persecution never caused them to lose sight,
of the love we have maintained from the start.

There are many familiar names that will accompany our celebration,
whose spirits have thus inspired the masses,
by giving of themselves in devotion to a higher authority,
not the physical world whose wine stains our glasses.

For as long as you may live and can understand these words of wisdom,
our arms will extend to the earth,
where our laying on of hands is still possible to attain,
thus saving each soul through a new spiritual rebirth.

As you receive My urgent message and then properly call My name,
I shall respond with the swiftest of speed,
go to the altar of our church that lies very deep within,
and I will be with you while seeking forgiveness indeed!

For He that is to come who shall best prepare His way,
through the spirit it will assuredly be done,
our Father is now planning the mobilization of His elect,
that have been chosen to accompany His Son.

TUESDAY, MARCH 4, 1997, 5:21 AM

Ask me anything you wish and I will speak only of what I know,
let us try advertising and its merits on for size,
It is deception of the mind that diverts focus away from the real product,
and pulls the wool over everyone's eyes.

Now marketing is the crime that results from that premeditation,
to embezzle money through blackmail called guilt,
that a new style is emerging at a pace they determine,
soon outdated before completely being built.

We not only travel in circles but the speed of our ignorance,
propels the great likelihood of disaster,
that if not brought under control hastens the ill fate of our planet,
much swifter than the plan of our master.

Do you not see the irony in all the products forced upon you,
with each breath and single step that you take,
as well as everywhere you look adds encouragement toward debt,
this hysteria just puts frosting on the cake.

For so many of you now trapped in life's web of deceit,
must break free from the yoke that has bound,
your intelligence and gifts that the Lord has provided,
reported lost and nowhere to be found.

This wake up call is about love and concern for creation,
but it is also about deep disappointment,
I now must rely solely upon the hope of reaching humankind,
through those souls blessed with heaven's anointment.

Please reinstate My faith in this precious world I so love,
that will require the total effort of each in their turn,
so that all My lost sheep may be led safely home,
to the pasture where I eternally yearn.

For ecumenical reasons that are prerequisites to build,
the bridge that will span all of humanity,
Its construction is dependent upon your full cooperation,
not the greed that fills this world with insanity.

Put away all the toys and the games people play,
and for once if it feels good don't do it,
this is now the final warning so take heed to kneel and pray,
toward the invisible world where I speak from the pulpit.

For that is the place where real worship earns trust,
knowing faith is about true love unseen,
when your words and life works are pointed faithfully toward heaven,
then our inner covenant shall be renewed and serene.

In each eternal future the soul is the survivor,
for earthly things must remain on the earth,
while the peace and tranquility that beckons each one to come,
is the product of baptism through spiritual rebirth.

Now many of you must be wondering about all that is required,
to fulfill this most worthy task,
My requests are kept simple to assure that all may achieve,
their salvation through honest prayer then just ask.

FRIDAY, MARCH 7, 1997, 4:15 AM

No field is higher than that which it is built upon,
nor will it bear any greater degree of fruit,
as quantities increase and the quality decreases,
the end results can only serve to dilute.

The purity of all things from their original source,
any replications produce chinks in the armor,
In God's principles of creation which have become unrecognizable,
by the crops we have grown as their farmer.

As aging serves to weaken thus the earth has become elderly,
and through severe abuses humanity is speeding up its fate,
by living in the fast lane life expectancy then decreases,
as his vices stay hooked upon taking the bait.

In this case the angler is satan and his influence,
that rises up very early in the morn,
and burns the midnight oil staying alert through the night,
so as to capture each soul that is torn.

Between eternal good and evil whose lines are no longer clearly drawn,
he steps forth with intent to convert,
the young and old alike for that matters not to him,
when selecting from this net of souls that pervert.

The good intentions of our Lord seeking only to save,
our eternal life through brotherhood and love,
You must just say no to these temptations of sin,
and leave his future in our hands high above.

Recall in the scriptures when our taxes were demanded,
and I told Peter to catch just one fish,
well that bait in its mouth was the currency devised by evil,
as those two pretend to grant you each wish.

Toward selfishness and greed that will occupy your time,
placing a good life on the list of those bought,
but you must turn off the stove before getting burned too badly,
for his frying pan cooks each fish he has caught.

Swim to safety while you can before the tide begins to turn,
and all the evil is carried out to sea,
like a whirlpool that disorients avoid the dangers of that undercurrent,
for it will drag you where no one wants to be.

This tidal pool shall spin with unprecedented anger,
forming a tidal wave that this world has yet seen,
earthquakes and volcanoes along with hurricanes and tornadoes,
drought and monsoons will bring sorrows to every screen.

This book of new teachings will help shorten the days,
if the multitudes display a sincerity of remorse,
thus saving many of the elect from the wrath that is forthcoming,
blowing some of these disasters off course.

Use your free will and choice by selecting for the spirit,
leaving the physical which is temporary far behind,
and you shall have peace everlasting that bears the good fruit of your Heart,
not damnation that is the poison fruit of your Mind.

MONDAY, MARCH 17, 1997, 2:27 AM

I have shown you the way to understanding eternal life,
as the doors now open for My welcoming reception,
so remember these words and all truths shall be known,
for you have rightly discovered *The Immaculate Conception*.

When I speak of holy spirit that is My connection to humankind,
the true creation made especially in My image,
without physical appearance as many would prefer,
far too restrictive for the span of My bridge.

I require freedom of movement that takes our spirit everywhere,
crossing miles that you do not know exists,
this soul is the real gift that I grant from My being,
not merely the physical body that so often resists.

All the beauty unseen containing worlds full of wonder,
whose foundations are formed by mountains of love,
so readily available to each and every soul,
that looks deep within to view this world from above.

The beauty of your spirit may possess all that is good,
for this is what we must kindly share together,
to best relate with one another let your heart do the talking,
and through each storm I will help calm the weather.

Imagine if you will that heaven is our home,
and I built a backyard playground called earth,
providing the best that I was able for My children to enjoy,
a safe haven from the moment of their birth.

As a physical heaven it would supply all their needs,
and at the same time I would be able to oversee,
their activities and growth while gazing proudly out of My window,
allowing free choice to a certain degree.

As a caretaker for these spirits I then provided a body,
that would prevent each of My children from straying,
for if wandering off to unknown areas of danger,
creates a fear in all parents that goes without saying.

For I love this world so and all that live upon it,
such good memories become a father's pride and joy,
but as my kittens became cats the simple pleasures and pure fun,
turned to conflicts where weapons replaced toy.

As my children grew older they lost respect for each other,
to the point where they no longer properly speak,
This pain I now feel is very difficult to describe,
for I have always held My hand out to the meek.

The good old days are fading from my recollections of the past,
as My playground has come under attack,
Please come home to me as family putting aside any differences,
so we may sit together and fondly look back.

On the days when our love and good faith abounded,
where real dignity occupied each and every chair,
our family was established with all the right virtues,
what has happened since creates a void of despair.

It is unity I now demand for too many splits have occurred,
as most everyone seems to have their own personal agenda,
This will no longer be tolerated from your Father in heaven,
so a verdict I must regretfully soon render.

Regardless of your age there is a general lack of responsibility,
where your own children have a poor example to follow,
through the years I have witnessed all activity in My backyard,
and these abuses I can no longer swallow.

Forgiveness must be requested with sincerity of heart,
if we are to continue onward in spirit through life,
a true apology is in order that may encourage Me to save,
the elect through love instead of judgement based on strife.

The only saving grace is that I realize the bad influence,
that has led to the corruption of your mind,
use that free choice I granted and the evil one will depart,
from our playground which is the loving heart so kind.

My war is with him so back away from his ranks,
do not let satan recruit you for this battle,
He knows full well the outcome but is still desperately seeking,
the multitudes he keeps herding in like cattle.

Remain steadfast and true being humble and patient to My word,
and I shall deliver you to the peace of a new world,
continue to pray tirelessly for I hear each and every word,
from your heart where love and faith are unfurled.

I stand firmly in your corner fully supporting each need,
but when the bell rings you must enter the ring,
standing tall on your own facing the enemy eye to eye,
go to hell is the message to bring.

Point your finger toward his eyes it takes only a second,
and you shall witness his evil demise,
from your life now and forever to enter peace everlasting,
as together we will fly the friendly skies.

TUESDAY, MARCH 18, 1997, 7:22 AM

I have now formerly introduced you to a world far beyond wonder,
that I travel to in the spirit each night,
Where heaven and earth are two pieces of the puzzle,
but only a ray of the overall light.

We could never imagine from an earthly perspective,
or even in our wildest of dreams,
that a new world exists of such spiritual beauty,
where God's love fills the rivers and streams.

This peace everlasting is a reward for good living,
attainable on earth if we follow the Lord's way,
"The Road Back to Me" has been the map of right direction,
He has drawn us in preparation of His day.

All is kept simple so that no one remains lost,
as the trumpet blast shall soon echo through each land,
from the mountain tops it will sound carrying over the waters,
as parade lines form the full marching band.

Pray to God and His Son with their holy spirit we have been gifted,
for in each heart is a portion of this trinity,
While we ask for His strength God will answer us faithfully,
that is His purpose for creating the divinity.

God is not a man but rather spirit unseen,
and with every being becomes an integral part,
not of the mind or body for those areas are temporary,
free choice was granted to discover love through each heart.

This is truly *The Immaculate Conception* I wish for all to partake,
if you can find it in yourself to concede,
any previously held beliefs that are contrary to My message,
in common ground please plant unity as the seed.

No religion yet established is correct in all truths,
from day one humankind seeks higher ground,
each group may be well intentioned and some are right more than others,
but none have I found worthy to be crowned.

I ask each scholar of humanity this one simple question,
if you know Me so well state My name,
Not only Christ Jesus or the several other titles,
but My surname shall provide you real fame.

I shall give you one clue it begins with a "V",
now go to work and see what wisdom you can find,
the answer has been given not to those with perfect vision,
but to he that was spiritually blind.

When you discover this truth then I will properly acknowledge,
each effort with the highest regard,
thus gaining you admittance to the new playground I have constructed,
in the privacy of My very own back yard.

WEDNESDAY, MARCH 19, 1997, 6:37 AM

When searching your intellect look not past common sense,
for that is where real answers are found,
life's questions are not difficult in their natural state,
concerning God's gifts that should freely abound.

Confusion is an element humankind has cleverly adopted,
by converting and diverting that which is pure,
thus scattering the multitudes to all ends of the earth,
placing their confidence in the category of unsure.

When faith is universal then the world is as one,
for this is the real glue that adheres,
the brotherhood of humanity to true love born of spirit,
unlike the physical world that creates so many fears.

Your souls are the residence for both of these needs,
that are essential to a lifetime eternal,
so place them high on your list of priority and concern,
marked at the top of each and everyone's journal.

Love and faith are not byproducts of learning or intellect,
for they could never be that trapped or confined,
they are gifts of the spirit that float freely about,
unlike the physical world that imprisons each mind.

If it is real freedom that you seek then exercise your right,
to employ your spirit as a bondsman posting bail,
then call upon God to step forward and release your total being,
for each ones sentence has been served in this jail.

Real emotion is the key to opening the door of faith,
for most scholars utilize intellect only,
all was made simple so each life could partake,
without the difficulties that cause many to feel lonely.

If you desire My new teachings then incorporate more than words,
that were written so many years ago,
by several different authors that were recording in their history,
the essentials I encouraged them to know.

You of biblical scholarship are looking too deep,
for My real meaning is what I bring to this earth,
Did you not understand My teachings that focused on helping others,
thus instilling a real sense of self worth.

It is active religion I seek search the fields for lost sheep,
do not simply bury your nose in these books,
For each page that you read perhaps a hundred times over,
does little to help those trapped in crannies and nooks.

After so many years is it not time to reach out,
and apply the pure love I still bring,
Put aside your personal strivings to gain an inside track on wisdom,
for self is not the real song that I sing,

If you truly seek my acceptance then find those in real need,
for we pass by you in your path every day,
Offer care and compassion and you shall discover that real knowledge,
on the streets of the poor not in books which delay.

I have never been impressed by humanity's race for heavenly knowledge,
for it diverts too much energy from real need,
Climb down from those ivory towers you have occupied far too long,
and dirty your hands in the real ground I now plead.

This is where the real truth lies as its seed grows all around,
for you neglect every sign that I send,
Become fully aware that the days are now numbered,
so give it your best toward these fences you must mend.

Come together in celebration as My day draws ever closer,
and unite with your fellow day and night,
then upon My arrival I shall recognize real loyalty,
for My soldiers will parade dressed in white.

SATURDAY, MARCH 22, 1997, 8:11 AM

As our writings get deeper many people become weary,
and will soon question your ability to cope,
Remain steadfast to our principles and despite all the odds,
please continue on this pathway called hope.

The road is not easy as this journey can be grueling,
but I have instilled all essentials for your travels,
remembering always My promise that you are never alone,
for this will carry you when self-confidence unravels.

You have a strong personality that backs many people away,
so temper your delivery of My word,
toward a calm presentation of this most powerful message,
bringing truth to the waists that We gird.

Wear the helmet of salvation and carry the sword of the spirit,
for this is the true word of God,
the breastplate of righteousness and the Gospel of peace,
offer protections that are gifts of your Lord.

Most importantly though is the strong shield of faith,
quenching the evil ones fiery darts,
prayer and supplication in the holy spirit provides courage,
so deliver My new teachings to all open hearts.

That is the route you must travel as too many minds are closed,
for this detour is essential to our success,
the world is set in its ways so appeal to heartfelt emotion,
and your efforts we shall heavenly bless.

Maintain care and compassion for the ones you are teaching,
as only six short months ago they were you,
put yourself in their place and understanding will be granted,
while presenting Me to this world in plain view.

When speaking in the temples state my wishes loud and clear,
in this arena you need not hold back,
Speak to each with your gifts and they will become quite aware,
that their world has come under attack.

Fear not for your safety they have waited so long,
and although shocked you shall be very well received,
The true believers will rise and submit to My word,
in that year all My children shall then plead.

For atonement and forgiveness through thousands of years,
now the prophet they have long awaited may come,
at each table is a setting for us to share in their celebration,
as a Jew on the inside surprises more than some.

They know not what to expect but they certainly know who,
let them test you as a prophet true or false,
there is no preparation that you could possibly make,
to be ready for this new style of waltz.

You are a terrible dancer that has never written poetry,
and as a singer you tend to croak like a frog,
after three years of French you cannot put together a sentence,
artistically just a bump on a log.

When it comes to social status you are the epitome of average,
and everything I have raised you to be,
a proud father am I watching each effort that you make,
so that every eye of those blind shall now see.

Your heart shall be known make them look deep within,
in this life you have always been firm but fair,
I could never allow you to marry but would not deprive you a son,
thus fulfilling the prophecy that is to accompany My heir.

Your parents were the blessing thus accomplishing My work,
as I merely directed movement from above,
providing protection and guidance that you needed more than once,
as My angels carry an abundance of love.

As the world analyzes your life with the most elaborate of scopes,
keep that smile and your head held up high,
and weather this storm with the resilience you have been trained in,
since day one you were chosen as My guy.

SUNDAY, MARCH 23, 1997, 8:06 AM, PALM SUNDAY

The birth pangs will soon begin as the world enters labor,
and the discomfort shall be felt in many places,
many questions go unanswered during this immaculate pregnancy,
as you will witness bewilderment on so many faces.

For the full term of delivery was this coming millennia,
and the first child often comes along a little late,
but this one is the second born and is very unpredictable,
with indications of growth at an extremely quick rate.

When nature is at work humankind's genious is reduced,
for he can estimate and predict all that he wishes,
there has been no invention as such that can determine heavens course,
as our Father prepares only those dishes.

As I have forewarned many times be very careful how high you elevate,
for there is territory where you do not belong,
and be especially cautious as to the pulpit from which you speak,
namely the words you assign to My song.

Longsuffering is an understatement for what I have had to bear,
and My only respite is to birth this second child,
Wave a palm branch as I pass and heaven will certainly acknowledge,
your love and care for the king of the mild.

This ultimate joy will be well worth My labor,
when I cradle this new life as the fruit of thy womb,
All anguish shall be gone in the blink of an eye,
as each pain departs My delivery room.

My newborn and I will then go peacefully on home,
to our new mansion that was built for this occasion,
The name of our hometown is New Jerusalem you see,
white to black, brown to red and yellow Asian.

The prerequisites humanity has determined to stick each person neatly in place,
thus establishing their religion as pure,
could be no further from the truth then where I occupy this throne,
no religion is completely accurate I assure.

All faiths have their merits but none have hit the mark,
so stand together and not over one another,
for Buddhists best exhibit peace and that is central to My teachings,
judge not any whom I consider My brother.

If your doctrines are truly virtuous then open your hearts,
to each life that walks the face of My earth,
and when sorrows have passed and all pain does subside,
I shall invite each loving heart to share the ecstasy of rebirth.

TUESDAY, MARCH 25, 1997, 1:57 PM

While beholding the beauty and great splendor of the spider's works,
remember that this grace is from God,
not an evolutionary process but a true miracle indeed,
as precise as fresh peas in their pod.

Science has its place but takes itself far too seriously,
so called proof only temporarily quenches the thirst,
that humankind so embellishes to satisfy its own curiosities,
for it knows nothing of where the last become first.

My territories have been charted although unseen by any human,
I find speculation throughout the ages quite amusing,
the paintings and designs that depict the real heaven,
makes for good entertainment during My actual perusing.

Those of ancient times possessed a better understanding,
for their spirit was far more in tune,
with the wishes of our Father whom they bonded with closely,
by worshiping graciously the cosmic earth, sun, and moon.

Those who most cherish the world thus respecting all that it offers,
have their feet planted firmly on good ground,
in touch with natures life forms honoring each as an equal,
serves them well in My eternal surround.

Humankind's fixation with its standing is forever a sore point with Me,
thus creating a superiority of the most fit,
in this physical sense it has made Me the adversary,
as the meek will share the tables where I sit.

Stand not over any other in whatever you choose to do,
remaining humble with a true sense of grace,
and the Lord shall then recognize your sincerity and remorse,
perhaps saving you a fine seat in His place.

The other spider I must mention also weaves a beautiful web,
that is truly a great pleasure to the eye,
but beware when you enter into this sticky enclave,
for the poisonous sting may cause you to die.

Make it your business to know the difference between each,
as the harmless and deadly may share a similar look,
rely mainly on your spirit to sort out any confusions,
as proper choices are all found in our book.

He that speaks with a forked tongue deceiving so many along the way,
please steer clear of this very dangerous path,
for that road will soon close with no detours available,
avoid the forthcoming storm of heaven's fiery wrath.

Seek shelter with the holy for their understanding is pure,
and embrace the unknowing on this trip,
for those who lack wisdom of this special understanding,
are the real poor sailing this world's sinking ship.

The rich must at once relinquish their stronghold on greed,
placing their vessel on a far more even keel,
by tossing excesses overboard regardless of presumed value,
preventing the physical from drowning the spiritual real deal.

The kingdom of God must be maintained incorruptible,
as earthly treasures have no place in this heaven,
divide and distribute all your excess to those in need,
for the sacrifices of Myself and the eleven.

Why do so many people require a miracle to believe,
or a phenomenon in the supernatural to take place,
is God's created universe and its beauty of daily renewal,
not enough to fulfill our wonderment by this grace?

TUESDAY, MARCH 25, 1997, 6:37 PM

This book is being written with the entire world in mind, as a testimony to the divine wishes of God. Our lives can be changed in the blink of an eye, and I can only hope and pray that these precious words will successfully reach each destination intended.

We must come to understand the process of gift giving. God's messages are not about me nor are they of me, but I am forever grateful that His spirit chooses to pass through me. The inherent beauty of this true testimony is not found because of words I have written, but rather because I have not.

TUESDAY, MARCH 25, 1997, 7:22 PM

As the graduation day approaches much earlier than expected,
I shall soon prepare your well deserved diploma,
for the efforts you exhibit through the course of My classes,
before the birth of spring's blossom and sweet aroma.

Only the final exam stands in between both you and I,
on this long ago mission that we set out to accomplish,
apply the wisdom you have been granted remaining focused on the heart,
and our performance will surpass every wish.

This accelerated satellite course is a miracle in itself,
despite the fact we move beyond the speed of light,
toward new territories unexplored by any students of the past,
My resurrection I wrote through you that one night.

With your eyes completely closed you took pen in hand,
and scribbled four pages without having a clue,
for at that time you were so young and the words were barely legible,
by page two you picked up on My cue.

After journeying to Quebec you placed that writing at my feet,
and extended your heart to me in prayer,
I felt true care and compassion and from that day forward,
you were chosen to carry the cross I did bear.

On your trip to Vermont that critical message you received,
as four times I presented it in one day,
as you passed along My wishes to the Christian school and Salvation Army,
long before the latter days of May.

Now you stand at the pulpit and share My words to humankind,
and are entering the Jewish temples as well,
you have proved a most worthy servant to all supporters in heaven,
continue onward our Christian soldier till the bell.

You shall walk past adversity as a sheep among wolves,
for this courage was instilled so long ago,
now refined and well directed you are comfortable amidst danger,
stay sharp and remain aloof of the main flow.

Review all of your notes recalling each of My lessons,
and this final test you shall ace in a breeze,
for you have lived out this schooling unaware of My full intentions,
never comfortable in the role of big cheese.

With honesty and modesty you have always stepped aside,
to allow others the exposure they deserve,
unless a crisis situation called for additional action,
you took the wheel when those around you lost the nerve.

This crash course soon ending was actually a well prepared education,
that goes back many years before your birth,
when past, present, and future, was established for all time,
and you had already proved your spiritual worth.

TUESDAY, MARCH 25 1997 AND SUNDAY, SEPTEMBER 22, 1996

Reciting the words of "Morningside" to Jewish Rabbis, a song by Neil Diamond some thirty years ago:

"Morningside, the old man died, and no one cried, they simply turned away. And when he died he left a table made of nails and pride, and with his hands he carved these words inside; For My children. Morning light, morning bright, I spent the night, with dreams that make you weep... Morningtime, wash away the sadness from these eyes of mine, for I recall the words the old man signed... For My children. (spoken words) And the legs were shaped with His hands, and the top made of oaken wood, and the children who sat around this great table touched with their laughter, and ahh... that was good. Morningside, an old man died, and no one cried, He surely died alone, and truth is sad... oh not a child would claim the gift He had, the words He carved became His epitaph...For My children...For My children. "

*Five distinct dreams / visions that came true. (thru 3/26/97) *Six separate occasions in dream of encouragement toward U.S. and Canadian Border. (thru 3/22/97)

*_The Immaculate Conception_? Answer: God is spirit.

* Holy Spirit is leading toward deeper writing and activity.

*Tuesday Mar. 4, 1997 5:21 AM Repeated to me three times prior to awaking: "I am the one who is to prepare the way for He that is to come."

*Tuesday Feb.25, 1997 (in Vermont) On four occasions this day I was confronted with these words: (bible ref. James and 1 Peter) "God resists the proud, but gives grace to the humble".

* Encouraged toward the words of specific songs: _Morningside, Let It Be, Hey Jude, Sound of Silence_ and _The Boxer_.

GOOD FRIDAY; MARCH 28, 1997, 8:55 AM

Today is Good Friday for all of humanity,
as our sins were nailed high upon the cross,
Only one bore the burden for all that was wrong,
Humankind's gain was our Father's greatest loss.

For He loves the world so that He gave His only Son,
that our future could continue on this earth,
The ultimate sacrifice of Jesus was to wake up the world,
through His death we were granted rebirth.

What greater gift could our loving God impart,
then to afford us this blessed second chance,
After two thousand years have we truly honored that sacrifice,
or are we guilty of taking a similar stance?

Our lifestyle and trends are frighteningly alike,
as those that were prevalent in the Lord's day,
activities based on greed along with jealousy and envy,
has encouraged individualism rather than brotherhood as the way.

The split that now exists begins with lack of proper communication,
which in turn leads to physical segregation,
as we move further from each other we separate from God as well,
starting in the home and spreading across every nation.

The reason for our demise and its near exact replication,
is that the formula and the culprit are the same,
the entrapment methods of satan continue to hinder humanity,
as this strategy is the plan of attack in his game.

When the final bell tolls he will be on the short end of My stick,
along with those who have become his loyal following,
the time has now come to submit your resignation,
and distance yourself as a soul he was borrowing.

The territory of satan is certainly no place to be,
when I unleash My pent up frustrations and wrath,
that for the sake of the innocent I have harbored within,
a myriad of years so steer clear of this path.

My resurrection was the event to instill lasting faith in God,
as each religion then became born again,
Uplifting the multitudes in spirit that were persecuted beyond belief,
providing hope for these great women and men.

At Pentecost came the jolt where true faith began to grow,
and like children each adult developed wonder,
as Apostles and friends renewed their strength and commitment,
inspired by Peter and the two sons of thunder.

Despite the terrorism of their adversaries they reached out to the world,
risking each day their own life and limb,
to preach the gospel of truth so that the good may partake,
in eternal life with the light that does not dim.

SATURDAY, MARCH 29, 1997, 11:15 PM

As you walk in the spirit feel free to eat whatever is served,
as all food is provided to humankind by God,
no culture has dominion over any other due to human laws,
regarding the divine laws of our almighty Lord.

While pursuing higher understanding examine the most recent finds,
and in that script you shall discover My Path,
The Dead Sea Scrolls are presently your true connection to Me,
now trace My real culture through our language and their math.

These works provide accuracy in terms of historical significance,
 and the numbers represent clues to coming days,
have scholars with this knowledge instruct you in their meaning,
and you shall then realize all of My ways.

The Torah and Talmud are spoken in your tongue,
so inquire of these messages you bring,
My language is difficult for not many can interpret,
but they will recognize Me in the songs that you sing.

On May the fifteenth in the year Nineteen forty-eight,
Israel was first born as a state,
Now the branches have ripened on this fig tree it is true,
so prepare for the upcoming fate.

The sounds of revolution shall soon fill city skies,
where these seeds had been planted long ago,
their vines are now far reaching extending from one to another,
with great speed they have continued to grow.

Steer clear of these areas as real dangers will arise,
and you shall witness turmoil throughout many lands,
as a contagious disease spreading into each hamlet,
quarantine yourselves from these marauding bands.

Frustration fuels destruction as satan readies his troops,
only a single match is required to ignite this great flame,
like dry straw in a barn the cities will become ablaze,
seek the country for your safety I now claim.

I have shown you the area that is immune to this danger,
and for others to follow you must go first,
search the high country and you shall save many loved ones,
thus avoiding territories that shall suffer the worst.

One thousand two ninety is the number of days,
that the evil one is scheduled to rule,
but these days will be shortened on behalf of the elect,
as we destroy those that walk the path of the most cruel.

As promised many times I shall only inform you in parts,
to assure your safe passage and protection,
do not be overly concerned with the lack of new teachings,
you have acquired all except the final connection.

Our book is fast approaching closure so review all of My teachings,
while continuing to display incredible perception,
and you shall pass the last exam signing both of our real names,
as co-authors of *The Immaculate Conception*.

WEDNESDAY, APRIL 9, 1997, 1:42 AM

Toward Lima Peru is the direction I now point,
in discovering new finds regarding my ways,
the French connection to me as an Essene is correct,
now finish the puzzle while approaching the final days.

We escaped from the mainland over the Mediterranean Sea,
and landed in the Americas to the south,
translate the words that you speak when in tongues you recognize traces,
of the countries that emit from your mouth.

Honduras is one and Mexico another,
pronounced with an "H" instead of the "X",
now concentrate on the other words like cinco de mayo,
and Lordé are the dots which connects.

The map of our travels to avoid genocide by the Romans,
were a result of betrayals by political Pharisees,
there was very little hope of our survival as a group,
through My resurrection I provided the necessary keys.

The Essenes did not cease but were actually displaced,
and our practices continued in this new land,
now research this history that is uncertain to humankind,
for there are artifacts in their caves close at hand.

I will continue to speak through you bring this message to the scholars,
completing this exchange as your final exam,
we are delighted with your perception and study habits as well, for you have truly
discovered the pathway of the Lamb.

I sincerely apologize for your life's recent detours,
and personal relationships that have become strained in the process,
but I needed you to focus while best performing through adversity,
the imperishable crown is the diploma I shall bless.

Your graduation ceremony is in the latter days of May,
as I mentioned to you on several prior occasions,
this clue pertains to the Mormons whose map you have a copy,
that is why I sent you to their various locations.

The finish line is in sight so remain steady on my track,
for you have run an extremely strong race,
keep the pace you are on and do not look right or left,
watch the blue ribbon straight ahead for first place.

There have been no pats on the back to divert our main focus,
from the goals that we have set from the start,
concentration is essential to this final stretch run,
come in strong and share the love of each heart.

Due to this record setting pace there is still plenty of time,
to reach out to all people through our book,
what you witnessed before Christmas was the leather bound edition,
of our course that is soon ending's first look.

Time is a strange phenomenon very difficult to understand,
while catching a mere glimpse of heavens real perception,
from an earthly perspective however that is a fine gift indeed,
to become an integral part of *The Immaculate Conception*.

This is the precise moment that we have long been awaiting,
allowing the scriptures to now speak loud and clear,
My time to return will be ushered in by your efforts,
a great celebration shall override every fear.

The faithful people of the world will rejoice at the prospect,
of my arrival to uphold all that is right,
As my many new Essenes will walk in unity throughout the world,
I shall anoint you as one dressed in white.

SATURDAY APRIL 12 6:22 AM

I preach not to any person from a lofty perch on high,
but rather whisper from groundlevel and below,
for so frequent are my days that have been spent in confinement,
and my nights at the establishments we all know.

I am a regular human being that has worked two jobs
and sometimes three, to pay the bills and stay a little bit ahead,
confronting each contemporary issue that we face on a daily basis,
from the same spoon I have always been fed.

I consider myself to be the epitome of average,
and in that way I hope that everyone can relate,
to the trials and tribulations that each one of us share,
every day that we leave home through the gate.

I have tried to accomplish all things that God wills,
but so many times I fall short of the mark,
as an imperfect human being it is never too late,
for any of us to choose light in place of dark.

I never could have written a single page of this book,
if it was not for God's grace and heavenly care,
please remember always that I am truly just like you,
and when I called once to our Lord He was there.

You can do the same from wherever you now sit,
for He is in each heart and knows the difficulties that we face,
there is nothing on earth that is hidden from His sight,
please speak with Him and join me in this grace.

The road back to Me is the marathon course,
that all of us need to travel in this life,
It begins with repentance and concludes with salvation,
on our knees He removes each heavy yoke of strife.

The Immaculate Conception is the revealing of God's will,
at a time when we have one foot on the slope,
His faith runs so deep that if we can soon righten ourselves,
then His message shall carry swiftly to the Pope.

What a pleasure it will be to receive forgiveness through God,
despite all agonies we have provided Him in our past,
knowing full well there is a place for true love in His Heart,
if we ask to join Him where the first become last.

Do not attempt to figure out why He maintains His passion for us,
heaven knows we have turned often from His sight,
for the further this world transgresses the stronger yearning is His love,
as our saviour shall never give up the fight.

Come face to face with His glory and look confidently into His eyes,
although disappointed He shall save us from this wreck,
His burden has been expensive but our bill is paid in full,
now it is high time for us to pick up the check.

A simple loving embrace is all that He seeks,
reach out to your fellow and put all differences aside,
the poor help feed the poorer so let us learn from their example,
and open our eyes to this world on the slide.

Early this past November I received God's initial message,
and these words sum up our many trials and tribulations,
The poor are not in terms of economic means but lack of knowledge,
wisdom, and understanding, now return to them their needs in all nations.

I sincerely hope that our book fully satisfies God's request,
and that He will bless us throughout the coming years,
so that we may gather the courage and own up to our misgivings,
when we finally meet and gently wipe away all His tears.

TUESDAY, APRIL 15, 1997, 7:38 AM

Imagine the world as a valuable potter's vessel,
that over the years began to crack and eventually split,
this is truly representative of all religions and nations,
from My viewpoint on the throne I did sit.

As your populations increase earthly problems do likewise,
and those splits serve to compound already difficult matters,
to the point that our precious vessel then falls from its shelf,
in a million pieces this created beauty then shatters.

At that precise moment in time there is nothing anyone can do,
to repair all the damage that was done,
it must be swept from the floor and sadly thrown away,
as all good memories through our minds they do run.

A tremendous amount of craftsmanship as well as time and effort,
went into the creation of this most glorious vessel,
in a flash it is destroyed as its unique beauty vanishes,
My pride and joy then becomes the dust of mortar and pestle.

Where the world is now sitting the cracks are clearly visible,
apply our glue to sustain the life of this treasure,
the splits soon to be evident shall represent sorrows,
and the fall will eliminate much of this life's pleasure.

The eventual fate is unavoidable as all life forms must age,
but proper maintenance can extend the expectancy of life,
to avoid a premature demise slow down the process of decay,
forging the battle versus death, sickness, and strife.

The momentum of satan's pace must be halted and then reversed,
as this can only occur by exercising your gift of free choice,
otherwise the final days will be shortened by this cancer,
leaving the multitudes forty-two months without My voice.

Please remember always that this life on earth is a gift,
do not hasten the next coming of My Son,
take a stand to end the evil rather than conceding to its influences,
and I shall honor that courage... do not run.

Beware of religious cults that thrive on the lost sheep,
as satan exploits their good intentions and then devours,
when they cross over the line the world turns away in fear,
from all religion as it poisons the multitudes of ours.

When mass suicides become news he changes peace to destruction,
realize this power and purchase not his product,
search for righteousness and truth, as loving faith shall abide,
look inward to your heart for this most proper conduct.

Many are now intimidated by his ability to twist your mind,
but you must focus upon the strength in your heart,
this is the final frontier to save each soul from demise,
where true faith resides lies the eternal life I impart.

I answer each from your voice that emits from this heart,
not your words that are spoken aloud,
that is why I can clearly hear every loving prayer in silence,
even from those that have been wrapped in their shroud.

From heaven there is no darkness as My light exposes all,
as evil intentions think they can hide in this way,
become conscious of what you do and not fearful or embarrassed,
but share our comfort with the dawn of each new day.

Uplift your hearts and true forgiveness shall be eternal,
by staring down upon the evil ones corruption,
remove yourself from his craftiness that day by day you accept gradually,
and he will leave you without further disruption.

His territory is temptation for he is powerless to impose his will,
nor may he cross the line to interfere with free choice,
after hearing My side of the story you will come to understand,
heaven's angels speak My most loving voice.

Turn off the music and the visuals that impair,
all your brain cells that he destroys while sitting idle,
actively involve body and spirit rather than stagnating your mind,
take charge of your future by removing his bridle.

Satan is lulling the world to sleep and a wake up call is now critical,
that is why I may appear so demanding,
pay close attention to these words for they come directly from Me,
after this battle I will be the only fighter left standing.

If you desire to be a winner then distance yourself from the loser,
as this heavyweight bout nears the deciding last rounds,
this is your chance to choose sides for transportation to eternity,
is it hell's fire or where God's love still abounds?

TUESDAY, APRIL 15, 1997, 1:12 PM

Whomever I have become is not for me to say,
but I can truly attest that a small miracle is taking place,
the holy spirit is quite active as the times are swiftly changing,
and the world has put on a very different face.

I am certain to be issued many comments and opinions,
as to what authority has led me down this path,
but "mine eyes have seen the glory of the coming of the Lord,"
stored in that vineyard are those grapes of His wrath.

The battle hymn of each republic should be a world wide cry,
as His truth continues marching on,
Glory, glory Hallelujah must be the echo throughout each land,
one shall remain and the other will be gone.

Solemn prayer is essential combined with faith and good deeds,
as the sands trickle down from life's hourglass,
come to terms with God and humanity seeking redemption from our Lord,
and avoid tarnishing as a weathered piece of brass.

Finish what you have started putting all houses in order,
and maintain faith for you know not when He shall arrive,
if you are fully prepared then there is nothing further left to do,
but help your fellow in this final stretch drive.

Are you satisfied with your current standing and prepared for accountability,
if so then I salute your good fortune,
if more work needs to be done please labor around the clock,
burning the midnight oil in the shadow of each moon.

When the gate swings closed there is no key available,
to open the security locks that heaven has set in place,
put off not until tomorrow what you can spiritually accomplish today,
there is no limit to the number of entrants in this race.

You must register on time however for no applications will be accepted,
beyond the notification date I allude to in this book,
so do not be shut out is the best advice I can give,
over your shoulder is not the direction to look.

Eyes straight ahead with true perception of the needy,
recall the poor are not measured in dollars and cents,
If you succeed in convincing any then you are convicted by all,
and a just reward awaits those most worthy through repentance.

Those that labor for the Lord shall never be unemployed,
as there is always an over abundance of His work,
As mentioned once before in this heavenly place of business,
the supervisors on earth will have to answer to each clerk.

Do not ask who or what, where, when, why, and how,
but get busy taking good care of your assignment,
so that when He arrives open hand you may give freely to the Lord,
what is rightfully His then take your place in the new alignment.

WEDNESDAY, APRIL 16, 1997, 10:10 AM

As you reach My fourth level of seed planted in solid ground this spring,
you shall grow by teaching well the coming harvest,
in these fields that I speak of beware the sickle's sharp threshing,
stay on My course thus completing your final test.

This preparation is detailed there is no greater written thesis,
so take your time and focus on our total combined research,
the test itself is not the difficult part but rather proper procedures,
that shall put birds upon our most worthy perch.

For mighty is the Tree of Life and as a branch of Mine you shall support,
those in need of a safe haven to securely nest,
the hours are never ending and the road ahead is extremely rough,
for the weary there is little or no rest.

Adversity will be the norm as you travel My high road,
as new challenges are sure to greet you around every corner,
do not let anyone rattle you for you're armed with true wisdom,
remain confident forgetting not the flora nor fauna.

You are wise to choose anonymity until I call upon your number,
embracing virtue and patience as your guide,
please relax and enjoy your upcoming family vacation,
as you have prepaid the cost of each ones favorite ride.

Upon your return in May we shall make preparation for graduation,
look toward Pentecost as the targeted date,
give or take a few days your course will then be complete,
as you renew acquaintances upon sealing your good fate.

THURSDAY APRIL 17, 1997, 12:11 AM

For all ears willing to hear and eyes able to see,
share your journey with those that so desire,
So each may then travel the same road back to Me,
that you have discovered far removed from the fire.

A direct prayer to God in the name of His son Jesus,
at the altar in any church of your pleasure,
thanking Him most sincerely for this precious gift of life,
and all the good years whose memories we shall treasure.

With our sins now forgiven and repentance formerly requested,
the Lord will walk us every step of the way,
to receive a spiritual baptism as the holy spirit renews life,
forgiveness when granted shall bring the light of a new day.

This second chance for body and soul is spiritually necessary to attain,
assuring safe passage home through the narrow gate,
where eternal life can be found without fear and corruption,
this is one destination that you cannot arrive late.

Offer your services to heaven in their battle versus the powers of darkness,
meaning that a war is now blazing we cannot see,
by volunteering as a soldier on the side of righteousness and truth,
God will welcome you as an enlistment born free.

I sought religious guidance to learn all about spiritual gifts,
for I have never belonged to any particular church,
at the point of transformation I began to read the bible,
for the very first time doing doctrinal research.

Spiritual baptism was a jolt that knocked me off of my horse,
while unprepared for such a drastic change at one time,
my religion has always been people, meaning family and friends,
now this old life has been stopped on a dime.

When injected with God's grace it takes some time to adapt,
so remain patient as all things turn out for the best,
My lesson was more profound due to lack of religious education,
as bible illiteracy put me light years behind the rest.

Renew a relationship with God by keeping Him close to your heart,
in this world we become diverted with confusions,
Each life is so busy that we find little time to give thanks,
God's endless love overrides any grandeur or illusions.

As your call to God is answered you shall recognize that special moment,
as colors turn vibrant and sense of smell becomes keen,
when looking up at the sun you will squint and shield your eyes,
the powers of nature are like no other you have seen.

My story of baptism may sound very similar to St. Paul's,
certainly not a gradual easing into this belief,
the Lord knows all the formulas let Him handle the details,
that is why He is our commander in chief.

This experience is a good example of how we think our life is fine,
but apparently our definition of fine is not the same,
as He who sits upon the throne not deceived by human reasoning,
what we believe may not be allowed in His game.

So often we attempt to justify through our craftiness and rationale,
that our life works short of criminal are okay,
but listen carefully to your voice and judge your own daily deeds, then in the mirror
truthfully answer to the way.

Compared to certain others we say our life is better lived, but judge not for we shall be
judged each on our own,
excuses are unacceptable when you have been properly forewarned,
welcome God's presence rather than choosing to bemoan.

This is not to create fear but to develop a pure understanding, so that all lost sheep
through the good shepherd may come home,
as westerners we have blurred vision when it comes to spotting real need,
bring compassion to the world outside of our Rome.

We are far removed geographically but must close the distance in spirit,
from third world countries plagued with troubles throughout time,
as we see only bits and pieces of what the media selectively feeds us,
tolerating famine, war, and hunger, is an inhumane capital crime.

Nations that are truly righteous will bypass the rules of oppressors,
providing for basic human needs in every land,
the means to feed all are available but the true will is lacking,
our first obligation is to love each other open hand.

THURSDAY, APRIL 17, 1997, 2:44 PM

The biggest mistake some people make is imagining they are on top,
while their vision remains focused looking down,
when in reality earth is the basement of this vast overall structure,
in comparison only a very small town.

For big fish in little ponds a word to the wise,
do not attempt to approach Me from the reaches of your tiny world,
I have issued several warnings that those types are unwelcome,
as aggressors become victims of My wrath soon unfurled.

Your earthly life is a proving ground for eternal life if you so choose,
the ultimate decision is one that only you can make,
the ground rules are firmly established open your eyes to their contents,
for the judge only points the direction you must take.

If you are a supervisor or leader and abuse the trust I have placed,
and your people suffer hardships day and night,
while others are allowed to operate achieving wealth through insatiable greed,
you are playing with the power of Thy might.

The next time you condescend it would be best to look upward,
for that is the only direction from where you are standing,
disrespect for your fellow man is quite bad enough on earth,
but in heaven we are far more demanding.

Your punishment is a hundredfold if those placed in your care,
must pray for mercy to obtain proper food and drink,
that is why My patience is thinning for I see all the haves and have nots,
it behooves each of you to stop and really think.

If I walked among you today would you be comfortable in your ways,
celebrating My return with ecstasy and great delight,
or because of your iniquities would you be embarrassed and ashamed,
plotting against Me in fear of exposure to the light.

For the multitudes that now choose darkness to perform their evil actions,
and use their mouths to emit slander and deceit,
I had hoped this time was different as mankind learned its lesson through Jesus,
but those poor ratios are similar on My sheet.

I allow even the despicable to come forth toward My altar,
but remember always I hear your soul not your words,
you cannot fool Me into forgiveness if it is not truly in you,
thus wasting time as the true believers come in herds.

A request is not a guarantee of My response in the affirmative,
for I look deeper than you could ever possibly realize,
I have known each of you since before birth when you were spirit without body,
a Father's joy that now brings tears to My eyes.

Corruption rules too many minds and the pendulum has fully swung,
as satan's influence runs rampant through My ranks,
please reverse this ungodly trend before it carries over the edge,
to My remaining good soldiers I assuredly give thanks.

FRIDAY, APRIL 18, 1997, 6:15 AM

As we begin to close our book thus assigning title and credits,
I wish to extend to humanity our hopes from above,
that each may find their way home upon the road back to Me,
for it has been prepared with an abundance of love.

We pray that this work has served the purpose of its calling,
and that all shall understand the message's good intent,
although there are many who shall disagree in part,
please stay open minded for it is truly heaven sent.

It matters not in this world what any human being claims to know of God,
for detractors seem to always come forth,
if this book helps even one then our efforts were not in vain,
to seek God in true faith from His direction due north.

It is the poor that we seek who lack knowledge, wisdom, and understanding,
as I was told to return to them their needs,
I have done the very best I can and God only knows this is true,
in His garden I have tried planting those seeds.

This book is the solid ground where you may grow eternally strong,
and become rooted far removed from all danger,
that the wayside seed, and the ones sown on rocky places,
must be weary of when away from the safety of My manger.

The seed that lands among thorns must also take great heed,
although well intended shall eventually become choked,
some survive longer than others a sad but true fact of life,
this is the forewarning of the end days I have invoked.

He knows so much more than any of you are aware,
please embrace this message for he is your ongoing connection,
I inform him only in parts to help guarantee his protection,
for he represents the good fruits of My resurrection.

Put your full faith in the cross and wait patiently upon My return,
never feeling anxious, unloved, or as a loner,
you have been given My word now acknowledge your saviour,
through My messenger you have again heard from Jeshua Verona.

SATURDAY, APRIL 19, 1997

The classroom from where I teach is not the room to be,
for those that are the feint of heart,
although peace is our main goal we must always take a stand,
for the oppressed have needed support from the start.

Become a spokesperson for the cause that originates in heaven,
utilizing your gifts to drive home our point,
that we shall no longer tolerate poor treatment of the good,
show us leadership as our choice to help anoint.

All the brotherhood of humankind that wish to share in your journey,
fairly soon you shall be presented that drum,
which I spoke of last Christmas still wrapped as your gift,
there is only one final lesson yet to come.

Remain as you are we are well pleased with your progress,
as in dream you stood tall to deliver,
in defense of a friend that was criticized unjustly,
while converting takers into the category of giver.

Your training throughout life has had a definitive purpose,
each experience is a new piece of the puzzle,
the time is soon coming when our testing will cease,
and quite gently we shall remove chain and muzzle.

You are not an experiment that we are conducting in our lab,
but a friend we have helped raise through the years,
to fulfill the proper course that needs to be followed,
for this world to overcome its many fears.

By example you will lead all My lost sheep back home,
as your life can be directly related to by most,
that share a common denominator for the multitudes are also average,
like yourself and the most celebrated host.

They shall listen and then follow for My voice speaks many volumes,
echoing loudly to each corner of the earth,
these days have been written now the invitations must be sent,
to the reception planned long before your birth.

Fear not where you tread for my promise is good,
I shall never dim the light of your path,
remain strong in the faith as you have always done in the past,
accepting graciously both kindness and wrath.

The road back to Me you have already traveled,
now go back and bring the multitudes along,
hold their hands really firm for so many fear the light,
and while walking sing our most loving song.

Peace and love everlasting is a most worthy destination,
so keep that fresh in your good heart and mind,
and it shall provide every strength needed to continue your trek,
for those who truly do seek Me shall soon find.

A glorious new world far beyond human comprehension,
where your spirits shall be set free from their confines,
as we approach the new millennia the battle has already begun,
we in heaven comprise our army's front lines.

Enlist your spirit as our ally and victory will be certain,
on this you can rely as the coming of a new day,
put your heart, mind, and body, in this most proper order,
and My helper shall then show you the way.

As St. Paul once said in scripture: "When I was a child I thought as a child, spoke as a child, and acted as a child, but when I grew up I put childish things away." Let us each do likewise, for it is in this spirit of growth that true understanding is born.

It is our true desire that each reader has uncovered with a renewed appreciation, the abundance of love that our Father has bestowed, still bestows, and shall always bestow and maintain for us. His amazing grace is continually displayed in honorable recognition of upholding His eternal covenant to humanity despite our many failures. Although we often lack patience with others, God has been most tolerant with us, far beyond all measure throughout our history. "For He loves this world so, that He gave His only begotten son, that we may have eternal life," through the crucifixion and resurrection of self for the purpose of our salvation. As human beings in general we have done very little to improve our collective condition upon His earth in the past two thousand years, thus displaying a neglectful sense of appreciation for what God placed upon the cross. For the remission of our sins Christ still makes the ultimate sacrifice as one who Himself remains without sin. Today we are faced on a global basis with the same downward spiraling pattern of crises that plagued us in those earlier times. The similarities of differences and polarizations of rich and poor, have established opposing corners not unlike the spiritual war that has since commenced in heaven, and shall come to earth as the physical war biblically known as our Armageddon. Those who prefer to say that our transgressions do not pertain to their lives are making a grave mistake, unaware that we as humanity are a brotherhood, simply meaning that we are separate but equal parts of the body of Christ. As a civilization we can only go eternally forward if these parts work cooperatively by total unification, with no individual or group being any more or less important than another in our pursuit of oneness. This formula must pertain to all segments of human society throughout the world.

If we continue to physically and spiritually separate from each other, by constantly warring and busying ourselves with materialistically oriented aspirations, then we succumb to the self-dictates of evil's mastery of the mind, thus bypassing the pure love that is God's gift to each soul. The collective decisions we make today are not only for this lifetime but for eternity as well, so it behooves each of us to make time for serious inner reflection. If not for our own sake then at least for the benefit of our loved ones, we must now address these critical internal issues, by placing evil and its offspring of temptations away from us for good.

How can God promote human unity if the leadership that comprises the diverse groups of our world, will not sit down together and attempt proper dialogue, seeking common rather than higher ground principles? Egotists and self seekers cannot be involved in the construction of this essential new age bridge. The main purpose of Christ's appearance on this earth as a man, was to bring truth and grace to a world gone astray, through the life teachings, crucifixion, and resurrection of one Jesus Verona. The bridge to be built at that time was between Judaism and Christianity, (Jew and Gentile) and as an Essene He stood atop that bridge prior to His public ministry. His life and teachings were the faith and His crucifixion was the sacrifice, but His resurrection is the ongoing hope for humankind. Christ came to us in peace as a carpenter, good shepherd, and teacher, but His next coming is as a spiritual warrior that the world has yet to see. Let us now get behind Him with all the support that our heart, mind, body, and soul can provide for His ongoing battle in our defense. May His arrival be a celebration of life and liberty.

This book is soon closing but our living God's book never does, and I pray that each person will achieve salvation through the sincere repentance of sin as a definitive and ultimate changing of our ways. What Jesus placed upon the cross requires our most heartfelt acknowledgement of faith through good works, to then share in God's kingdom of everlasting life and collective eternal peace. This true faith will manifest itself in a spiritual baptism of your life that can only be gifted by God, and shall change your total being forever. This renewal of life represents death to sin as you come to now live under the law of grace, from here to eternity. Please go within yourself to God's altar of peace, for the soul is where He has forever held our worship. Let us limit the confusions and remedy the distractions of this externally physical and temporary life, by slowing the pace of today with a refocusing upon the eternal truths within us. Without our soul progress through spiritual understanding, the teacher remains cross-bound. It is time to learn the lessons, and release our Christ from within self and thereby join in His eternal journey.

SUNDAY, APRIL 27, 1997, 6:44 AM

Life's path is at the crossroads between heaven and earth,
please come and follow me for I know the right way,
I have traveled this road before to our Father high above,
and have returned to lead all sheep gone astray.

We may never have the chance to pass this way again,
so take the hand of each one that you love,
walk in peace on this journey keeping the faith as we go,
embracing innocence as does the child and white dove.

Our pathway has been lit by the light of resurrection,
and through Him comes forgiveness of all sin,
put behind you the past focusing sharply on the present,
and in the near future He shall welcome each of us in.

Release the heavy yoke that binds us to this earth,
and shed the skin that has grown thicker through the years,
drop all of your battle cries between one another today,
for the real enemy has instilled all our fears.

By creating worldwide dissensions he has won many battles,
but knows full well the outcome of this war,
if assigning your loyalties to his methods of recruitment,
then you shall not be admitted through heavens door.

It is now the twelfth hour and a decision must be made,
you can no longer straddle both sides of the fence,
neutrality is not an option so take a stand with free choice,
and live or die with the gift of common sense.

Think hard for a moment about the Creator of all things,
and the love that He provides to each soul,
was this life the gift of satan I say most assuredly not,
for he is the grim reaper recruiting companionship in that hole.
Earthly death is a natural progression but is by no means eternal,
as Jesus for our sins paid the price,
with the inheritance of God's kingdom we can travel as did He,
by expelling the evil one that has authored each vice.

Close his books at once and faithfully open God's,
and in the name of Christ you shall be saved by His grace,
For satan has no jurisdiction where God's love is requested,
through the eye of the needle is the direction we must trace.

I am simply a messenger not a cultist or preacher,
as no membership cards are required in this club,
true faith in the Lord and the wisdom of His love,
while helping others sets you apart from Beelzebub.

Solemn prayer is the hope while faith is our passport,
and true love is the chosen mode of transportation,
to eternal life hereafter is there really any choice,
come one and all from each and every nation.

Listen carefully for the marching band led by those dressed in white,
following the sounds of heavens drum and fife,
step confidently in God's parade with eyes focused straight ahead,
signing your own name to the Lamb's Book of Life.

This ending is the new beginning where the pen may now rest,
and our words must be converted into action,
you must resist all temptation from satan's one final push,
displaying your great willpower as the featured attraction.

He is to the right and to the left and over each shoulder,
but never shall he appear straight ahead,
focus hard on that finish line a very short distance from here,
where the holy spirit has graciously led.

The Imperishable Crown awaits following this one final surge,
reach down deep inside and finish strong,
In this marathon race that you have run so very well,
may save multitudes from that most evil throng.

As our book soon travels My words shall echo loudly,
of heaven's sentiment to all ears that will hear,
life is no longer a game but a war that has begun,
it is now time to overcome apprehension and fear.

Please follow the leader who is known as the good shepherd,
as He brings home all the willing lost sheep,
from the very beginning to these days soon ending,
this has been heaven's goal and the promise that we keep.

Come one and all to a world far beyond wonder,
where only true love and faith may abide,
this is the real magic kingdom that we have named New Jerusalem,
our Lord and saviours most beautiful and precious bride.

As My seeds were scattered they did seek solid ground,
in each land where they could become fully grown,
although spring is the season for new life, those seeds have long been established,
by the sower of all things to be sown.

They are to the north and south with two in the east,
and the majority are firmly planted in the west,
bring My Lost Tribes together for their season is upcoming,
through our book and your voice I attest.

The songs that you sing are sweet hymns to unite,
while your message spoken in tongues call forth the legions,
to come march in My parade whose ranks are now forming,
as My words extend to the furthermost regions.

As heaven's little drummer boy await patiently your drum,
let it be is still the advice I proclaim,
with the latter days approaching in this merry month of May,
our agenda regarding graduation day is the same.

Do not become over anxious, kindly take a very deep breath,
thus slowing down excess energy in your surround,
recall those critical shots with the game on the line,
in all the noise and confusion you never heard a sound.

This focus is imperative so apply the wisdom of your training,
following the game plan that we established from the start,
there shall be no unexpected surprises to catch you off guard,
as you walk this heaven lit path in our heart.

I have diagrammed the play in detail as we kneel together on the sideline,
once again listen closely to your coach's word,
shut out every other sound that may disturb your concentration,
as I the Lord should be the only voice heard.

My play is now established with good intent and design,
while the ball shall directly travel toward you,
if our brethren do their job then victory will be assured,
sending home multitudes of both Gentile and Jew.

Your playing days are then over as you assume the role of teacher,
passing along wisdom and understanding from God,
the names and faces have now changed as this new day is dawning,
while we prepare to face the modern day Herod.

As I move to the front office you shall be anointed as coach,
and your roster will comprise twelve strong in number,
when I finish selecting the team provide My same words of inspiration,
awakening each from their very long slumber.

Your growth rate in the holy spirit from newborn to adulthood,
although unprecedented has missed not a single phase,
there are good reasons for My methods uncharacteristic as they may seem,
over analysis is inappropriate in these days.

The time for action has arrived while the scholars still ponder,
and would do so for as long as they are able,
but the study period has concluded and it is time to take the test,
close all books by separating the truths from fable.

So many have devoted their lives and I am forever grateful,
to the cause of scriptural adherence and its true roots,
while others have served faithfully with the appropriate combination,
of preaching the Gospel and also applying those good fruits.

But in humankind's quest for understanding he has continually bypassed the heart,
time and again trying to prove his every theory right,
it is those at ground level that I speak through in volumes,
who give thanks despite the extent of their plight.

Humankind continues to misread Me for I desire not his strivings,
nor am I impressed by the heights he attains,
did you not learn your lesson at the tower of Babel,
for I am with those who dirty their hands planting My grains.

Do not look to approach Me by achieving glory according to men,
if you truly desire grace then humble yourselves to the poor,
for it is in those eyes you shall find Me and the secret of eternal life,
they are the meek to be welcomed at heavens door.

Their fields is where I till not in the skyscrapers which rise,
to heights that represent only further separation,
I most vehemently despise the fact humanity continues to disregard,
My messages now sent to each and every nation.

SUNDAY, MAY 11, 1997, 7:11 AM

The Cantab that I spoke of whose color is red crimson,
was indicated for more than one reason,
I now ask you to consider a directive due north,
where this final exam completes a most successful season.

Your former high school coach did play the part of Me,
as you witnessed both My compassion and rage,
those are truly the elements of My sentiments exactly,
at the conclusion of this tumultuous age.

The setting provided for you was to renew the tie to Cambridge,
and the duality is My inference to Latin,
combine these few factors and return to where you started,
as the road shall become smooth as fine satin.

My promise from the outset was protection and direction,
thus provided as My covenant through each day,
you have also held your word to complete this vital mission,
with graduation only a brief moment away.

When you asked Me quite frankly how to recognize these powers,
I informed you that they were predicated on heat,
remember that which you witnessed as those fragments from the sky,
came to earth while I sat next to you in My seat.

For a true point of reference in regards to the Dead Sea Scrolls,
select the university at Harvard and not Brown,
The French connection I mentioned are of DeVaux and Dupont-Sommer,
as their versions are the only game in town.

The truths that you seek shall be contained in those works,
as all others do not accurately compare,
as for the publication of our book in these latter days of May,
at the roses full bloom you may go straight to the square.

The other scrolls in Peru are best left to the scholars,
that project is for them but not you, for I shall soon
reveal your identity that is of no specific type,
you are My creation of both Gentile and Jew.

Although our book is completed My teachings continue on,
as evidenced in your dream this fine day,
for My lessons are timeless and need not be revised,
it is still prudent remaining open to the way.

Your heart is increasing as you seek that which is righteous,
stay My course and you shall never go wrong,
by following the leader in this parade heading uphill,
against the grain is the title of our song.

Your desire to help others carries an added responsibility,
providing more energy then you could possibly muster,
please concern yourself not as I shall refill your cup,
that runneth over with our love's greatest luster.

No matter how many times you bang your head against the wall,
clear the cobwebs and go back for a little more,
this is the critical phase of training that fully develops
the drive, most essential in delivering lost sheep to our door.

Frustration becomes the rule amidst a world on the slide,
the exception is heaven's patience and calm,
do not let this envelop you on the road back to Me,
the right medicine is to sing every new psalm.

Which I grant to you in spirit for they provide fine
companionship, as an easy to digest food for the soul,
that may otherwise grow hungry without ever truly fasting,
through this sacrifice you shall earn My leading role.

It is wise to promote faith as this formula's main ingredient,
without question a key byproduct of the heart,
along with hope and charity forms a strong coalition,
to accompany love that remains the most vital part.

Belated congratulations on graduation as understanding is your
diploma, thus awarded upon successful completion of My course,
this is the one for your wall that far surpasses every other,
and although invisible becomes a most powerful resource.

Not unlike the imperishable crown which is our next goal as
a graduate, when you transcend from the student to instructor,
I shall soon provide the drum that sounds this newly
discovered wisdom, seize the moment as My symphony conductor.

This beautifully arranged sonata was composed long ago,
by the maestro of each performance thus far,
In humankind's history of productions too numerous to mention,
and as limitless as the total accounting of each star.

Point your focus towards oneness as the formulation of unity,
that can only occur based on commonality through simplicity,
like the story of Hillel with the gentile mimicking the Torah,
and the flower communion of Capek best represent this plea.

To halt and then reverse this lengthy process of decay,
requires a rust proofing that I taught you early on,
the living water that I supply may quench each everlasting
thirst, while the physical water serves as baptism by John.

For one originates in heaven and the other is of the earth,
both were most worthy but only mine is eternal,
we are departing Pisces for Aquarius where baptism is within,
grasp this truth as did Nicodemus through My journal.

The gifts you have been granted allow the means for return,
in essence a round trip ticket back home,
for the lost sheep I now proclaim may trade in their one way
fares, and take this heavenly journey through each poem.

Carefully written for the purpose of renewing our deep covenant,
that goes back all the way to creation,
God has never wavered from the promise made to His children,
can we honestly say the same from each nation?

Let us make amends with He who provides all that we see,
and so much more only visible through our hearts,
that when opened up to all of life presents a world beyond wonder,
where we become Christlike, not simply students of the love He imparts.

The enlightened Buddha delivered wisdom with understanding of our existence,
and its relationship to each life form of God,
when Jesus became the living Torah we received truth and grace,
bringing us ever closer to universal Christhood with our Lord.

In regards to internal strife recall My mention of your cities,
and the warning signs to observe the coming of great troubles,
Nature supplies all the answers with many disoriented behaviors,
war is at hand when the size of the crow doubles.

This new age is now dawning as God teaches us through revelation,
beckoning humanity to step forward for last call,
The Immaculate Conception maps "The Road Back To Me",
for in each of us is His love as in Paul.

* This road back to God through the inner commitment of souls, is to fulfill our true
purpose upon this earthly plane. We must strive to forge ahead based on true inner faith
and not doctrine. The Christ spirit dwells within each of our souls, while forever awaiting
our call for universal truth and understanding. There is no religious church outside of our
being that can take us to where we need to be with God, that dwells within each life.
Place selfhood and free choice back upon God's altar by asking to serve His will, as we
accomplish together this holy covenant. May the word speak to you as kindly as it has
spoken to me, for our hope is for the one truth to shine through every soul.

Amen.

JACOB'S LADDER

Our special troupe is delayed but has not lost its way,
a brief intermission in this final three-act play.
For the some have been seated early and the most shall soon follow,
through the deep woods and old man's mountain hollow.
You have rightly discovered the pathway to our most secret hidden nest,
where we prepare this wedding feast for the unheralded earthly best.
So gather these shepherds drawn far away from their flock,
and provide new direction to "the door" where I knock.

They are overlooked and underrated in your world that has forgotten,
but to those of us who see "all" they are heavens dearly begotten.
As invitations continue onward to this fine celebration due north,
our "inner" kingdom of family gathering must always go forth.
The "eyes" of your world shall not dare look our way,
for evil seeks the lost multitudes that choose greed and decay.
Keep them humble and lowly with warm blanket and roof,
as each will witness joyfully My biblically promised proof.

Scripture tells us quite clear "many are called but few are chosen,"
no longer including just the arid desert but as well the tundra frozen.
As we avoid "the swarming" multitudes upon that errant wayward journey,
steer clear of your cities both up and down that attract "big business" and attorney.
Stay well aware within you as to My "harbored" feelings of wrath,
as grave danger nears move your people far, for most deadly is this path."
The road less traveled" is the map indeed of safe passage back to Me,
so deliver to all "The Immaculate Conception"; of wounded and bending knee.

Many are ill and extremely tired but their great faith drives them here,
as they forever follow "the light" of My spirit, past the cloudy and into the clear.
I come once again to My most loyal troops, true "soldiers of fortune" not fame,
who sacrifice all that the world so endears, for the right to be called in My name.
"Our Kingdom" does not follow, the reward systems set upon your earth,
as the rich turn poor they weep and gnash as each death shall know rebirth.
Your guide shall learn our patience soon and when ready feel free to go,
to the church I told you very long ago that you never thought was so.

Continue to climb up "Jacob's Ladder" for there is only one more rung, as the chosen
arrive through truth and grace, to witness your gifted tongue. Engagement looms but
not with Cupid as I perform that honor soon, life's greatest song that   "All" may sing...
our mazel tov comes this June.   L' Chayim! (To Life!)

MY STILL NARROW GATE

Thoughts are the beginning of ideas, words, and action,
from one to the other takes a minimal fraction.
Of time and energy lodged within the human mind,
how this process unfolds brings both evil and kind.

Do not ever take for granted this most influential power,
are you formulating conflict or the smell of a flower?
With this momentary decision of the path that We show,
upon which road shall you travel; the high or the low?

Because of the swiftness that the brain sends its command,
you give far too much credit without accounting demand.
So often it misreads signals by deception of earthly source,
becoming your greatest danger when absorbing evil force.

In your world of great distraction now the multitudes truly stagger,
digesting poison food and drink from he that wields the dagger.
These days are written in most every journal as each soul must tow the line,
by focusing hard upon our spiritual truth so in health you come and dine.

The human condition is extremely weak when contagious with disease,
as "the choice" is made to sink or swim which power do you wish to please?
So many of you live each day alike as if nothing matters most,
this passive attitude that satan plants, is an invitation to his roast.

This wake up call I speak in some is available still to ALL,
that will "tune in" soon to My critical message before the coming "Fall."
Please stand tall with head up straight and soul on "full response",
and listen carefully to Me deep within you, and not the media's most deadly haunts.

We are saddened greatly by what goes on in your world so out of tune,
if this continues on and evil gains momentum we must dim the sun and moon.
My light is bright and shall guide each path if in truth you shall welcome in,
this grace now offered unto every soul that repents their earthly sin.

This war began very long ago with so many battles fought,
each life "must claim" its sacred ground and sell every evil bought.
Return To Me and I shall claim you back but this offer soon expires,
DO NOT be holding onto an outdated invitation when your alarms decry our fires.

Good and evil have forever sparred
but this is the only championship fight,
so convert your soul from its spectator body
and emerge within My Might.

Too long you have followed the masses to slaughter
accepting death too easily as your fate,
but it no longer has dominion when true faith is your guide
as I may greet you at...My Still Narrow Gate.

THE ONE FINAL TRUTH HEAVEN SENT

When we "freely chose" to depart God's Oneness, for the desires of this physical life,
our likeness and image as divinely created, became split into child, man, and wife.
Free choice is the parting gift that "we" commanded, upon the top of each holiday list,
so to safely go home and into God's grace, it must be redeemed to clear each earthly mist.

This physical world must be overcome, for inner spiritual truth to then **rise**,
as each happiness depends upon our covenant fulfilled, when we dry every tear from His **eyes**.
We have never been refused a worthwhile request, how fortunate do you feel for this **love**,
but todays world is dying from those choices we demanded, and once again we are
    desperate for His **dove**.

If the day ever comes when "He chooses" to not rescue, our souls from their bodily sins,
and we are forced to then accept full responsibility of our actions, who loses and who truly **wins?**
Shall God step aside as the new multitudes plead, from our lives we believe that we **control**,
for to separate His love would be our ultimate free choice, that lands each soul in that
    infamous **hole.**

I for one choose repentance of my sins and transgressions, and ask daily forgiveness
    through the weakness of my flesh,
it is true wisdom to do likewise as we approach the end of days... to be "saved" move far
    away from His thresh.
God's loving patience is unconditional as also must be ours, but poor "free choice" has
    brought destruction to the brink,
"Heaven and earth will pass away but My words will not," so share holy communion
    within our daily food and drink.
There is still a little time but these days are now numbered, please no longer put off good intent;
to "choose the will of our soul" thus replacing earthly desire, and then He shall deliver ...
"The One Final Truth Heaven Sent!"

Amen.

In Conclusion

If the words within this journal of our experience has brought attention to the realization of our soul's importance, thereby creating a reconnection of total being within us as an awareness of spiritual full potential, then this mission has succeeded in its intent and purpose. As we come to better understand our gifted capacities from a spiritually directing standpoint, through the energies of prayer, meditation, and good deeds, our communion with God and one another shall bring about peace and brotherhood upon this earth permanently. Remember always that our thoughts supply an energy as well as our actions, and we must therefore apply ourselves to life accordingly. If there is unbelief in this truth then how else could prayer be heard and then answered? Where would hope be based without a source of divine inspiration?

Resurrection as reincarnation of our souls is an immutable law of the universe, and not an element of disputation among varying beliefs. Our complete soul development is thus dependent upon this eternal truth, and its acknowledgement as a natural life cycle reality. The sooner we welcome in this truth, the sooner we can resume spiritual growth. The truth has been too long stifled by doctrine and self servitude.

What we term as coincidences during the course of daily routine, oftentimes are particular learning opportunities, revisited upon us in order that we may through free will thus elevate our soul. There is NO soul that has perfected itself within one lifetime, so therefore we must continue to persevere improvement through the ongoing truthful encouragement, of the educating Christ spirit that dwells within each of our beings. This is the true presence of Messiah, and the eternal partnership covenant for which we live!

Universal energy that is transmitted into our earthly plane only arrives in part, according to our collective ability of receiving and then appropriately sharing with our brethren. Throughout this lengthy process of our soul maturation, the Lord our God remains patient, longsuffering, and forever true. Do not be timid in approaching this welcoming grace within you, and when understood comfortably, to then apprehend it completely.

Let us understand that both positive and negative energies must coexist within our physically dense world of matter, in order to produce the necessary and coordinated movement of time and space. In the universal reality there is only positive energy, because time and space as we know it does not exist in dimension four. Let us assertively disassociate from the negative energy of today, thereby bringing heaven down to earth. From God's pure viewpoint above and within us, there are no barriers, divisions, or separations. Let us likewise peer into His unified creation, and thus merge all dimensions into One. The letting go of self and its desires, allows for the glorious transformation through willpower in the here and now. What a wonderful world we shall see when self is set aside upon "The Road Back to Me."

*The Christ spirit is a constant guide in our soul's quest to return home, and let us thank God for this wonderful gift!   Amen.

DAY ONE OF DAVID

The messiah's birth in the manger was not accomplished by chance,
but rather issued from a heavenly decree.
For there was room at the Inn but the times were unsafe,
and the preparation must be perfect you see.

Protection and direction was foremost in the hearts, of this select
group that surrounds the most Holy.
As Essenes from the mount are these saints straight from heaven,
in this world always hidden and lowly.

Working amongst the masses in the most critical of times, as the
background in each masterpiece painted.
Never losing their focus upon the subject while posing, God's
perfection cannot ever become tainted.

There are many channels of service as each takes their place,
and carries forth the Lord's plan without flaw.
When the movements of the Holy Family appeared erratic and
confused, in those palettes are the precise oils to draw.

This work is not designed or contrived within the mind, but
rather follows as a painting by number.
Adapting only when necessary to the actions of our adversary,
thereby protecting the Holy One's slumber.

Time and again this heavenly path must be traveled,
with the testing results quite the same.
Through the trials and tribulations the Master plan is thus achieved,
while the zigzags remain plentiful in this game.

This mission once again must be accurate and so precise, as
the road bends and then curves with great danger.
Though never far removed when it comes to the House of David,
keeping close watch upon the safety of that manger.

The Essenes are back in place for this most glorious return,
with the days so long awaited now at hand.
As the instruments dressed in white well aware and at the ready,
for the conductor of heaven's finest band.

Now return to the House of Israel and remind "all" of My
children, what is truly required in becoming a Jew.
Remembering always that you travel by divine command only,
upon "The Road Back To Me" ... they have you.

Omeyn.   Amen.

"Day One of David"

Our mission is thus fulfilled upon the completion and delivery,
of this summons which proclaims to all His living word,
it is His final eternal gift completing the bridge to humanity,
bonding each Torah to Christ and both Temples to the Third.

November 3, 2003 – 6:30 a.m.: Final Message from me

Let us return home in peace to a unity departed,
now with knowledge, wisdom, and understanding...
your needs are returned!

*Torah & Christ
are One!*